The Waterfowl Man

of Sylvan Heights

To Terri

Hope enjoyed your
visit _

The Waterfowl Man of Sylvan Heights
Mike Lubbock's worldwide quest to save waterfowl.

Copyright © 2014 by Dale Alan True

Garden Wall Publishing
1806 Hunterwoods Drive, High Point, NC 27265

ISBN: 978-0-9913719-0-7

Printed in the United States of America
First Edition

To Ali:
*For your sustaining love and support in my travels
and fascination with birds.*

Mike Lubbock

CONTENTS

ACKNOWLEDGEMENTS

So many people are necessary in drafting the content required for any work such as this book. With due respect to those unnamed, yet whose numerous contributions are appreciated, there are several notable individuals who truly merit recognition.

Gary Dean, owner of Dean Studio, provided the graphic design, cover art and photographs. A substantial portion of his work was donated so the birds at Sylvan Heights Bird Park could benefit from the book's proceeds.

Jennifer Harrington, author (as Jennifer Delamere) of the Love's Grace Trilogy historical romance series, generously offered her time to proofread the book.

Katie Gipple Lubbock provided the illustrations which appear in the book.

Frank S. Todd, a recognized authority on waterfowl, author of *Natural History of the Waterfowl,* and a long time friend of Mike Lubbock, made available the content of his published works as reference material for the writing of *The Waterfowl Man of Sylvan Heights.*

INTRODUCTION

Revealing The Waterfowl Man

With all enticing legends, there are myths associated with the truth. The legend of the Waterfowl Man is no different. As often is the case, the facts prove more interesting than the myth. *The Waterfowl Man of Sylvan Heights* is the factual account of Mike Lubbock's life with birds, his journeys through the world's wild places, and his over 60-year career as a pioneering aviculturalist, culminating with the opening of the Sylvan Heights Bird Park.

Fortunately for the reader, Mike wrote copious field notes on all his journeys and missions going back to 1962. His journals depict treks to raging mountain rivers, arid wastelands, arctic ice flows, lush tropical forests, and vast marshlands. Anywhere in the world waterfowl could be found, Mike planned an expedition to find them and observe their habits in the wild in order to protect their species from the possibility of extinction. His notes record information as minute as what time he woke up each day, what he ate for meals, the weather conditions, and birds observed, as well as specifics of his daily activities, thus preserving a richness of detail often lost over time. The seemingly innocuous details in those journals held the key to unlocking the memories that make up the basis for this book.

DISCOVERY

As a volunteer at Sylvan Heights Waterfowl Center, I was nosing about Ali Lubbock's office one evening and found some notebooks upon a shelf. I inquired of their significance and Ali told me they were Mike's journals from his trips, and that there were many more scattered about in other places.

My first reaction was to carefully take one of the well-worn books from the shelf, open it gently, and glance at the notes Mike had made on an expedition to the Arctic. I was struck by the significance of the collection of notebooks. I knew they needed to be preserved, placed somewhere they could be better protected from the elements and from prying eyes such as my own. Though I would never willingly damage or abscond with one, others might, and these were too important to be left to that fate. These were the background stories of the legend of

The Waterfowl Man, a catalog of the many challenges to his physical endurance, a record of successes and failures, a testimony of the providence he experienced in the wild.

From the point of my discovery, I felt personally responsible for preserving the content of the journals. I needed to do more than merely place them in a protected place; I also had to transcribe and archive them digitally so the content would not be lost to the ravages of time. For some reason, I knew this was my charge to perform.

WRITING THE BOOK

Archiving the journals was a natural extension of my volunteer role with the Lubbocks. Since 2002, I had worked closely with Mike and Ali to promote the conservation mission of Sylvan Heights Waterfowl Center in the small rural town of Scotland Neck, North Carolina, developing the preserve's original website and working in various capacities as their media writer and historian.

One would think that with my nature writing experience and the discovery of Mike's journals, the idea for authoring a biography of Mike Lubbock would have come to my mind immediately. But that was not the case.

While the journals represented crucial documentation of Mike's career and achievements, they were not that exciting to read and did not initially seem to be a basis for a book. A large portion of the entries consisted of routine matters regarding the trips, such as airline flight times, a long list of equipment packed for the expedition and often how it was acquired, expense logs, and information on obtaining the necessary permits for travel or for collecting birds or eggs. Mike was also very liberal in noting things I would consider incidental, such as describing the meal he had on a flight, whether the airline hostess smiled at him, good or bad features of the transportation system in a given country, and background on the hotels he stayed in or the hosts with which he roomed. This level of minutia was often maintained through the entire trip, and while there were some very interesting parts in the journal, it was nothing I considered book worthy. Archiving the notes for Sylvan Heights' library was the only purpose I initially had for transcribing the journals.

That would have remained the case, except for a twist of fate. After I had taken home the first batch of notebooks and began to read them, I was immediately confronted with a problem I had not noticed during my initial encounter with them in Ali's office. The fact was I could not read Mike's handwriting. It was pure chicken scratch to me.

I called Mike and told him I could not make out more than 15 percent of what he had written. He told me to keep reading and eventually I would figure out his "code." I knew that would not be the case, but I went back to the notes and tried again to decipher the scrawl. It was useless.

There was only one way to solve the problem. I would need to go to Lubbocks' home periodically and record Mike reading his journals, and then later transcribe the recordings in my office. This was a major inconvenience for both me and Mike. For me it was an extra step in the process that included a six-hour round-trip drive from my home in High Point. Initially Mike was reluctant to spend the extra time with me to record him reading the journals – valuable time he would be away from caring for his birds. But we both agreed it had to be done, and this is what we did over the course of four years.

I particularly remember the first reading session with Mike in the den of his home. I had set up the tape recorder and a video camera as a backup. Mike read aloud the journal of an expedition he made to Alaska in the early 1970s. It began with the usual list of minutia I've already described. After an hour, I began to wonder if there would be any interesting highlights.

Eventually the journal described his experiences in the wild, although it was still very dry. Then something happened that changed the course of the whole project. While reading about a predicament he faced crossing an ice flow, he put the journal down, took off his glasses, gazed into space and began filling in details of the incident from his memory. For thirty minutes or more, the story came to life. Animal encounters, nefarious characters, health issues with his expedition partner, a brush with danger, all came to light as his memory began firing on all cylinders. Throughout the rest of the journal, Mike continued to periodically fill in marvelous exploits of the trip between the details logged in the journal.

The same thing occurred when he read the second journal on his trip to the Canadian Arctic. This expedition was filled with the kind of adventure I remembered from Raiders of the Lost Ark. It was at this point that I suggested to Mike that we should write a book on his life and experiences in the wild. That was the genesis of the book project.

BIRD SENSE

I believe it is important for the reader to recognize that Mike Lubbock learned his craft through self-study, hard work, mentorship, and experience. He has never taken a single course in biology, ornithology, natural history, or any of the natural sciences. His knowledge has been nurtured with an ingredient sometimes missing in the world of academic science – passion.

Mike has something else in his repertoire that sets him above most others. Mike calls it "bird sense." It is the intuitive knowing of what a bird needs to be protected and have the proper environment for good health and breeding. This characteristic is different than just having knowledge of birds. It's an awareness that supersedes natural knowledge. Mike does not believe bird sense can be taught – one either has it or they don't. This gift has been especially helpful in achieving the avicultural success Mike has garnered over the years.

In addition, it should be noted that most of his expeditions occurred during a time not so long ago when many modern conveniences were yet to be invented or deployed. While in the remote Arctic landscape, Mike had no cell phone to call and let someone know of the perils he faced. In the wilds of Botswana, there were no major roads to the remote places where he searched for birds, only rutted trails, if he was lucky. This was when the wild was still largely inaccessible to all but the most prepared and hardened explorers. Today, some of these venues have become destinations for family vacationers.

THE JOURNEY BEGINS

A substantial portion of the book is presented in Mike's own words, taken either from interviews I conducted with him or directly from his field journals. My role is simply that of a storyteller. Determining which adventures to put in or leave out of the book was a daunting task. The stories included here will immerse the reader in the adventures of Mike Lubbock and the journey he has made from young bird enthusiast to avian breeder to conservationist.

Men such as Mike Lubbock only come along once in every generation, if that. I am honored to have been the author selected to share the astounding story of The Waterfowl Man with the world.

The Prologue contains a brief look at the conservation mission to Guatemala in 1984. This was the mid-point of Mike Lubbock's career, the momentous event that changed his approach for how to best save birds from extinction. As the book progresses, you will see why this was such a significant discovery.

— Dale True

PROLOGUE

Lake Atilán, Guatemala
April 9, 1984

Mike Lubbock climbed agilely into the boat and tossed his diving gear to Madelyn. Getting settled in the cramped, outdated watercraft was difficult for the lanky avian specialist. Discomfort was a familiar state he had learned to tolerate on his many expeditions to the far-flung corners of the world. Guatemala was no exception.

He gunned the throttle of the ancient outboard motor and sped toward a lagoon he had spotted while searching the area by helicopter earlier that morning. The lagoon was tucked away on the far side of the vast lake and difficult to see unless you knew it was there. But upon arrival he discovered the little canal was too shallow for even the small boat to navigate. His search for the Atilán Grebe would have to wait. On the way to the lagoon he had spotted some fishing nets that might hold a clue as to why the flightless grebe was disappearing from the lake – and more importantly, from existence.

The course was immediately altered to Santiago Bay. Upon arrival, he slipped off his short trousers, revealing his swim trunks underneath, and pulled his snorkeling equipment from under the seat. Sliding silently from the boat gunnel into the water, Mike closely examined the nets of the native fishermen. He found several set in the water and dove down the length of one of the lines to inspect it while Madelyn observed from the boat.

Mike knew the first net had been set for at least three days, because the one fish caught on the line was long dead. The law specified that nets could only be left in the water for a maximum of twelve hours. But every net he'd checked so far on this lake had obviously remained deployed much longer than that. His main worry was that any of the few grebes left would drown if they got caught up in the nets put out by the native fishermen.

He snorkeled on the water's surface, observing how the other nets were set.

"Mike! Watch out!" Madelyn shrieked with all the volume she could muster. "He's trying to hit you with his boat!" She hoped her warning was able to pierce through the water.

A native Guatemalan was fast approaching in his dugout, making a target of the interloper trespassing among his nets. Mike stopped swimming and looked at Madelyn, who was desperately pointing behind him. He turned and saw the bow of the dugout a mere twenty feet away, clearly aimed for the space of water he occupied.

Mike dove deep out of harm's way and waited on the bottom until the dugout departed from the area. It was easy to observe the dugout's location in the crystal-clear lake water. After a minute near the shallow bottom, he swam underwater toward Madelyn and emerged almost completely out of breath.

Mike hoisted himself into the boat. "That guy seemed determined to drive us out of the bay!"

Not willing to find out if the man might come back with his friends, Mike started the motor and slammed the throttle to the maximum limit, heading back to Panajachel where he would rendezvous with the rest of the team to compare notes. He now knew why the Atilán Grebe was in danger of extinction, but time was running out to save it.

* * * * * * * * * * *

The large flightless water bird known as the Atilán Grebe no longer exists on our planet. Despite the heroic efforts of a small group of biologists and conservationists, this bird has joined a rapidly expanding list of extinction's victims. The details of Mike Lubbock's role in those efforts and many other rescue efforts around the world will be detailed in the chapters ahead.

The futile experience of attempting to save the Atilán Grebe was a major turning point in the career of ornithologist Mike Lubbock. He understood the grave error in waiting too long to begin captive breeding programs to increase the survival of endangered bird species.

Many in the conservation biology community consider captive breeding programs to be an effort of last resort for saving birds at risk of extinction. They prefer to manage the habitat and the behavior of man in order to support threatened species, and presume that taking birds in from the wild for a managed program of breeding only makes their task more difficult.

Prior to the 1960s, this cautious view of captive breeding programs had its merits, and it still has some merit today. Although the breeding of waterfowl had been conducted for many decades, there were enormous difficulties when the breeding techniques of the day were applied to birds brought in from the wild. The methods of wild bird breeding were frequently unsuccessful.

However, by the 1970s, the art and science of aviculture was going through a renaissance of new innovation, led by Englishman Mike Lubbock. It was the young and resourceful Lubbock who began applying some of the natural techniques he learned from years of intense study of waterfowl behavior, both in the wild and during his time at the Wildfowl & Wetlands Trust in Slimbridge, England.

Mike Lubbock became an avid outdoorsman, prepared to go on any adventure into the wilderness, often risking his life in order to learn the secrets of the birds. His missions were always focused on finding ways to help waterfowl survive in a world becoming increasingly bereft of suitable habitat.

From his childhood days in England to building Sylvan Heights Bird Park into the world's largest collection of waterfowl, Mike's single-minded passion has been breeding and studying birds. Throughout his career he made extraordinary husbandry breakthroughs that have paved the way in protecting threatened waterfowl species from extinction.

It all started with a young boy and his extraordinary egg collection.

CHAPTER ONE

Taking Wing

Birds played a major role in each and every season of Mike Lubbock's life since the age of three. Throughout his boyhood days in rural England he collected bird eggs. His enthusiasm for eggs became so intense and consuming that the massive collection he gathered now resides at the American Museum of Natural History in New York City.

He is considered by many to be the world's foremost authority on avian breeding and behavior. He has traveled from the Arctic Circle to the remote sub-Antarctic regions of Patagonia, from Africa to Australia, in search of wild birds. His expeditions are legendary; his conservation accomplishments profuse.

Success and accolades have been showered upon him – 17 World's First Breeding Awards, induction into the International Wild Waterfowl Association's Hall of Fame, recipient of the prestigious Jean Delacour Avicultural Award. He and his wife Ali were named Entrepreneurs of the Year in 2007 for the establishment of Sylvan Heights Waterfowl Park & Eco-Center, now known as Sylvan Heights Bird Park.

However, Mike has never chased after awards or sought tribute for his achievements. The dream he still chases today, after more than 50 years of work as an ornithologist, is the thrill of seeing rare and endangered species of birds hatch from eggs – whether in the man-made incubators at Sylvan Heights' immense waterfowl breeding preserve or in a nest built by wild parent birds along the free-flowing rivers in Brazil.

Mike's avian dream took him on a journey that started in his boyhood home of southwestern England, crisscrossed the globe several times on expeditions, and eventually brought him to the rural farming community of Scotland Neck, North Carolina. Here, with his wife Ali, he established the Sylvan Heights Waterfowl & Bird Park, a spectacular place for visitors to not only see birds in a natural environment, but also to witness conservation in action.

The birds of Sylvan Heights comprise one of the most biologically significant waterfowl collections in the world. Far more than merely an aggregate of ducks, geese, and swans, Sylvan Heights' public park and private breeding preserve is the site of an ongoing international work of waterfowl preservation. The magnificent ecological bird park and waterfowl breeding center speaks volumes with regards to Mike's dedication to the preservation of the world's waterfowl.

BIRD SENSE AND FEATHER FINGERS

Saying Mike Lubbock has a way with birds is synonymous with saying Mozart had a knack for writing music.

Mike's bond with birds defies categorization. Like most ornithologists, he engages in memorization of facts and applies the principle of observation. Observation of avian behavior in the wild is a major factor in his success with breeding birds. This is why his explorations to the wild and remote places of the world were so important.

Anyone who has seen Mike stroll the grounds of Sylvan Heights comes to the same conclusion – he spends an immense amount of time observing dozens of birds at once, waiting for them to reveal their secrets. Then he calculates how to apply his discoveries in ways that allow him to transform Sylvan Heights' pens and aviaries into the best facsimile of the birds' natural environment, regardless of which part of the world the species originally called home.

Mike: There are very few people that I can actually say have bird sense – it's something I can't teach someone else. You've either got it or you haven't. It's like in cattle farming. Say a farmer has a herd of 70 cows. He knows those cows and has a feel for them. He'll go out to his field, and even though he doesn't count them, he knows there's one missing. I have that sense for birds. When I go around the aviaries, I know if there's a bird missing. I can't tell you how I know; but when I count them, sure enough there's one missing. It seems strange, but I've always had that kind of thing.

People ask me, "How do you know all those birds?" I look after the bird park and the breeding preserve – thousands of birds. Yet I'll go around and ask the staff, "Where's this one? Where's that one?" I have a feel for it; that's what I mean by bird sense. I've been fortunate to have that feeling for birds all my life. I guess it's like a green thumb in gardening. I must have feather fingers.

Bird sense best describes the connection Mike has exhibited with birds throughout his life – as a young boy tracking down bird nests, as a young explorer who found eggs when others could not, or sensing the needs of the birds at Sylvan Heights. It's that kind of mysterious man-to-bird connection a young intern at Sylvan Heights noticed some years ago, and made the first reference to Mike Lubbock as the "Waterfowl Man." The name stuck with the interns who come each year to learn advanced avicultural techniques and avian behavior from the expert. It has since become a common moniker for those who recognize the avian bond Mike Lubbock has established.

Mike's fascination for nature could have steered him toward any type of bird or animal. During his youth, he was especially intrigued by owls and hawks, but he loved and studied all animals and their natural environments.

Throughout his entire career, Mike gained his awareness of the natural world from books he read and from his experiences caring for animals. Nowhere in his résumé is listed a college degree or even a single course on natural history or biology. Everything he learned about bird behavior was by observation. Often, he would sit in front of a nest location for hours at a time, just watching the birds as they came and went, recording all their natural tendencies in his head. These learning experiences began early in his life and continued throughout his career. Immersion in the natural world has given him mastery in many areas, including ornithology, aviculture, botany, and zoology. He is arguably the century's most esteemed and successful self-taught naturalist.

POST-WORLD WAR II ENGLAND

Mike was born in Taunton, Somerset, England on the 17th of January, 1944. His parents met in London during World War II. Ralph Hugh Lubbock was in charge of the barrage balloons that hovered over London to confuse the enemy's attempt to bomb the city from the air. Alfreda Vavasour Dawson was a WRAF (Women's Royal Air Force) and worked in the home office, mapping out aircraft routes for the Royal Air Force. Ralph was considerably older than Alfreda.

After the war, the couple moved to the Blackdown Hills of rural southwest England, where they established a dairy farm in Churchstanton. This was a very small village without even so much as a single shop in its boundary.

Alfreda Vavasour Dawson of the Women's Royal Air Force with dog, Raffles.

Mike: The war had been a difficult time for everyone in England. Rationing was still going on for years after the war. How my parents were able to take up farming has always been a little puzzling to me. My father, who was then in his early sixties, had never farmed before. My mother, who had just turned thirty, had spent most of her life living in London. She also knew nothing about farming.

The West Country was still very backwards then compared to London. Why did they choose the rural Blackdown Hills as a place to settle down? They were either foolhardy or adventurous. However, what I remember of those seven years on the farm influenced my life forever.

BIRDS' NESTS AND EGGS

While Mike's adventurous spirit appears to have been inherited from his parents, his passion for avian husbandry clearly stems from his early years growing up on the family farm.

Mike's mother was his greatest influence at this early age. She was not only a mother, but also a friend. They would go on long walks through the farm, down to the woods. His love of birds grew from these mother-and-son excursions to look for birds' nests. Through these early contacts with nature, Mike developed an avid curiosity for birds' nests and eggs.

Mike: In those days taking eggs was not illegal. I would only take one egg from any nest I found and move on to the next one. It was in this manner that I began studying

20

birds, learning to identify them and observing their habits. There weren't many bird books around then, but I had an old one that I used to identify birds such as a Black Cap, a type of warbler. I used my book every time I saw a nest or a bird I didn't recognize.

My mother never prevented me from climbing trees. In fact, I remember a kestrel's nest built in an old Magpie's nest at the top of a holly tree. My mother was on the ground directing me to the next branch as I ascended the tree. She also helped me rear a Jackdaw (a member of the crow family) when I was six years old. I do not remember what happened to the bird, but I do remember collecting it from an old hollow apple tree.

One day my mother and I went into the woods where there was a badger den. We found a young badger that had been kicked out of the set, probably because he was ill. We took the youngster home to see if we could nurse it back to health, but it did not survive the next day.

There was also a hollow tree at the far end of the woods near a badger set. A tawny owl nested in the hollow. There was a small hole that one could peer into from the back of the tree. It was too high for me to see into, but my mother would hold me up for long periods of time to watch the incubating owl eggs. Later we watched the young owls grow and eventually fly.

LIFE ON THE FARM

In this pastoral setting, Mike learned the value of work and the requirement to always be readily available to the unabated needs of animals in his care.

The disciplined life of farming was the perfect preparation for the rigorous tasks he would face many years later when he founded Sylvan Heights Waterfowl Center.

The Lubbocks' dairy farm had a herd of handsome Ayrshire cattle, which needed to be milked twice a day. A local man was hired to be in charge of all milking activities. The milking machine had an engine which produced a vacuum on the suction cups placed on the cows' udders. This process always fascinated Mike, who watched intently as the white liquid made its way through the pipes and then fell down over a

Ralph Lubbock exercizing bull with long pole.

cooling device that had cold water going through it. The milk would then go through another pipe to be collected in a big glass jar before running into a milk churn, which would later be picked up and taken to the milk factory for distribution.

All the cattle had horns, which is a husbandry practice rarely seen these days. They also had a bull with large horns. He had a large ring in his nose to which his father would attach a long pole to guide the massive animal around the yard. This afforded the bull the exercise needed during the winter months when he was kept in a small stall and could not be let out into the pastures.

Mike: I was with my father one winter's day while the bull was being exercised in the corral. My father slipped on the ice as he maneuvered the huge animal. The bull was very quick to react. He put his head down, picked up my father with his horns and tossed him over a six-foot wall. I remember running as fast as I could to the nearest gate, which had a hinged latch holding it closed. The latch was too high for me to reach. My father was still down while the bull roamed free and then headed right for me. I gave up trying to open the gate and managed to climb over it to safety with the bull in hot pursuit. I ran in panic to get help.

My father was taken to the hospital. He had some nasty injuries to his head, nearly losing an ear and suffered a punctured lung and broken ribs. He was lucky to have survived. As a result of this incident, the entire herd was dehorned.

To this day I treat bulls with great respect, even if they don't have horns.

Mike treasured all the farm animals, except for one. A domestic goose gander cornered him once and thereafter would always chase young Master Lubbock at every opportunity. He was terrified of geese for a long time. It seems so ironic that the Waterfowl Man's first encounter with a member of the waterfowl family was far less than ideal.

Farming in those days was very hard work. There was no electricity and very few machines, so horses were used for many tasks. The farmers around the Churchstanton area had a strong sense of community. Everyone knew each other and would always help out should anyone have a problem or a need.

One essential need of nearly every farm family occurred during the harvest. Threshing one's crop, the process of removing the grain from the stalks of barley, wheat, or oats, was a bigger chore than a single family could do alone, so the whole community pitched in to help.

Threshing days in autumn were a big event. The threshing machine was large and was towed behind a tractor, which in those days had a steam engine. The tractor and threshing machine in Churchstanton were owned by two brothers. One brother controlled the tractor while the other was pitching the wheat into the machine.

The threshing for one farm would take all day. All the local farmers would come and help the family. That family would return the favor when it came time to thresh the others' harvest. There was only one threshing machine that would go around to the different farms in the area.

Mike: In the evening, everyone involved in the threshing would stay for a big ham supper, which was accompanied by lots of rough cider called scrumpy. This was a very strong apple cider, poured out of earthenware jars. The cider was brewed locally by one of the farmers.

The ham was also brought by one of the farmers, butchered locally and then cured by the local baker. This was illegal to do, but many of the farmers that kept pigs usually butchered at least once a year and shared the meat and sausage with their neighbors.

BOARDING SCHOOL

Living in the isolated Blackdown Hills can cause a growing adventurous boy to become restless. The village had only a small school.

Mike's parents were very worried as to whether or not this school was best for the rambunctious lad. One very apparent problem was that Mike began speaking with a broad Somerset accent, which sounded out the "Z's" and "R's," plus picking up swear words from the local children. His parents were concerned Mike would end up speaking in this local dialect. The only other school with a kindergarten and a good reputation was a convent in Taunton, which was run by nuns. It was decided that the five-year-old Lubbock would attend the convent school rather than the one in the village.

Every day after classes were over, the bus dropped Mike off at a stop nearly a mile and a half from home. His mother would always meet him and they'd walk the road home looking for birds, birds' nests, or just admire the beautiful English countryside.

Mike: I learned to read and write and do arithmetic by the time
        I reached the ripe old age of seven. But I was becoming
        very inquisitive. I imagined, for instance, what the nuns
        looked like without the habits they wore on their heads.
        Since they always had them on at school, I couldn't be
        sure they had any hair. This was something I desperately
        wanted to know.

        My mother read stories to me quite often and one of
        my favorites was Winnie the Pooh. In one of Pooh's
        escapades, he and Piglet dug a deep hole and covered it
        with leaves in order to catch a heffalump. They baited the
        trap with a jar of honey. I thought this was a great idea,
        so with the help of another boy, we dug a big hole
        (though not very deep) and covered it with sticks and
        leaves so the hole could not be seen. The idea was for the
        nun to fall in, and while floundering, her habit would fall
        off and we'd then know if she had hair or not. The plan
        actually worked, except I was not around when she fell
        into the trap. Luckily she was not hurt.

        Straightaway I was summoned to the Mother
        Superior's office. Sister Mary-Michael had seen me earlier
        that day on the convent grounds with a beach shovel. My
        actions made her suspicious and she decided I must know
        something about this freshly dug hole. Soon after this my
        father was sent for, and following a short discussion I was

dismissed from the school.

After this incident, my parents decided to send me to boarding school. I remember wondering how my parents could hate me so much as to send me away. But I soon learned that sending a young English boy to boarding school was the normal thing to do in those days.

The boarding school chosen for the high-spirited Lubbock was called Kestrels, which is named after a species of hawk. It was located in East Anstey, situated in the scenic countryside of Exmoor, about fifty miles from the Lubbocks' farm in Churchstanton. The school was once a very large gabled house. The owner of the school was Mr. Stapleton, who was also the headmaster. Mr. Stapleton had purchased the large estate house and turned it into a prep school. The vast property included a main gate, a sizable stable, and another house that had once functioned as a servants' quarters.

Mike: I don't know why my parents chose this school except it had only 65 students and my father liked Mr. Stapleton. Mr. Stapleton had gone to Rugby School (where the game of rugby was invented) and played cricket, two sports on which my father was very keen. My father was once a very good cricketer and kept wicket for Eton. He played for the team during a very famous match against their archrival Harrow. It was called the Fowler's Match. The score cards for this match are still on display in the Long Room at Lord's. In return, Mr. Stapleton also liked my father because of his cricket skills.

Prior to his relocation to Kestrels School, Mike's mother took him to a shop in Exeter to buy a variety of items needed for his new life away from home. This included a tuck box, which holds a student's personal property at the school. These were fairly large and had a domed top that one could lock. It rather resembled a small Davy Jones' locker.

It was with great trepidation and melancholy that Mike faced his future at Kestrels. The thought of leaving behind his animals and the woods where he and his mother searched for nests was unbearable.

Abandoned in Exmoor

A cold and bleak day ushered in the winter term of 1951 at Kestrels. Attempting to delay the approach of this sinister event, a solemn Mike Lubbock sat in the back of the family car, hoping the remaining miles left to East Anstey would never come to nil. Mike could not appreciate the beauty in the gently rolling Exmoor hills. Only dark thoughts swirled in his troubled mind. The first day of prep school had arrived, and with it the abrupt and sorrowful end of his joyous, carefree life on the farm.

Mike: I was dropped off with my apparel, tuck box and some pocket money. There were several new boys who, like myself, were looking very dejected and upset. My parents made ready to leave and I clung to my mother for all I was worth. I did not want her to leave me at this place in the middle of nowhere with 64 boys I didn't know.

As I watched my parents disappear down the drive, I sobbed heavily, but to no avail. No one took any notice of me as they carried on with what they were doing. I was only seven and absolutely terrified, having no idea of what would happen to me. I felt I had been abandoned in Exmoor.

Mike Lubbock at Kestrels, age 7.

Crying did little good, so after a while young Lubbock had no other choice but to pull himself together. He plucked up his courage and asked one of the older boys what he should do. The boy was very kind and showed Mike the cellar where his tuck box was to be kept. This would be the only place to store all his valuable items, including the highly prized weekly ration of candy. He then took Mike to the dorm where he'd be sleeping with ten other boys, pointing out the location of the bathroom and lockers along the way.

The matron called for all the new boys to gather. She laid down all the rules, such as not talking after lights out. The matron's quarters were opposite Mike's dormitory, requiring her to come through his room to get to hers; therefore, his every move would be observed. The matron was also in charge of handing out the sweets.

Mike: Every day after lunch, the whole school would form a line and file by the matron, standing by a big cupboard which held 65 tins of goodies, one for each boy. When I finally got to the cupboard, she would reach up and grab my tin and give me a candy or chocolate bar.

In the early '50s, sugar was strictly rationed and chocolate in particular was hard to get. As such, I needed to get a candy request to the matron every two weeks in order to keep my tin full. Having a chocolate bar every day was a sure way to find your candy tin empty when you got up to the cupboard. Being the first boy to run out was especially embarrassing. It would be at least a week before the candy rations flowed again. So, I often ordered pear drops, mixed toffees or fruit lollys, which seemed to be far less rationed.

The first winter term was very traumatic. There was no one to turn to for comfort or solace. Almost immediately the bullies attempted to exert their dominance on the younger students. The only alternative was to stand up to them. Mike went to work to make friends, who would stand together against the ruffians.

Rugby was the only sport available during the winter term. Mr. Stapleton was a big fan of the sport, having gone to the school where rugby was invented. Despite being only seven years of age, Mike played with the juniors. He was a good runner and could kick the ball, so he tried out at fly-half, which is a key position that gets the ball first after a scrum. Mike excelled at fly-half position and played through his senior years.

Within a year of Mike's enrollment at Kestrels, his parents gave up farming. They moved to Webbington in Somerset, about a hundred miles from the school. Mike's father worked for Avery's Wines in Bristol.

Mike Lubbock front and center holding the ball.

RETURN TO NATURE

As far as Mike was concerned, one of the few redeeming features of Kestrels School was it was named after a bird. Even the school's three houses were named after raptors, Mike's being the Eagles House. Birds were the common thread that kept him connected to his treasured memories of life on the farm. As he became accustomed to the routine of Kestrels, he began to find more and more time to pursue his first love – caring for animals and egg collecting.

During his time at Kestrel's, Mike made a good friend in Simon Hellings. They were both interested in the natural world. Simon was a fantastic tree climber. Every Sunday afternoon during the summer they would sneak off to new terrain in the countryside to find birds' nests. They always returned to school with their clothes dirty, pants stained green from tree moss and shirts torn from being caught on limbs and briars. The matron was never pleased with the school boys climbing trees.

The entire time Mike attended Kestrels he could barely concentrate on lessons. He was merely counting down the hours and minutes before he could get out of class to be in the woods, look for nests, collect eggs, and care for his animals.

Mike: Sunday afternoons were my favorite time. We could hike anywhere on the grounds, as long as we were back by four o'clock in the winter and by five o'clock in summer. There were wonderful woods everywhere with lots of birds. The early summer was my favorite season, as many birds were nesting then. Climbing trees was one of my most enjoyable pastimes, though I'm not sure it was allowed. Egg collecting was my hobby, and many times I climbed up to a buzzard's or a magpie's nest for a prized egg.

Simon's father was often out of the country in the marines. Since Simon had no family close by, he often came home with Mike during breaks in the school year. Even though the family no longer worked on a farm, Webbington was very much a farming community in an idyllic country setting. Mike was always thrilled to return home, especially with his good friend Simon who enjoyed the outdoors almost as much as did Mike. They gleefully explored the local farms, woods, and even ventured into the caves in the area. They climbed nearby Crook Peak, which can be seen from many miles. This distinctive crest on the western edge of the Mendip Hills is covered by open gorse and scrub. Mike's mother would often take the dogs up the peak's sharp incline.

Although his initial admission to Kestrel's School was one of dejection and sorrow, Mike eventually learned to not only make the best of the situation, but also to thrive. He was able to make his passion for nature and animals a major part of his life at school.

Mike: Animals were always a part of my life. From the time I can remember I kept various mammals and birds. My mother had encouraged me. I still did such things at prep school, from the age of 7 until 14. In the later years at Kestrels, I got away with a lot regarding pets.
I had ferrets and rabbits, birds, eggs, and lots of other things. The headmaster allowed me to keep an owl at school. In the school photo, I was the head boy, and I'm shown in the picture holding an owl on my finger.

As his tenure at Kestrels came to a close, it was time for Mike to discuss his future with his father. Becoming a farmer was not an option, as his parents didn't own the farm on which they worked. C.S. Forester's nautical series on Horatio Hornblower had intrigued Mike greatly. He thought sailing the seas in the navy would allow him to discover and study whatever wildlife lived in the vast world outside of England. Wherever the navy sent him, he could set off into the local countryside and find animals and nests, exactly as he did on the farm and even at Kestrels.

Mike decided that attending the Nautical College in Pangbourne was his next step. He figured he would join the Merchant Navy after graduation and see the world.

Mike: Pangbourne was the elite of the nautical colleges in England. I had a good interview with them. But I was one of the first Lubbocks not to attend school at Eton. It would have been very easy for me to gain entrance there with my lineage.

Playing sports became as helpful at Pangbourne in occupying his mind as it had been at Kestrel's. Mike was good at cricket, especially, as a bowler. There was also a natural history society that he was allowed to join during his second year at Pangbourne. There were not many members, but the society offered opportunities to observe nature or go fishing. He even managed to keep his ferret at school under the guise of a natural history project.

THE WILDFOWL & WETLANDS TRUST

Schooling at Pangbourne turned out not to be as intriguing an idea as Mike had hoped. Being a military college, there was lots of discipline and marching all the time. None of this interested him. Nor did the school work, which was essential to advancing in the navy. During class, he always chose a seat by the window that looked out over a piggery in the countryside, not far from the college. While the master taught subjects that held no interest to him, Mike would stare out the window and watch the pigs. His naval career was going nowhere.

After completing only his second year of college, Mike went to his father and pleaded with him to leave Pangbourne. Instead of donning a sailor's uniform, he sought sage advice from his father on how to begin a career working with birds. It was then that the door to the world of waterfowl opened wide and beckoned young Mike Lubbock to step inside.

Traveling the world to study wildlife became the plan in which Mike would pursue his passion for nature. This was exactly how his hero Peter Scott observed and studied animals in the wild.

Mike: I enjoyed watching Peter Scott's TV series on nature. It was similar to David Attenborough's show. Peter Scott went around the world and looked for animals and birds. It was called the *"Look"* programs. Seeing him in New Guinea, or someplace like that, studying wildlife really caught my attention. Those programs fascinated me.

Peter Scott was a hero to me because of where he traveled and how he presented animals to the public. I wanted to discover birds and animals on distant continents like he did in those shows. From age 14 to 17, watching Peter Scott on television enticed me more and more into the natural world.

Mike has no idea how his father knew of the Wildfowl & Wetlands Trust, most commonly referred to as the Wildfowl Trust. Mike certainly didn't know much about it or even that his boyhood hero, the explorer and ornithologist Peter Scott, had founded the conservation preserve in 1946 at Slimbridge, England on the estuary of the River Severn. Within a short time, however, Mike's father had arranged an interview for his son at the Wildfowl Trust.

Mike: Ducks, geese, and swans were not my favorite birds at that time. If there had been a hawk trust, I may have veered toward that; I'm not sure.

I didn't know very much about the Wildfowl Trust, but my father wanted to take me up there. Before that, it was thought that I might work at the Nature Conservancy, which was a government-run organization where you could go and study birds in central England or study grasses somewhere. That wasn't what I wanted to do.

But my father got me an interview at the Wildfowl Trust, and that was the start to the whole adventure. I had never been there before, but we went and looked around. It was much smaller then than it is now. It was only about 30 acres and much wilder. I remember meeting the controller there. I always remembered him because he was called Brigadier Sparrow. I thought that was a fitting name for a man working at the Wildfowl Trust.

Mike didn't meet his hero, Peter Scott, during the interview. But he toured the facility and met many of the approximately 30 staff members working there, including the curator, Tommy Johnstone. Once all the formalities and been dispensed, Brigadier Sparrow summed up the situation by saying, "Well there are no openings on the grounds staff. There are no openings anywhere." But he said, "If you want to volunteer, we could fit you in. Maybe you could help out in the laboratory."

Becoming a volunteer for the prestigious Wildfowl & Wetlands Trust in Slimbridge, England is how Mike Lubbock began his life with waterfowl. It was 1961 and he was 17 years old.

Mike: My father could tell that working with birds was doing something I really wanted to do. He told me I may have problems in the future because I would never make any money at this. But he reckoned if I stuck with it and if I became an expert, and if I could make a difference in this field, then that would be something worth doing.

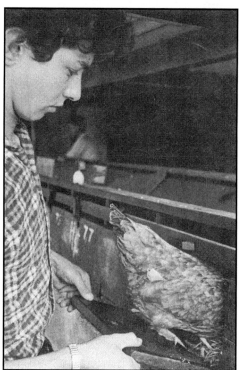

Mike with broody hen.

Six months after I started at the Wildfowl Trust my father died. He was a man of few words, but I can hear his voice right now telling me, "When the hard times come and you don't know how you're going to carry on, you have to stick to it." I always remember that and I have told my son, Brent, the same thing.

Mike's first assignment was weighing eggs with Dr. Janet Kear. Dr. Kear was a research scientist who had been recruited to the

Wildfowl & Wetlands Trust by Peter Scott to work in the laboratory program. She was doing research which some years later would result in the formation of conservation programs and the writing of several important books on birds. But being stuck inside a lab recording measurements on eggs wasn't what Mike wanted to do.

Mike: I ventured outside and came to Tommy Johnstone, who was the curator. I asked if I could volunteer with the grounds staff. He told me, "There are no openings, but sure you can." So I did that.

As a volunteer, he was allowed to stay in a local guest house, for which his father paid rent. But Mike's tenure as a volunteer only lasted about six weeks. Tommy Johnstone had observed Mike's tenacity and determination and offered him a paid position with the grounds staff.

Mike: I must have impressed Tommy Johnstone, because I learned to identify every bird species in three weeks. I knew every bird in the place. I even knew how many birds were in each pen. I was keen on every detail. When five o'clock came, I wouldn't go back to the guest house; I just stayed on the grounds until dark, taking it all in. I certainly felt this was the life for me.

Mike's wages were only 7 pounds per week. At first there was no room for him in the hostels provided by the Trust, so he had to pay someone out of pocket to stay at their place and provide a meal at night and a sandwich for lunch.

DANCING DAYS

During Mike's early years at the Wildfowl Trust, he was cast as a dancer on a teen dance show called *Discs a Go-Go*, which was recorded in Bristol and hosted by Kent Walton.

Developed in 1962 by the Westcountry Television Network, the show very much mimicked Dick Clark's *American Bandstand* in the United States. *Discs a Go-Go* featured music and dances that were popular in England as Rock and Roll became prominent during the late '50s and early '60s.

Eighteen-year-old Mike Lubbock had a knack for dancing, especially the unrestrained and energetic dance called the Jive. Dancing was his preferred method of letting off steam during his time off from the Wildfowl Trust. One night after winning a Jive contest in the town of Cheltenham, Mike and his dance partner were approached by two talent scouts from *Discs a Go-Go*.

Mike: A guy and a girl came up to us and asked if we wanted to try out for *Discs a Go-Go*. I had heard of it, so I said, "Sure! Where do you do it?" He said the show was filmed up in Cardiff, Wales. Well that was a little difficult because I had to get down to Bristol and then get a train to Cardiff.

But we went to the audition. Ten couples had been selected from around the West Country. They only wanted five couples, but we were chosen.

Mike on set, pictured center back.

Fortuitously, the filming of the show was soon moved to Bristol, which was close to Slimbridge. This allowed Mike to work six days a week at the Wildfowl Trust and spend his day off dancing on the show.

Mike and the other dancers were tasked with learning the popular dances in America, such as the Twist, Hully Gully, Mashed Potatoes, the Jerk, and the Fly. The producers would get a dance film from the United States. After watching the film on the day of the show, the cast worked with a choreographer and had only two hours to learn the new dance before performing it that afternoon.

One of the perks of being on *Discs a Go-Go* was that Mike rubbed shoulders with some of the great British bands of the Sixties. The Beatles, Rolling Stones, Dave Clark Five, Yardbirds, Kinks, and Animals were among a litany of rock royalty that performed their hit songs on the show. These were the groups that ushered in what is known in America as the British Invasion.

After a show, the cast and performers would get together at a country club in Bristol where they were entertained by a singer or magician. This venue gave Mike even more opportunities to meet face to face with current and future rock stars.

Mike: When the Yardbirds came to *Discs a Go-Go*, we went over to the club after the show. I was sitting on the stairs right next to Eric Clapton [lead guitarist for the Yardbirds]. We were just talking away. And I'll always remember, he turned to me and asked me a question in a very Cockney accent that he had in those days. He asked me what the producers thought of the Yardbirds. I said, I think they thought you were really good.

The Beatles were on the show. It was 1963 and they were just hitting it big in England. We would talk to them a bit during rehearsals, but they never came with us to the club. I forget the all songs they did, but one of them was "Please, Please Me," their first big hit. They came on the show twice, and then we could never book them again.

Jimi Hendrix came on the show. During his performance, he set his guitar on fire. That was

Picture of Mike from Discs a Go-Go

spectacular, and everyone took a step back and said, "Wow!" That became a signature feature of his act, but our show may have been one of the first venues where he did it.

The Dave Clark Five did the show often, even after they became famous. For a long time people thought Dave Clark was the singer, but he was actually the drummer. They shot a film, *Catch Me If You Can*, in the Mendip Hills, which is just outside of Bristol. We were invited up there while they were filming. We became extras for the movie.

None of these people sang live on the show. They always mimed the words to their record. A funny incident occurred when The Who came down to do the show. Their first record had a keyboard part that was played by a studio musician. The producer asked which one of them played the piano. They said, "None of us." The producer said, "Well, I know it's mimed, but we need someone to play the piano." In the end, he wouldn't allow them on the show and they never came back.

Ironically, no one, including Mike, really knew anything about the British bands that appeared on the show in those days. It was just before the Beatles made a full-scale invasion of the United States, ushering in a new style of Rock-and-Roll music to the world.

Mike: It's funny, you look back and realize these groups are so big now and yet they weren't back then. I was more excited when we had singers from America, like Gene Pitney, Roy Orbison, and Lorne Greene (from the TV show Bonanza).

Plus we had big singers from England, like Frank Ifeld, who was bigger than the Beatles at that time, and Tom Jones. In fact, the first TV show Tom Jones ever did was our show. I remember talking to him and I noticed he kept a lucky rabbit's foot on him all the time. His big hit was "It's Not Unusual," which he performed on the show.

Mike's celebrity rose along with the popularity of *Discs a Go-Go*. This became a problem when the public discovered where Mike worked at his "day job."

Mike: There was a newspaper article printed about me meeting the Duke of Edinburgh. The headline was, "Disco Dancer Meets Duke of Edinburgh." That's how people knew I worked at the Wildfowl Trust.

After that article appeared, I couldn't go out on the grounds because the kids would recognize me and cause a commotion. It was decided that I should stay behind the scenes, especially on weekends when it was crowded. It wasn't the best situation for me, but I guess it put more visitors through the gates of the Wildfowl Trust.

Mike performed on *Discs a Go-Go* for nearly five years. Eventually Mike walked away from the spotlight and the thrill of the show.

Mike: It was a lot of fun, but hard work. I was working six days a week at the Wildfowl Trust and doing TV one day a week, plus going to clubs in the evening to finds kids for the show. I was really burning the candle at both ends. But it was very good money for back then – 250 pounds per show. All my clothes and travel expenses were paid.

I didn't regret my decision to stop dancing – it wasn't what I wanted to do anyway. Plus it took a lot out of me; even though I was very young, it was tiring. But it was quite an experience, and sometimes I look back and wonder, "Did I really do it?"

During his time on the show, Mike never lost focus on his work with waterfowl. Once he stopped dancing, his celebrity quickly faded and life at the Wildfowl Trust returned to normal.

Mike: I owe the Scott family a tremendous amount of gratitude. They really gave me a lot of confidence. They let me do my TV work. I mean, they could have said that I could either work at Wildfowl Trust or dance on *Discs a Go-Go*. But they didn't make me choose.

I remember going up to do rocket netting for Greylag Geese in Scotland. I had to come back all the way to Bristol on a Wednesday to dance on the show and then go back to Scotland again. They let me do that. There were a lot of things that when I look back on it, I really owe them. That's life and things happen, but I just think sometimes I don't give them enough credit.

Mike was in the right place, doing the right things to position himself as an expert in waterfowl husbandry. He was living his life's dream. Soon the focal point of his dream would shift to another continent. The saga of the Waterfowl Man was ready to take flight.

CHAPTER TWO

Coming to America

"Doing what you love is freedom; loving what you do is happiness."

Mike loved working at the Wildfowl Trust. It was the realization of his boyhood dream. Every day he searched for eggs, cared for the birds, and learned more about their mysterious ways. Not only was he on the grounds staff, he was also part of the education staff. Anytime a school group or tour came, he would show them around and tell them about the birds.

Mike became involved in projects outside the grounds, such as rocket netting birds in Scotland for the purpose of banding and tracking them. (Rocket netting is a method of trapping a large number of birds or other animals. One end of a expansive net, folded like an accordion, is staked to the ground, while the other end has charges attached that propel the net up and over the flock when detonated.)

He was also selected to go on expeditions in the wild to collect birds important to the Trust's conservation projects.

After a few years he had worked his way up to the position of assistant curator for the Wildfowl Trust, accumulating more and more responsibility for the birds in the collection.

Mike: My big thing was breeding birds. I really enjoyed collecting eggs and breeding birds because that's what I used to do when I was young. Setting up the birds, bringing them back after an expedition and hatching them, this was to me very, very interesting. There were long hours, but it didn't seem long to me because it was so fascinating.

THE FIRST EXPEDITION: ICELAND

Expeditions would become a major component of Mike Lubbock's life with birds. Throughout his career, he has made more than 20 journeys for the purpose of collecting birds or eggs, or as a consultant to governments and conservation organizations.

In the early years he was sent on expeditions to collect species of birds that were needed for special breeding programs conducted by the Wildfowl Trust. In those days, the only way to obtain some species of birds was to go into the wild and catch them. Today this practice is not only frowned upon, but is illegal in many countries.

However, had these birds not been collected when they were, several species of birds might have become extinct. Survival breeding programs, such as those currently employed at the Sylvan Heights Avian Breeding Center, are at the forefront of protecting waterfowl and other bird species. Interestingly, some of the birds at Sylvan Heights are descendents of birds Mike and other explorers caught in the wild during the 1960s and 1970s.

Mike: There has always been excitement in collecting for me. Going to a remote place, collecting eggs, then bringing them back, hatching and rearing them, and then breeding them. That whole sequence was a challenge I enjoyed. For my life, that was *the* challenge.

The most important outcome of this was that by learning more about these species of birds, we could help them to survive in the wild if a problem developed, such as a declining population or loss of habitat. The more I learned about certain birds, the more I could help others that were in trouble.

My expeditions were not just about going into an area, finding a nest, collecting eggs or catching up birds. There were incredible amounts of time spent on observation of bird behavior. I learned a great deal in the wild. And all that came into play during my life – it's all I've wanted to do.

Mike was chosen to be part of the Wildfowl Trust's Scientific Team, which utilized rocket netting in Scotland to identify banded geese and provide important census data. He also organized several other trips to Scotland to collect eggs of European Eider, Goosander, Red-breasted Merganser, and European Scoter.

Mike's first expedition to collect birds for the Wildfowl Trust was to Iceland in 1969 when he was 23 years old.

Mike: I was still wet behind the ears. The mission was to catch Long-tailed Ducks and Harlequin Ducks. Along with me on this trip were Christopher Sellick and Peter Gladstone.

Peter was related to the Gladstones, a famous family in English history. (William Ewart Gladstone was the prime minister of England four separate times from 1868 to 1894.) Chris Sellick had been on trips with the Wildfowl Trust to South America and various other places, including Iceland.

Mike: I had known Chris before the Iceland expedition. He had gone to Argentina and India and brought birds back to Slimbridge, so he had experience. Peter was a master at Shrewsbury School, where he also kept a bird collection. There were some really good students there who later went on to work with birds. I knew of several students who studied with him. I wish I had gone to that school!

Chris and Peter didn't work for the Trust, but they liked doing expeditions. They had their own nets. We agreed that any birds we caught would come to Slimbridge.

The plan was for Chris to fly ahead to Iceland and make arrangements for the expedition. Mike and Peter loaded the Wildfowl Trust's Land Rover and their equipment onto a large passenger-cargo boat, the Gullfoss, which left from Leith, Scotland.

Mike: The voyage to Iceland took three days. The weather started off with nice, calm seas. We were all enjoying ourselves, but soon were hit by a force 9 gale. It got even worse that night. We made sure the Land Rover was battened down securely.

The next morning no one had the stomach to eat breakfast. Everyone was sick. The seas remained rough all the way to Iceland. That was my first experience with a bad storm at sea. I remember thinking I was glad I didn't join the navy!

After making port in Iceland, Mike and Peter disembarked from the Gullfoss and made their way inland to rendezvous with Chris Sellick. The team established a base and began catching birds soon after. The Harlequin Ducks were located along various rivers. They were caught by setting nets at one end of the river and then pushing the ducks down the river toward the nets.

Mike: Chris Sellick taught me different techniques for catching birds with nets. This experience helped me when I went to Africa and other places.

Acquiring Long-tails was more difficult and time-consuming. The nets had to be set across lakes. Mike had to get permission from some of the farmers in the area to access the lakes where the Longtails resided.

Mike: I remember we were on a farmer's property. He had these wonderful lakes below his house on a hill. There was a little rubber boat we could use to get out to the nets. Late one night while we were all drinking scotch, the farmer told us the story of a Viking that was killed at this particular lake. The legend is that every so often the Viking would come up out of the water with his sword raised, and then disappear back down into the lake.

When my turn came to go out on the lake late that night, I got in the boat and paddled out to check the nets. Suddenly the whole night sky started to shimmer with colors – absolutely amazing – just like a curtain effect dancing across the sky. I thought – "My gosh! That big Viking fellow could be coming up with his sword at any minute and pierce my boat!" I had never seen the aurora borealis before and that's what it was – the northern lights. But I'll never forget how concerned I was about that Viking coming after me.

The team managed to catch Longtail Ducks on the farmers' lakes. They had brought collapsible boxes so the birds could be shipped to London by air and picked up by Wildfowl Trust staff at the airport. Peter and Chris flew back to England and Mike went home on the cargo ship with the Land Rover and equipment.

The experience in Iceland was great fun for Mike. It was a short and straightforward adventure and provided a basis for knowing what to expect in the future. The Iceland trip was just the beginning of a long series of demanding, grueling, and sometimes frightfully dangerous expeditions on which Mike Lubbock would journey over the next 15 years.

PETER SCOTT & JEAN DELACOUR

The saga of the Waterfowl Man began in earnest when Mike was promoted to Curator of Birds of the Wildfowl & Wetlands Trust in Slimbridge. It was during this time that he developed two professional relationships that helped propel his career to astounding heights. Sir Peter Scott and Jean Delacour became essential mentors for Mike as he studied birds and gained an appreciation for the need to preserve them for future generations to enjoy.

Shortly after arriving as a volunteer at the Wildfowl Trust, Mike met Peter Scott, who became famous for his wildlife adventure television shows and documentaries on BBC. He was knighted by the Queen of England in 1973. Many visitors came to the Wildfowl Trust not only to see the birds, but also to catch a glimpse of Peter Scott.

Sir Peter Scott was an outstanding naturalist and wildlife artist. He'd become interested in nature through hunting, which was his hobby as a youth. He was one of the original founders of the World Wildlife Fund, became the organization's first chairman in 1961, and designed the famous black-and-white panda logo that is still in use today.

It was no secret that Sir Peter Scott's main interest and greatest expertise was as an ornithologist. He loved to study birds, paint them on canvas, and collect them at his home, Long Bridge, in Norfolk, England.

One day many years before, Scott had visited Berkeley Castle Estate in Slimbridge with Lord Alan Brook to observe the wild geese that migrate to the area every winter. He observed White-fronted Geese among the other species of waterfowl and became enamored with an idea to preserve the marshes for perpetuity. The massive waterfowl collection at Slimbridge resulted from his first encounter with the idyllic wetland. In 1949 he approached the owners of the estate and asked to lease the estuary and adjoining land that became the Wildfowl Trust.

The satisfaction of working alongside the great Peter Scott was a major reason why Mike Lubbock loved his job at the Wildfowl Trust. Although his mother had introduced him to the natural world, it was Peter Scott whose spark ignited Mike's passion for birds.

Mike: He was always an icon in my eyes, and I was a little nothing at the bottom of the hierarchy. Yet despite his fame, it was never any trouble to him if I wanted to see him about something. He was very encouraging and a great influence on which direction I took in my career in those early days.

As a young boy, Mike frequently imagined himself replicating Peter Scott's journeys to the far corners of the world, observing wildlife. Now he was on a mission parallel to that of his hero. In fact, it was often Peter Scott himself who selected Mike to represent the Wildfowl Trust on expeditions to the wild.

A colleague of Sir Peter Scott was the famous ornithologist, Jean Delacour. Born in France, Delacour was considered one of the world's greatest breeders of birds. Known for his collecting expeditions to Africa, Asia, and South America, he maintained a large private zoo for many years which contained some of the rarest birds in the world.

Scott and Delacour teamed up to write the seminal work on water-fowl, the four-volume classic, *The Waterfowl of the World*. Jean Delacour wrote most of the text, and Peter Scott provided the elegant illustrations that grace the pages. This became the most important set of books on waterfowl available in those days.

Mike had great respect for Delacour because he had tragically lost his bird collection during each of the two world wars yet had the resolve to recover from the setbacks – both times starting from scratch. Mike considered that kind of resiliency and passion for birds to be characteristics he wanted to develop in himself.

One week each year Delacour would come to Slimbridge to visit with Peter Scott at the Wildfowl Trust. It was during these special vis-its that Mike Lubbock developed a personal relationship with Delacour, whom many considered to be the world's greatest expert on avian husbandry.

It's difficult to imagine how Mike could have possibly been in a better position than to be the curator of birds of the world's largest waterfowl collection and have the two most renowned ornithologists and adventurers as his mentors.

For eight years Mike worked for the Wildfowl & Wetlands Trust at Slimbridge, learning and growing into the role of an ornithologist and waterfowl breeding specialist, reaching the position of assistant curator at the world's most prominent waterfowl preserve and research facility.

AMERICA BECKONS

Mike Lubbock was becoming a rising star in the avian husbandry profession. As the calendar rolled into 1969, there was no reason to believe anything could persuade him to leave his dream job at the Wildfowl Trust. Yet an opportunity was brewing at an estate 3,000 miles from Slimbridge, England. Someone in America was actively seeking a waterfowl breeding expert.

It was on one of his annual visits with Sir Peter Scott that Jean Delacour delivered some direct yet simple advice to Mike Lubbock that forever influenced his career.

Mike: Winston Guest and his wife, a young couple at the time, came to the Wildfowl Trust in 1969. They approached Peter Scott about finding a curator for Duck Puddle Farm in Oyster Bay, New York. The farm was home to Winston's private waterfowl collection. Tommy Johnstone, my boss, asked me if I would be interested in the job.

Mike had a myriad of conflicting thoughts running through his mind as he considered Winston's offer to go to New York. His recent marriage to his first wife Joanne topped the list of concerns. Their nuptials transpired a scant one year prior to the offer to relocate in America. It would be a disruptive change for the young couple (Mike at age 23 and Joanne just 18).

America seemed to be another world altogether. Everything he knew about it was from movies – cowboys, the Mississippi River, the Grand Canyon. He had no idea what it would be like to work in a new country with new customs.

He already had the best job he could ever imagine at the Wildfowl Trust. Why should he leave it?

Mike: I wasn't certain about taking the job. It would be a big upheaval for me to suddenly leave England, which I had known all my life, and move 3,000 miles away.

As I pondered what to do, I knew that Jean Delacour was with Peter Scott on one of his summer visits. He spent a lot of time in America, had an office in the American Natural History Museum in New York City, and also lived in Los Angeles for part of the year. I thought he'd be the one to ask whether I should take this job being the curator of this private collection.

So I went up to him in front of Peter Scott and said, "Excuse me, Professor Delacour." (I didn't call him Jean in those days, being an upstart.) "Can I ask you a question?" He said yes. I said, "I have an opportunity to go to America to run a collection of birds owned by the Guest family. I'm at a dilemma as to whether I should stay here or whether I should go."

And he looked at me and said, "You have no choice. You have to go."

That was it! I'd asked for Delacour's advice, and now I truly had no choice but to head off to America. Peter said it would be beneficial for me, even if I never returned to England. However, if I did return at some point, he thought I would have much more to offer the Wildfowl Trust.

America had waterfowl collections that were being built up rapidly, along with new ideas on husbandry that needed to be brought into England. So that was the decision, and I never regretted it. It changed my whole life from there on. But it was really Delacour's advice that swayed me the most.

Duck Puddle Farm

The Lubbocks landed in New York in the early spring of 1969. He had never met Winston Guest, not even when he and his wife, Helen, had come to Slimbridge to make inquiries of Peter Scott concerning someone to run his collection.

Mike: The Guests were to pick us up at the airport. I asked how I'd recognize them and was told they would be wearing daffodils in their lapels.

Arriving on the grounds of the Long Island estate in Oyster Bay, Mike didn't know what to expect. There was a nice old house where the Guests lived, and on the grounds was a cottage where he and Joanne would reside. The estate, named Duck Puddle Farm, was a sizable property at 150 acres. Winston Guest had inherited the estate, which had a significant history attached to it. King Edward VIII, who abdicated the British throne to marry Wallis Simpson, had stayed in the house, as had Sir Winston Churchill.

Mike: The Guest family was tied into the Phipps family. Their money came from Carnegie Steel and Woolworths. Barbara Hutton was part of this family. Winston Guest's godfather was Sir Winston Churchill, the former British prime minister. Winston Guest's father was a well-known polo player and a second cousin to Winston Churchill.

Some of the Black Swans that were at Duck Puddle Farm were from the stock of birds that Winston Churchill had at his Chartwell estate. I had told Winston that Peter Scott had received Black Swans from Churchill and was breeding them at Wildfowl Trust at Slimbridge. They were still there when I was at Slimbridge. Winston wanted some offspring from that particular pair. I did manage to acquire some of Churchill's Black Swans and brought them to Duck Puddle Farm.

The Lubbocks' arrival at Oyster Bay coincided with the zenith of large waterfowl collections that had sprung up on so many Long Island estates. At least seven were on Long Island, and there were more within the area of New England. With Mike now the curator of Duck Puddle Farm, it wouldn't be long before Winston Guest's collection was among the finest in all of the United States.

Winston already had the ponds dug, and a nice collection of birds were housed in the various pens and aviaries. Many birds had been imported from Europe. He had not bred any of them, because he lacked the fundamental knowledge of avian husbandry, which was the reason he brought Mike to New York.

Large ponds and open-air pens were the main feature of his collection. One of the largest open-air aviaries housed geese, swans, and ducks and included two ponds. Other ponds on the property included the House Pond, Henrietta's Pond, and the Middle Pond. The water from the House Pond, so named due to its proximity to the main house, ran downhill into Henrietta's Pond, which was named after a Magellan Goose.

Winston had also built a magnificent roundhouse pheasantry, the first one Mike had ever seen. It was a spoke-and-wheel design with the pens coming together in the middle for easy servicing. While Mike was impressed with the facility, he told Winston he wasn't familiar with breeding pheasants. About a week later most of the pheasants were sold, and from that point on they raised primarily waterfowl.

Throughout the spring and summer of 1969, Mike worked endlessly setting up brooders, small areas for hatching eggs, with duckeries on the outside of the building. The first year of breeding was very successful, even though much of Mike's time was spent getting the collection's infrastructure established.

Mike: I had Robin Clifford as my curator, whom I brought over with me from England. But I needed extra help during the summer. I frequently went to a nearby 7-11 convenience store. Almost every time I went, I saw a guy who just hung around at the store. He had a wooly head of hair – a real hippie type. But he was always nice whenever I talked to him.

Eventually, I learned his name was John De Jose, and he had an interest in what I did at Duck Puddle. He said, "You know, all those birds down there at the farm? I'd really like to see them sometime."

So I arranged to have him come for a visit, although I kept him out of Winston and Helen's view because of his hairiness, which I knew they would not appreciate. But after that first visit, he volunteered to help out at the farm. He was a hard worker. He didn't live too far away – up the road somewhere. I eventually met his parents. They were also very nice people.

John had attended a university but couldn't get a job. He was very bright. By sometime in 1972, I actually employed him. I got him off the street, so to speak.

Duck Puddle Farm was an exciting challenge for Mike and allowed him to flourish and test his own ideas in avian husbandry. He had carte blanche to attempt any advancement or innovation he wished. Winston Guest had faith in Mike's abilities, giving him full control over breeding the birds, plus monies for building the new brooders he designed.

Mike: While in America, I came up with all sorts of ideas. For instance, in England there were only three types of nest boxes and they were all the same – no real differences. When I got to America, I decided to try different designs for different species. I built different-sized boxes, added a porch to some, and placed them in different spots in the pens, all sorts of things. Now wherever they breed waterfowl, you'll see a porch box. That was one of my ideas.

I built a duckery with a door to an outside pond. I was the one who came up with sexing young ducklings. Nobody had ever sexed them before – ever! So I sexed them, then pinioned the males on the right and females left. Everybody does it now, but that had never been done before.

Porch Box.

I came up with nest box designs, pond designs, and perimeter fence construction to keep predators out of the aviaries – completely new ideas. I contributed to advances in incubator design, hand rearing without a chicken as an incubator, and wet brooders – rearing birds in water. Prior to this time, waterfowl were fed chicken feed, but I developed the nutritional formula for waterfowl feeding pellets.

Today most of these things are old hat, but in those days, they weren't. If I hadn't gone to America, I doubt any of this would have happened. All these avicultural advances allowed me to have the success I've had at Sylvan Heights.

His time in New York already proved advantageous for his career. Mike Lubbock's name became very well known within the annals of American aviculture. He became a frequent speaker at conferences held by waterfowl enthusiasts, accumulated numerous North American First Breeding Awards, and won a World's First Breeding Award for the European Black Scoter. He felt much more appreciated in America for his expertise in avian husbandry than he had in his native England.

Mike: One of the things I really enjoyed in America was the annual meetings of the International Wild Waterfowl Association (IWWA) and the American Pheasant & Waterfowl Society (APWS), where people from all walks of life who had an interest in birds would travel to a particular venue. Many of them wanted to find out more about this Englishman they'd heard so much about.

THE DUCK PUDDLE EXPEDITIONS

There were a lot of birds at Duck Puddle Farm. With Mike's management, Winston Guest soon had one of the best waterfowl collections in North America. But he also wanted species that had never before been brought in from the wild. Some of the species he desired could not be obtained through normal channels in Europe or the United States.

Mike: Winston Guest could afford to bring more birds into the collection. I went on an expedition every summer. It was good for me, as I accomplished a great deal in those four years [from 1969 to 1973].

The second year I was there I made a trip to western Alaska to collect waterfowl with Kerry Muller of the National Zoo in Washington, D.C. We brought back young birds and eggs to Duck Puddle – Spectacled Eiders, Red-Breasted Geese, Emperor Geese, and others. The following year I went to the Canadian Arctic.

A few years later, I went on the African expedition. That was a big trip – I really didn't know what I was getting myself into. It was successful, but quite daunting.

The African Pygmy-geese were bred from that particular trip, and the Maccoa Ducks were established as well from that trip. Winston Guest paid for me to go on all those expeditions.

I asked Winston once why he was interested in preserving waterfowl. He told me he was trying to make up for all the pheasants his father had shot over the years on hunting trips. His father actually held a record for the most pheasants bagged during a pheasant shoot on Gardiners Island, a private island just off Long Island.

Exploring remote and wild habitats for birds was a difficult and dangerous business in those years. Transportation into the wild was not as readily available then as it is today. Mike had arduous treks through territories in places like Botswana and the Falkland Islands, whereas today, roads easily allow those journeys to be made by a family on an adventurous vacation.

Collecting expeditions in the 1960s and 1970s were not considered conservation missions. Their purpose was to collect birds or eggs for aviculturalists to breed wild waterfowl.

Decades later, biologists discovered that bird populations were declining rapidly in the wild on all continents, with some species dropping to frightfully low numbers. Because Mike and others had collected birds when they were plentiful, aviculturalists now have the ability to preserve these species should any of them become extinct in the wild. Methods have been developed to release captive birds in the wild (breed-and-release programs), whenever habitat reclamation makes it appropriate.

Remarkably, many of the waterfowl species living at Sylvan Heights Waterfowl & Bird Park today come from the original generation of birds Mike and others brought in from the wild 45 years ago. Those crucial gene pools have been preserved over the decades by the men and women dedicated to maintaining managed populations and survival breeding programs, such as those at the Sylvan Heights Avian Breeding Center.

Expedition Gone Fowl

Mike Lubbock made four expeditions during his years at Duck Puddle Farm in New York. He brought back eggs and birds for Duck Puddle Farm, the Smithsonian National Zoo, the Wildfowl & Wetlands Trust, and several nature centers.

One of the Duck Puddle Farm expeditions afforded Mike the opportunity to explore the Canadian Arctic to find waterfowl and eggs. Mike's 1971 excursion to the Arctic Circle was an epic journey which became far more adventurous than he had anticipated.

BAD OMEN IN EDMONTON

The 1971 expedition to the Canadian Arctic was a joint birding expedition to collect waterfowl eggs and hatchlings around Victoria Island in the Northwest Territories of Canada. At the time Mike made his journey, Victoria Island was considered part of the Northwest Territories. However, in 1999 the northern tier of the Northwest Territories became the separate Canadian territory of Nunavut.

Al Oeming, owner of the Alberta Game Farm in Edmonton, Alberta, wanted to increase the number of waterfowl there and needed someone who knew how to collect eggs and properly transport them. He had successfully applied for and received the Canadian permits required. Al also hired a pilot and a small plane to fly him and Mike to the Northwest Territories.

Mike arrived in Edmonton on July 4, 1971. This is late in the breeding season to begin an expedition, but it's when the ice starts to break up in the arctic. The team's primary destination was Cambridge Bay on Victoria Island. From this location, they could use the small float plane to explore the surrounding area.

Clouds and rain showers greeted the exploration team the next morning. Mike and Al went to the airport to look over the Cessna float plane and meet the pilot, Charlie Fix. Bush pilots like Charlie are rugged individuals. They know every inch of water in the territories they fly and which lakes are big enough to land the plane.

As the day progressed, the weather conditions in Edmonton turned from messy to foreboding. Charlie checked the weather reports along the route they planned to take to Cambridge Bay. The forecast was not encouraging along the entirety of the route through the Northwest Territories.

To Al, this news had an ominous feel. Rain and low-hanging fog were predicted along the corridor leading up to and including Cambridge Bay. These conditions could cause navigational problems and make landings far more dangerous. Waiting a few days in Edmonton wasn't going to help matters. Bad weather was forecast for the remainder of the week.

The trip was already paid for and planned. If they didn't go now, another window of opportunity to collect these birds would not open until next summer. A decision needed to be made.

The plane was designed to carry four passengers, but with the substantial amount of equipment needed, that was a stretch. Considering the weight of the cargo and possibility of weather problems, Al decided only two of them should go on the expedition. Mike would be the explorer and Charlie the pilot. They would leave Edmonton that evening in hopes of staying ahead of the worst weather.

Charlie and Mike fueled the plane and loaded it in the pouring rain. They took off at 8:30 p.m. in hopes of making it as far north as Yellowknife or possibly Bathurst Inlet before stopping for some rest. However, the weather conditions worsened to the point that Charlie decided to stay overnight at Calling Lake, not far from Edmonton. The Cessna effortlessly made the landing on the water and taxied to shore. Charlie had friends staying at the lake, who gave them supper and a place to sleep for the night.

It was still raining intensely the next morning, but the daylight made flying possible. They took off again at 10 a.m., arriving five hours later to refuel on the southern edge of Great Slave Lake.

In the Arctic, bush pilots have extra fuel stored in designated places along their travel routes. The fuel is stored in large drums that are turned on their side when empty. If standing drums can be seen from the air, the pilot knows fuel is available. Before the ice comes at the end of the season, pilots fly out to resupply the fuel dumps. It's imperative for all the pilots to know where all these caches are stored.

Mike: The Cessna was equipped with long-range tanks, but it could still only fly six hours. You really have to plan out where you're going in this territory, because if you run out of fuel you're out of luck.

Despite the rain, there was enough visibility for Mike to spot birds on the ground. Between Calling Lake and Great Slave, he observed many White Pelicans, Buffleheads, American Green-wing Teal, widgeons, mergansers, storks, and Trumpeter Swans. He had definitely come to the right place to find birds.

The duo continued north, now heading for Yellowknife, on the northern edge of the massive Great Slave Lake, which was the next refueling station. They were making progress toward Cambridge Bay, but Mike could never get relaxed due to the conditions in the air and a prankish pilot.

Mike: We flew through such significant air turbulence that I was feeling lucky our plane remained in the air. The fuel tanks were located in each wing. When one tank runs out, the pilot switches to the other. I was tired and dozed off a little.

    Suddenly I heard the engine sputter to a stop. I snapped awake in terror, convinced a crash was imminent. Charlie stared at me for what seemed an eternity before reaching up and flicking a lever to switch to the second fuel tank. He laughed heartily as the engine came back to life. I guess this was his way of initiating me to the world of bush flying.

By 8:00 p.m. they had reached 64° latitude, 111° longitude. Mike caught sight of the first notable patches of ice. Later they flew over Contwoyto Lake, which had no open water. The ground at this latitude had considerable snow and ice.

Charlie set the plane down near the small lodge at Bathurst Inlet. The lodge is located 30 miles north of the Arctic Circle and within a few hours' flight of Cambridge Bay. Mike had some coffee and emptied a ten-gallon fuel drum into the fuel tank. The weather was looking bad, so they decided to press on rather than catch some much-needed sleep at the lodge.

They left Bathurst Inlet at midnight, yet due to their extreme northern location there was still plenty of light. Mike spotted more wildlife – Peregrine Falcons, Golden Eagles, Whistling Swans, and northern eider as they passed over some scattered hills. Mike noted in his journal that most of the lakes were completely iced over, and he recorded sightings of deer, falcons, eagles, and wolves. The weather was improving as they neared the end of their marathon journey to the arctic.

At last, Cambridge Bay came into view. The exhausted occupants climbed out of the plane and onto Victoria Island at 3:00 a.m. A throng of thirty or more Eskimos ran down to the landing dock to meet the weary travelers. Charlie knew the owner of one of the cabins, so they walked up the hill to get settled. Charlie's "key" to enter the cabin was a screw driver. Finally, at three-thirty in the morning, it was available to sleep after fifteen and a half hours of flying from Edmonton.

THE SEARCH BEGINS

Cambridge Bay was named for Prince Adolphus, 1st Duke of Cambridge, and is the center of transportation and commerce for the region. It is located at the western end of Queen Maud Gulf, where it narrows into Dease Strait, making this the main stop for ships traveling the Northwest Passage through the Arctic Ocean.

Mike intended to utilize Cambridge Bay as a base camp, from which he could conveniently fly to other areas in the region known to support flocks of ducks and geese. The airport at Cambridge Bay had regularly scheduled flights to Edmonton. This would be of great help in quickly getting any birds he found back to Al Oeming at the Alberta Game Farm.

Mike and Charlie woke from their much-needed sleep late on the morning of July 7 and prepared the plane for the first search. The temperature was cold, but sunny – perfect conditions for sighting birds from the air.

They left Cambridge Bay to search nearby areas of Victoria Island for waterfowl. Mike quickly spotted Lesser Canada Geese, Blue Geese (a dark morph of Snow Goose), Lesser Snow Geese, and Oldsquaw (Long-tailed Duck). These were not the birds he wanted.

Flying over a lake, Mike saw a number of Whistling Swan nests, massive flocks of King Eiders, and Brent Geese. There was just enough water to land. Mike signaled for Charlie to put the plane down.

On the ground, Mike found eggs in the Brent Geese and King Eider nests. He had candled the eggs to check how far they had developed. He knew there was about a week to go before any of them would hatch, so there was no point in taking the eggs. Mike walked back to the plane, leaving the eggs in the nests.

Mike: I wanted to get young hatchlings, not eggs. I went up there without an incubator, so we wanted to get babies that were hatched and load them on the DC-3 that came to Cambridge Bay twice a week from Edmonton. Al and the staff of Alberta Game Farm would look after them until I returned. That was the plan for this trip.

The air search continued west over herds of musk oxen and large flocks of Canada Geese. They reached a fishing camp and had supper there. The weather worsened, so they chose to stay the night at the outpost.

The wind blew strongly the next morning and the forecast called for more bad weather. Charlie and Mike determined it would be best to stay at the outpost. They went fishing with the camp owner's two boys. Cambridge Bay was well known for char fishing. A portion of the Ekalluk River on Victoria Island is named Iqaluktuuq, meaning "place of big fish."

Between them, they caught 23 char, the largest weighing 14 pounds. Later that day, they decided to go fishing again at the ice floe, this time catching 25 char and one lake trout.

Mike: On the way back to the fishing camp we discovered our boat had been cut off by ice. It became necessary to push the boat across the ice. This was a rather treacherous plan as the ice kept giving way, putting us in danger of falling through. But we made it back safely and my only discomfort was two very wet feet. We arrived back at the camp around five o'clock. It was bloody cold.

GEESE OF THE PERRY RIVER

Next morning it was on to Cambridge Bay for refueling. Today's activity would be special. The flight plan would take him to the famous Perry River. Mike's hero, Sir Peter Scott, had made several expeditions to this area, the first occurring in 1949. Finding birds in the same remote location in the arctic would be a thrill for Mike.

Mike's primary goal for this trip was collecting a particular species – the Perry White-fronted Goose. This rare waterfowl species is similar in size and morphology to the Tule Goose and is larger than the Pacific White-fronted Goose. The main breeding site of the Perry White-fronted Goose is located where the Perry River empties into the Queen Maud Gulf.

Once the plane was refueled, Mike and Charlie began a flight across Queen Maud Gulf, over seals and polar bears, to a completely iced-in Perry River. They began to cover 100 square miles of tundra in search of geese, seeing several flocks of Snow Geese. Mike spotted a small flock of Perry River White-fronted Geese, but none of them appeared to be breeding.

Eventually their quest brought them to a large lake with an island. They landed among hundreds of Snow Geese, Ross' Geese, Blue Geese, and Lesser Snow Geese, all breeding in this one area. Mike targeted the young Ross' Geese. As soon as the plane came to a halt, they jumped out and chased the young geese in a wild scramble upon the tundra. They managed to catch a number of them, along with a few eggs that were chipping.

Before leaving the island, Mike noticed hundreds of abandoned eggs and broken nests. There were big piles of eggs which had not even been sat on, becoming bleached in the sun. These piles of eggs caused Mike to question how they got stacked this manner. After Mike pondered the mystery, he believed he knew the answer.

Mike: When these birds first come up to the breeding grounds on these islands, ice still forms a bridge across the lake. Predators, like the Arctic Fox, walk across the ice to the islands. So when the first birds breed, the foxes come and take the eggs and pile them up in a large mound.

But when the summer thaw comes, the foxes must get off the island to avoid being stranded. They leave the mounds there until the lake freezes again, and then the foxes come back and eat the mounds of eggs, which have been conveniently stored for the winter. That's the only thing I could work out as to why these piles of eggs were there.

They took off again and only a few miles away found another lake with more islands. The biggest islands had far more Ross' Geese and Lesser Snow Geese. They both look very similar from the air, though the Ross is a smaller goose. It was difficult to estimate the number of Ross' Geese on the island, as there were so many. Mike collected as many goslings as possible, most of them having only recently hatched. This was perfect timing.

Mike: It's interesting that this area of the Perry River is where Peter Scott first found Ross' Geese on his 1949 expedition. The whole story is in his book, *Wild Geese and Eskimos: A Journal of the Perry River Expedition of 1949.*

Mike found King Eider nests on a nearby island. The eggs were further advanced than those on Victoria Island. He decided to take these eggs.

Mike very much wanted to find Perry White-fronted Geese. Back in the air, he searched for a considerable time. The Perry River area was where they should be. He saw scores of molting Snow Geese and Canada Geese, but no Perrys.

Charlie interrupted Mike's riveted attention on the ground below to emphasize the plane's critical fuel situation. They had been in the air for hours on this search for Mike's prized birds, but reality intruded on Mike's focus. Since the plane carried two spare fuel drums, which could be poured into the tanks at a nearby outpost, Mike convinced Charlie to continue searching another 10 minutes. However, even with the extra time, no Perry geese were discovered. It was time to refuel.

As the plane banked slowly south toward the outpost, Mike excitedly trained his binoculars on a small flock of birds. There they were! He spotted Perry River White-fronted Geese! Unfortunately, as before, there were no nests. He spotted a second group, then a third, but again none of them were breeding.

This was a major disappointment. He had come so far to the perfect place in the world to find Perry River geese, but unfortunately his timing was not as perfect. It would be extremely difficult to get adult birds all the way back to New York, especially this early in the expedition. For now he would have to be consoled by the sight of musk oxen and caribou herds roaming the tundra below.

The engine sucked in the last gallon of gas as Charlie landed on the Perry River near the old outpost. Mike loaded both spare drums of fuel into the tank. Charlie discovered the engine was low on oil. A search through the abandoned outpost uncovered a few cans of outboard motor oil. Charlie said, "It will have to do." Into the engine it went.

While Charlie worked on the plane, Mike checked the containers which held the birds and eggs he collected. The goslings wouldn't need any food in the boxes on the flight to Edmonton.

Mike: Because I took eggs with the chicks already pipping, I didn't need an incubator. The chicks were making their own heat as they chipped out of the eggs. We were due to meet the plane from Edmonton in a few hours. The birds we wanted to put on that flight had only just hatched, and they wouldn't want to eat for 24 hours. So the younger the birds, the less their eating would be affected by the long flight to Edmonton.

It was 4:30 in the morning. Mike and Charlie had been collecting birds through the night. Even with watches it was easy to lose track of time when you have 24 hours of light. Mike had lost his sunglasses in the Perry River during the scramble for birds, and now the intense glare reflected from the water and ice was burning his eyes. The loss of his sunglasses was taking a toll.

They needed to head back towards Cambridge Bay. Time was getting desperately short and Mike still needed more eggs to put on the ten o'clock flight to Edmonton that morning. Plenty of Snow Geese had been collected, so the search now focused on eiders and Brent Geese.

Prior to reaching Cambridge Bay, Mike spotted Black Brant Geese and told Charlie to land. He began collecting eggs. Some were close to pipping and others were close to hatching. He also found King Eider nests, but the eggs were still a ways from hatching. Even so, he decided to take some of the eider eggs – with luck, they would be in Edmonton in 15 hours.

Mike: I didn't have a portable incubator for the eggs I was collecting. My idea was to put the eggs among the warm goslings. This could work since the eggs were close to hatching.

With time running out, they raced to the air strip to meet the flight to Edmonton. The flight had not come in yet, so they repacked the young birds and the eggs to get them ready for departure.

While waiting for the flight to come in, Charlie cooked up some of the char filets they'd caught two days ago – the last time they'd slept. They enjoyed the delicious fire-grilled fish, especially because they had not eaten anything since breakfast the day before. As they consumed the last scrumptious bites, the DC-3 roared to a halt at the end of the runway.

Mike and Charlie took three containers full of eggs and birds to be loaded aboard. Mike said good-bye to them and hoped to see them all alive and well when he returned to Edmonton in about a week. The thought occurred to him that maybe he should get on the plane with the birds and get back to Edmonton. It was a thought upon which he later regretted not taking action.

BIRDS ON THE RUN

Finally came the time for sleep. The crew of the Cessna float plane had passed the point of exhaustion and slept until four o'clock in the afternoon. They had something to eat, refueled the plane, reorganized, and prepared to take off from Cambridge Bay to find more birds.

That evening they flew outside of the Cambridge Bay area and found more swan, eider and Oldsquaw nests. Soon Mike spotted something of interest. It was a pair of White-fronted Geese that were molting on a big lake, but from the air he couldn't be sure which species. Charlie recognized Mike's excitement from his body language and positioned the plane for landing before Mike could even ask him to do so.

Once on the tundra, Mike got a closer look at the mystery pair. They were Perry White-fronts! The birds were in molt, so they couldn't fly. These were adult birds, but this might be the last chance to collect Perrys. He decided to go for it.

Mike ran after them from one angle and Charlie from another, hoping to trap the birds in a pincher formation. Their pursuit of the birds drove them into the lake, where they repeatedly dived to avoid capture. Finally, Mike positioned himself where he thought the goose might emerge from under the water. Perfect timing! The male came to the surface and Mike caught him by hand – something he had never done before with a wild bird.

They took off again and searched the area for more Perry White-fronts. Mike saw many Canada Geese, but no Perrys. He was about to give up the search when he spotted a flock of 15 Perry White-fronts. As was the case previously with the smaller flock, all of them were flight-less, having recently molted. Charlie lowered the plane quickly and then pivoted above the lake, herding the birds onshore while landing.

Mike and Charlie bounded from the plane. The chase was on! Birds scattered every which way. This time they managed to keep them away from the lake, where the birds had the advantage. After an exhausting frolic on the tundra, Mike caught four and Charlie managed to catch one. Fantastic! Mike now had six of his prized Perry White-fronted Geese.

After this wild goose chase, Charlie and Mike were both physically exhausted. Even though there was still plenty of fuel in the plane, they flew back to camp in Cambridge Bay. It was eight o'clock the next morning.

Before they could stop for much-needed rest, they had to come up with a plan to care for the birds they had acquired.

From Mike's Journal:

> We converted the tail section of the Cessna into a holding container for birds. We didn't have anywhere else to put them, so this is how we handled it. After the young birds were all settled in the plane, we went to Charlie's friend's cabin where we had supper, or breakfast, or whatever. Time of day is an illusion now. Terms like "morning" and "night" have no relevant meaning.

> Charlie's friend is still away from his cabin, so I put the eggs and hatchlings by the heater. I rinsed my burning eyes in cold water. I must have a case of snow blindness, because my vision gets blurry on occasion. Finally we can sleep.

COPPERMINE RIVER

The hectic pace of the previous days came to a welcome respite, thanks to a friend's empty cabin in Cambridge Bay and a generous allotment of sleep. Mike once again was refreshed enough to plan out the final few days of the expedition.

The Cessna's tail section had become a waterfowl hotel for the older birds, while the cabin's heater served as a makeshift incubator for the eggs and hatchings. Mike needed to get all of these birds and eggs on a plane to Edmonton, along with anything else they might collect over the next two days.

Thoughts of the Coppermine River area swirled through Mike's brain. This area was home to colonies of breeding waterfowl. It was a place Mike hoped to explore on this trip, but traveling that far from Cambridge Bay would make it difficult to return in time to meet the flight to Edmonton.

Fortunately, Mike had a Plan B. He knew of another scheduled flight to Edmonton that originated out of a small air strip near Great Bear Lake. They could explore Coppermine River and still have time to meet the flight farther south at Great Bear Lake.

Late in the afternoon of July 11, Charlie made the plane ready for flight while Mike checked on the birds and eggs. Two Canada Geese and three Whistling Swans had hatched overnight. Once the birds and eggs were all safely tucked into the tail section of the plane, they took off southwest for the Coppermine River.

The Coppermine River was named for the copper ore that was discovered along the lower portion of the river. Mike was headed to the extreme northern waters, where the river widened as it flowed into Coronation Gulf within the Arctic Circle. Numerous migratory waterfowl species return annually to their breeding grounds on this part of the river.

As the plane arrived over the flats, Mike spotted Whistling Swans with cygnets. They landed and caught three cygnets. They searched another area; however, no nests were spotted.

Time for further exploration had run out. The fuel situation became a concern. The long flight from Cambridge Bay plus the extra time searching the Coppermine River area used more fuel than they had anticipated. Mike decided to head towards Great Bear Lake. He needed to get his precious avian cargo on the plane to Edmonton. To make matters worse, they ran into bad weather over the Coppermine River.

From Mike's Journal:

> 2 a.m. Monday, July 12. We are getting low on gas and there are no suitable lakes nearby to land on and refuel. We have two drums of gas onboard if we could just find a good bit of water to land. We're in thick fog, but Charlie is keeping his head about him. He says nothing is wrong.

Mike: Up there you have to fly by radio, not by compass. The
        magnetic north just makes a compass useless. If you fly
        high enough, you can fly from one radio tower to another.
        If you come down too low, you're out of radio range.

        In the fog, you either fly above it, although you don't
        know how high it is, or below it. This time, Charlie
        decided to fly below it. We didn't know where we were.
        But he kept his cool and stayed calm, which a good pilot
        will do.

Mike continued to make journal entries throughout the ordeal.
Charlie did not admit to Mike that he was struggling to find anywhere
at all he could safely land in order to refuel the nearly empty gas tank.
Mike kept his thoughts occupied by writing, which was the best way
he knew to cope with the matter.

From Mike's Journal:

        We now have to keep very low to the ground, as visi-
        bility is practically nil. Charlie has spotted a small lake to
        the right. It looks a bit small, but he circled it to see how
        deep the water may be. The heavy mist keeps us very low,
        but it's impossible to estimate water depth. Charlie says
        we have to land. Here we go! So far, so good!

Mike was still writing in his journal as the plane landed forcefully
on the small lake. The pen jolted on the initial impact, leaving a large
extended mark on the page. The plane was down, but not out of danger. Somehow, Charlie maneuvered the bouncing plane clear of the
large boulders protruding above the water. However, the floats clipped
a couple of the submerged rocks.

A wave of relief flowed through Mike's body as the plane emerged
safely from the maze of rocks. The engine sputtered. Both fuel tank
gauges read "Empty" as the Cessna quietly coasted to a stop without
power some thirty feet from shore.

Mike: Charlie was just a little man, but my God, was he tough.
        He knew how to fly that plane, he really did. Coming
        down onto that small lake, you couldn't see the rocks
        until you were about to land; but suddenly they just

loomed up out of the water – and he landed between the rocks. How he did it, I'll never know.

Charlie and Mike carefully waded on the slippery lake bottom to dry land and tied down the plane. Fortunately, their docking space was near a small cabin. It was a prospector's cabin with no sign of a resident. It had been well equipped at one point, except a bear had intruded and ripped the place apart. Nearly everything inside was broken or smashed. Mike was thankful he hadn't been an occupant during that particular bear invasion.

Mike went back to the plane to check the eggs and birds. They all seemed to have survived the hard landing. Charlie reported that the floats had a few small holes in them. After pumping water out of the floats, chewing gum was applied to the holes. The two drums of spare fuel were carefully poured into the fuel tank. They could not afford to spill even one drop. In this remote wilderness, fuel was literally a lifeline.

They returned to the cabin and waited for the fog to lift. The entire area was enveloped by swarms of mosquitoes. Mike needed to use the outdoor "facilities," but if he ventured outside, he knew the massive number of mosquito bites he would suffer would prevent him from sitting down afterwards.

GREAT BEAR LAKE

During the night, the fog lifted enough to escape the tiny mosquito-infested lake. They took off at four in the morning with only enough fuel for two hours of flying. Charlie figured they could get to Great Bear Lake. He knew some people at the fishing lodge there and was confident they could make it that far.

Takeoff from the lake occurred without incident. They got over the hills cleanly, but the fog was still heavy. After checking the maps, Charlie chose a series of valleys that would take them below the fog to Great Bear Lake. The only question was whether they had enough fuel to get there. Charlie said fuel wouldn't be a problem. Mike surmised it was.

When they arrived at Great Bear Lake, it was shrouded in heavy fog all the way to ground level. Visibility was only a few hundred yards. Charlie was sure it was the right lake, but didn't know exactly which part of the massive lake they were over. He decided since they were running on empty, they needed to land regardless of their location.

The plane landed safely, but after scouting around, Charlie determined they were at the opposite shore from the fishing lodge. Rather than taking off again and getting back into the fog with low fuel, he decided to drive the plane on the water like a boat to the lodge.

At seven o'clock in the morning, the battered plane taxied to the dock at Branson's Lodge with barely ten minutes' worth of fuel. Mike experienced the all-too-familiar feeling of relief following a brush with danger.

The lodge interior was grand and well stocked – an arctic paradise! The staff welcomed their unexpected new guests with a warm breakfast. This was a king's feast to the weary travelers, who had eaten mostly rations for the past eight days.

Mike: Branson's Lodge was operated by Canadians who catered to wealthy Americans wanting guided fishing tours. They would fly fishermen to different lakes in order to find the kind of fish a visitor wanted to catch. It was a very well-run, high-class place – with good food and luxuries one wouldn't expect this far north.

This pleasant change in personal amenities couldn't solve one major problem. The delay getting to Great Bear Lake caused them to miss the flight to Edmonton. The only way the birds and eggs would ever get there now was to be hauled to Edmonton in the crowded tail section of the Cessna float plane.

Mike rigged a homemade incubator with heat lamps in the lodge's boiler room. This was a perfect place for the young swans. He fixed up a nearby shed for the Perry White-fronts, which seemed to be doing well. All of this was at best a temporary solution. Keeping the birds and eggs here for any length of time would be very risky. They needed to get to Edmonton as soon as possible.

While Mike cared for the birds, Charlie monitored the lodge's shortwave radio for weather conditions. The next fueling stop along the route to Edmonton would be Yellowknife. The fog lifted around Great Bear Lake, but weather reports from Yellowknife were still very bad. Under these circumstances, they could not press on. Branson's Lodge would be their home for a while longer, at least.

With time on his hands, Mike needed to keep himself occupied. He went outside to get a good look at the surroundings now that the fog had lifted.

From Mike's Journal:

> Great Bear Lake is really beautiful – blue water, green trees and hills. It lies just south of the Arctic Circle, so the terrain is much different than farther north where we collected the birds. At least I'm better off being stuck here than the middle of nowhere. Everyone at the lodge was very helpful and would give us anything we wanted.

Mike walked around the lakeshore with his binoculars, hoping to spot birds. His birding excursion yielded sightings of American Goldeneye, Red-breasted Mergansers, Bald Eagles, and ravens – including a rare white one. He also came upon a black bear, which was startled and ran in the opposite direction.

Still restless, he tried some fishing and caught a five-pound Lake Trout. During this time, he had to go inside the lodge every so often to monitor the temperature of the incubators. He hoped the eggs would be okay, but he had doubts. It was difficult to keep a constant temperature inside the homemade incubator he had pieced together. At least all the young birds were eating well.

From Mike's Journal:

> Turned in feeling exhausted, though it was still light outside at 12:30 a.m. I had gone 32 hours without sleep. I wasn't sure what time it was, what day it was, and at times, where I was. My eyes were still burning and I bathed them in some type of concoction the folks at the lodge gave me. Despite my extreme fatigue, I still had to get up every couple of hours to check incubator temperatures in the boiler room.

During the night, two swans and one Canada Goose hatched. This was good, of course, but as the eggs hatched, it also meant that more baby birds were in need of extra attention at this critical time in their young life.

Mike was hoping Charlie would have better news with regards to their hopeful departure today. Wrong. The weather report from Yellowknife remained terrible – heavy fog. They wouldn't be able to safely land there.

This was disconcerting news for Mike. The trip appeared to be unraveling in slow motion. He was much better suited to controlling a situation by taking action. Waiting around a fancy lodge was not an acceptable response. He went outside to look for birds.

From Mike's Journal:

> The lodge's generator broke down for three hours, causing the egg temperatures to drop – I can only hope some will make it. The lights produce a very dry heat, so the eggs had to be watered quite often. The young birds are doing well and they are eating robustly. I brought egg crumble with me on the trip, so I had food for the birds with me. The Perry White-fronts in the shed had room to move around and drink. I also gave them lettuce and grass, plus corn from a frozen packet.

The weather reports received after lunch were starting to sound as if they were on a tape loop – rain and fog in Yellowknife, as well as at Great Bear Lake. Charlie went to sleep. Mike attempted to counter his boredom with a walk around the shore to see if he could find nests. Fighting swarms of mosquitoes with every step, he saw a wolverine, moose, a white wolf, and several signs of grizzlies, but no nests. The mosquito bites were getting through Mike's clothes. With his anxiety level at new highs, he returned to the lodge to rest.

BIG ROCKS AND CHEWING GUM

By evening the weather at the lake began to clear up. Charlie tried to get a report from Yellowknife, but could not make radio contact. It's decision time. Do clear conditions at the lake mean it's also clear in Yellowknife? Mike had enough waiting around to fill a lifetime. Taking action, even if it might turn out to be wrong, seemed better than sitting around. They needed to get to Edmonton.

The birds and eggs were quickly loaded on the plane, and a few minutes later they took off for Yellowknife. Within a half hour they encountered a low ceiling and thick fog. The veteran pilot decided this was too terrifying even for him. Charlie flew the plane as low as possible, skimming over tree tops, desperately seeking a place to land. After twenty minutes of hair-raising flight, he found water. Charlie had no idea how deep the water might be, but he decided to put it down anyway.

The landing progressed smoothly until they hit shallow water. That's when they saw the big rocks ahead of them. Contact was inevitable. At one point, Mike thought the plane was going to flip over. It sounded as though the rocks punctured every compartment in the floats.

The plane stayed afloat and Charlie guided it to shore. By some miracle, they found only two compartments leaking badly. They pumped the floats dry and patched the holes with the old standby – chewing gum.

There were better places Mike could think of to spend the night than in a Cessna surrounded by Canadian wilderness. Charlie had no idea where they were. The treetop flying could have taken them in any direction. He was just trying his best to avoid a crash.

They were miserably cold, and mosquitoes rushed in from everywhere. Mike didn't want to use much repellant in case it affected the young birds in the back of the plane. He managed to feed and water the birds, which all seemed to be doing fine. The eggs were retaining heat. The precious cargo was doing very well under the circumstances.

The fog lay thick all night until 12 noon the next day. It was clear enough to take off from the lake – but where would they go? Yellowknife was the destination, but not knowing exactly where they had landed, Charlie wasn't sure they had enough fuel to get there. Because they were transporting birds in the cargo section of the plane, they didn't have the extra fuel drums. He thought they should go back to Great Bear Lake. Mike concurred. Returning to Branson's Lodge would allow him to reheat the eggs and feed the young birds.

Mike: Before we took off from that lake, we had to account for the direction of the wind. The lake was long, but very narrow. Float planes are difficult to take off from water; you have to get up to speed in order to get lift from the wings. Plus, you need to take off into the prevailing wind.

Charlie was looking at the lake. He said in his Canadian accent, "It won't be easy to take off from here, because the lake runs this way and the wind is from the other direction" (meaning the short distance across the lake). "What I'm going to do is run down the length of the lake, and just before we get to the end, I'm going to turn quickly into the wind and pick her up."

I said, "All right, you're the boss."

That's what we did. We tore down the lake at full speed. I thought we were going to run straight into the trees. But then just a few feet from the shore, he twisted it 'round in the water and up into the wind. I don't know how he did it. It was just amazing.

After the incredible takeoff, Charlie climbed high enough to establish radio contact and set a course for Branson's Lodge. However, they soon encountered bad weather again and were forced to make another emergency landing on a small lake, scraping against more rocks. The plane came to a halt only when it hit the shore so hard the floats stuck into the bank. This time Mike's knees were hurt badly and he bumped his teeth on the instrument panel, even though he was strapped in by his seatbelt. Charlie was not injured.

After catching their breath, they emerged cautiously from the cockpit. Mike noticed he was bleeding from both knees, but told himself it wasn't serious. An inspection revealed the damage to the plane was not all that bad. The holes they'd fixed in the floats just a short time ago were open. More chewing gum fixed those. One of the struts was damaged, so they used their belts to tighten it and keep it from flapping in the air.

It took four hours to fix the plane, but during the repairs they noticed the fog beginning to lift. A window of opportunity presented itself. Mike and Charlie planned to make the most of it.

The battered plane, held together with chewing gum and leather trouser belts, gracefully lifted out of the water. Soon, the intrepid explorers were back to the friendly confines of Branson's Lodge, sitting down to a delicious meal. It was nine o'clock in the evening, July 15.

Mike: During the times when we were down on these remote lakes, no one in the States could get in contact with us. Over these three days, including the time we were living luxuriously at Branson's Lodge, people from New York hadn't any clue where we might be or how to reach us. We should have been in Edmonton several days ago. It was reported in the Long Island newspaper that we were lost in the arctic. The headline read: "Expedition Gone Fowl." We were fine, basically.

70

Charlie assisted Mike in securing the eggs in the incubators and feeding the birds. Mike later checked in with the nurse for a course of headache pills, sterile dressing for his bloodied knees, and ointment for his burning eyes. Finally it was time to go off for a good night's sleep.

The next morning brought clear skies. For once since this arduous return from the arctic began, the weather appeared cooperative. The radio reports south to Edmonton were equally good. Mike and Charlie packed the birds in the plane and were in the air by noon.

They were less than an hour from Yellowknife when Mike noticed that the mended strut had worked loose. This development required yet another hair-raising landing at the northern branch of Great Slave Lake.

Mike: In order to avoid the total collapse of the broken strut, which may have resulted in the plane capsizing in the lake, Charlie had to land on only one float. This amazingly difficult landing was complicated by the large waves rolling along the open expanse of the lake. Nothing seemed to faze Charlie; what an incredible pilot he was. I would have surely given up by this point!

After two hours of repairs, Charlie declared the strut "safe." They took off from Great Slave Lake and decided to bypass Yellowknife and take the shortest route to Edmonton. They were met with forcible winds that made the flight feel like a treacherous carnival ride. Mike, trying to keep his mind occupied on anything but the flight, looked at the lakes for waterfowl. But there were none to be seen.

By eleven o'clock that night, they landed at Hay River, a small outpost on the southern shore of Great Slave Lake. There was only one gallon of gas left in the tank.

From Mike's Journal:
Another close call! We seemed to be doing this all the time. I guess Charlie thought better of telling me this detail while we were yet in the air. We weren't carrying any extra fuel after leaving the Arctic Circle, due to all the extra cargo of birds and incubators.

Charlie had a friend named Sid, who was part Indian, at the Hay River outpost. Sid cooked supper and gave them a place to spend the night. Mike had quite a job convincing Sid not to eat the Perry White-fronted Geese.

71

Mike: At Hay River, we were finally at a place with good
        communications. We rang up Al Oeming in Edmonton
        to let him know we were okay and would be headed for
        his game farm in the morning. Al told us that they had
        organized a search party, which was about to get
        underway to find us.

Mike got up that night at 4 a.m. to check on the eggs, which fortunately were still warm. They got into the air early that morning and
arrived in Edmonton at eleven o'clock without further incident. From
the airport, they drove straight to Alberta Game Farm.

Al and his staff at Alberta Game Farm had already received the
Snow Geese and Ross' Geese from the Arctic Circle. These birds were
all doing well. Mike stayed a few more days at the game farm, hatching eggs and making sure the young were being reared properly. They
built shipping crates for the goslings and eider ducks. Mike put them
on the plane to New York once he thought the birds were ready
to travel.

Mike and his valuable cargo flew to Kennedy Airport in New York,
where he was met by a crew sent by Winston Guest. All the eggs and
birds were taken to Duck Puddle Farm.

Mike: That was a very hair-raising trip – flying in the wilderness
        in a small plane. I really learned a lot about bush pilots
        and how they fly by the seat of their pants.
            The unfortunate thing about Charlie Fix was that a
        few years later he was involved in a freak accident. He
        went up to the Arctic many times, taking people fishing
        for char and the like. He was by himself at one point and
        grabbed hold of the prop to start up the engine, for some
        reason. Most of the time you just push a button to start
        it up. That's what he did when I was with him. Anyway,
        the engine kicked into gear when he pulled down the
        propeller and it severed his arm right down to nothing
        basically. Charlie flew the plane back by himself with one
        arm. How he did that I don't know.
            What amazes me most when I think about the crash
        landings and the delay in getting back to Edmonton is that

the geese, eggs, and babies survived all that chaos. They went through hell, but they still came out of it all right.

Those Perry White-fronts were interesting. Since they were adults, I left them all with Al Oeming. I felt they had gone through enough traumas, so I didn't put them on the flight to New York. I said to Al, "Down the line I'll get some of them from you." Al bred those birds a couple of years later. Soon after that, he sent me two pairs. I believe the heritage of those birds may still be around. They were the first Perry White-fronted Geese to be brought into captivity.

The expedition to the Canadian Arctic was a success for Mike and substantially increased the size of the waterfowl collection at Duck Puddle Farm. A large flock of Ross' Geese, plus King Eiders, Lesser Canada Geese, and Brent Geese were bred from the birds brought back from his journey to the frozen North.

Today when walking the grounds of Sylvan Heights near the White-fronted Geese, Mike is reminded of the arduous chase he had trying to corral their ancestors on the Arctic ice. He also admits that as a young man at the time, he failed to fully recognize the peril he faced during those close calls on this expedition and jokes that he may have used up three of his nine lives on that trip.

In spite of the danger he experienced in the Arctic, Mike began planning his next adventure soon after his return to New York. He would seek rare species of waterfowl in the wild and mysterious continent of Africa.

CHAPTER FOUR

Africa

Happy indeed is the naturalist;
to him the seasons come round like old friends;
to him the birds sing:
as he walks along,
the flowers stretch out from the hedges,
or look up from the ground,
and as each year fades away,
he looks back on a fresh store of happy memories.

Sir John Lubbock
The Beauties of Nature (1892)

A relentless breeze tossed his long, curly black hair to one side. He gazed into the brushy grassland and took in a deep breath, noticing a wild scent in the air. The Dark Continent had beckoned Mike Lubbock from the time of his youth, and at last he stood within its borders.

He diverted his attention from the primeval landscape and looked down to stare again at the reason he had traveled so far off his route from Johannesburg, South Africa. Mike and Joanna stood in front of the stone commemorative plaque. This time he read the inscription aloud.

RALPH HUGH LUBBOCK
Game Warden
Kruger National Park

They stood in reverence only a short distance from the entrance of Kruger National Park, the first African wildlife reserve opened to tourists. Mike's father had served as one of the early game wardens for this historic South African park. As a boy, he relished the stories his father told him of Africa as the family sat around the dinner table.

As a young animal lover, Mike enjoyed hearing how his father would drive to a waterhole in the bush and wait quietly until dark. Then he would turn on the headlights and before him stood the legendary species of African wildlife – leopards, lions, cheetahs, cape buffaloes, elephants, giraffes, and zebras. Mike repeatedly asked his father to tell him about the enraged black rhino that charged the safari vehicle, turning it completely upside down, trapping him underneath. His father was injured and alone for many hours before another ranger discovered the scene – four wheels turned to the sky and muffled cries for help coming from the dusty earth.

Mike gathered from his father's stories that Africa could be frightening at times, yet the seven-year-old boy continually imagined a time when he would go there to see those animals for himself. He eagerly anticipated the challenge of surviving in the untamed wilderness.

Mike's lineage is steeped in a tradition of naturalists. In addition to his mother, who encouraged him to study and examine all aspects of the outdoors in the English countryside, the Lubbocks had other family ties to the natural world.

SIR JOHN LUBBOCK

Mike's great-uncle was Sir John Lubbock, a prominent banker in London as were a number of other men in the Lubbock family. In fact, there was even a Lubbock Bank at one point. Being a politician as well as a banker, Sir John instituted the Bank Holidays Act in 1871, much to the enjoyment of the English people. The holidays were initially called St. Lubbock's Days. At one point, John Lubbock was one of the most well-known people in England.

However, Sir John's talents were much more than that of a politician and banker. His greatest contribution to society may have been his study of nature. He was an ardent student of biology, entomology, geology, anthropology, and botany. He was a major contributor to the establishment of archeology as a disciplined science.

When John Lubbock was a boy, he learned from his father (Sir John William Lubbock) that the famous biologist Charles Darwin was coming to live at the Down House, near the Lubbock estate in Kent. For over 40 years, the younger John Lubbock had frequent conversations with Darwin, receiving encouragement and guidance until eventually becoming a colleague. In fact, Darwin's seminal work, On the Origins of Species, quotes portions of Sir John's work in anthropology.

Lubbock published *Ants, bees and wasps: a record of observations on the habits of the social Hymenoptera* (1882) and *On the Senses, Instincts, and Intelligence of Animals* (1888). In these books, Sir John investigated the sensory capability of insects and discussed animal intelligence and other topics concerning natural history. He also wrote The *Beauties of Nature*, a collection of essays and observations on animal life, plant life, and geology.

RALPH LUBBOCK

Mike's father, Ralph Lubbock, was the eldest of four siblings and went to school at Eton, as did his uncle, Sir John Lubbock. Eton is a large boarding school for boys founded in 1440 by King Henry VI as "The King's College of Our Lady of Eton besides Wyndsor." The school is located in the village of Eton, near Windsor, England.

Mike: There were lots of stories about my father. As a boy, he got into big trouble with his uncle, Sir John Lubbock. One day, he was outside Sir John's home in Kent and shot up one of his ant farms with his air gun.

It's said he shot the Head Mistress of Eton in the bottom with an air gun while she was bent over picking up potatoes. He had to own up to it.

It seems he was always shooting that air gun at something.

He eventually left Eton, didn't go to college and married fairly young. His wife was an heiress in Scotland. He married her and moved up north to her Scottish estate. Soon he discovered that she had a very nice-looking sister. He grew to like the sister more than he should, and a very big problem ensued. The papers got to hear of it. Of course the Lubbock family tried to avert a scandal, but the story got into the Times anyway.

My father's parents took hold of the situation. They removed him from the house in Scotland and put him on a ship to South Africa with a hundred pounds in his pocket and instructions to never return to the shores of England. That's how he got to Africa in the first place.

Ralph Lubbock continued his bounder ways in South Africa. However, with the help of some well-positioned and wealthy South Africans whom he'd originally befriended at school in Eton, he eventually settled down and spent many years as a game warden at Kruger National Park.

His change of character was sufficient enough that in the end, the Lubbock family welcomed Ralph back to England, where he ultimately met Mike's mother, Alfreda, and started a dairy farm in the Blackdown Hills.

While his father told young Mike stories of charging rhinos and stalking lions, Mike's grandmother also helped to instill a longing to visit Africa.

Mike: I always remember the stories my father told me about Africa – they were vivid and deeply rooted in my mind. My mother would on occasion take me to the local zoo in Bristol, but other times my grandmother took me to the London Zoo, where she was a member. The keepers allowed me to throw cabbages to the hippos. They had every kind of African animal you could imagine. I would watch the elephants and just dream what it would be like to come upon a wild herd of them on the savannah. I knew one day I would go to Africa.

BOTSWANA

Duck Puddle Farm; Oyster Bay, New York
SEPTEMBER, 1972

This was the trip Mike wanted to make. Once it became clear that his boss, Winston Guest, was willing to finance the expedition of his dreams, he began arranging the journey to Africa.

Mike: I may have been guilty of twisting Winston's arm a bit in order to justify the expedition to Botswana. However, bringing back African pygmy-geese and Maccoa Ducks was something Winston wanted almost as much as I did. We were prepared for pygmy-geese before I ever went to Africa. We built a tropical house specifically designed for pygmy-geese. The aviary had water inside and there was a big door so the birds could go outside in summer.

Getting prepared for the trip was far more difficult than Mike had anticipated. He didn't know what to expect. He planned to catch birds, but was prepared to get eggs at the end of the trip. He had to acquire the proper nets, but he could only find the waterfowl nets he wanted in England.

Mike: I remember the nets were a problem because I ordered and paid for them well in advance of my trip. But just before we had to leave for Africa, we still had no nets. The company said they had already been delivered, so we went to Kennedy Airport to look around and found them stuck in the back of a warehouse.

Another matter that concerned him was his travel partners. Sam Weeks was going to accompany him, representing the Smithsonian National Zoo in Washington, D.C. Mike had never traveled with Sam before. Even though he was curator at the zoo, Sam's skillfulness in field work and living in the wild were unknown factors.

Sam Weeks was an important part of the package Winston Guest needed to make the African expedition. As a private citizen, Winston was not able to secure the permits to collect waterfowl and other birds in Botswana. Sam, being associated with the National Zoo, applied for and received the necessary permits.

Complicating matters further was the fact that Sam Weeks decided to take his wife, Gloria, along on the expedition. That opened the door for Mike to invite his wife, Joanna, who did at least have experience working with waterfowl. Mike needed Sam to help him with the nets and care for any birds they caught. The women could also assist and help out in the camp. Still, there were real concerns as to how these relationships would play out once they reached Botswana.

Mike: Joanna had experience. She'd been on trips with me catching birds before. We had to have someone along from the National Zoo because of the permits. I figured Sam being curator of the National Zoo would have some experience in the field, but Gloria had none at all.

Botswana held a smorgasbord of rare waterfowl species, and Mike was eager to begin the expedition. He would search especially for the African Pygmy-goose, Maccoa Duck, and the African White-back Duck.

The African pygmy-goose is not a goose at all, but rather a small duck with a goose-like bill, from which it derives its name. Many consider this to be the most beautiful of the waterfowl species.

The Maccoa Duck is an African species that had never been brought in from the wild. It is a member of the stiff-tail family, though it is not overly plentiful in Botswana. The males are a rich chestnut color with light blue bills. Prior to Mike's trip to Africa in 1972, Maccoa Duck nests had never been observed by ornithologists.

He also wanted the African White-back Duck, a small diving duck that is almost grebe-like in shape. Their mottled brown-black and white appearance does well to camouflage this duck, which tends to feed in the dense shadowy vegetation on the edge of lakes and rivers. The African White-back does indeed have a white back; however, this can only be seen when the bird is in flight, at which time the white flashes prominently.

Any other waterfowl species acquired during the trip, such as Spur-winged Geese, Red-billed Pintail, Comb Duck, or White-faced Tree Duck, would be a bonus for Duck Puddle Farm. The National Zoo needed African birds such as the Jacana, cranes, and shore birds. Finding those would be easy enough, because when nets are placed over waterholes, various non-waterfowl species that come in to drink the water will be caught, such as Sand Grouse or Wattled Cranes.

BOUND FOR SHAKAWE

After initially landing in South Africa to visit Ralph Lubbock's commemorative plaque in Kruger National Park, Mike and Joanna flew to Gaborone, Botswana, where they met up with Sam and Gloria Weeks. Here Mike and Sam endured the prolonged administrative process of securing bird permits. The permits had already been granted before they left New York, but they still had to go through all the bureaucratic red tape and double-stamping to get them issued.

Mike: The only bird the Botswanan authorities wouldn't let us catch was the Fulvous Tree Duck. It seemed they thought the word "fulvous" indicated it was a rare duck, though it isn't. Nor was it a bird we wanted anyway.

Once business was concluded in Gaborone, they flew 250 miles north to Francistown, often call Botswana's "Capital of the North." Mike had established a contact there in Peter Becker and his partner, who owned Botswana Game Industries. The company provided lodging and guides for hunting safaris.

Peter didn't know much about waterfowl, but he knew the Okavango Swamp area would be a good place to find African Pygmy-geese and African White-back Ducks. He suggested Mike and his party stay at one of his camps far to the north, near Shakawe. Peter assigned Howard, one of his guides, to take them all to Shakawe and offer suggestions of where to look for birds in the area. Peter also provided a team of Botswanans who could help set up camp and perform other tasks.

With the guide and Botswanan helpers added to the team, they were ready to leave Francistown. Everyone pitched in to load supplies, nets, and other equipment into the Land Rover supplied by the safari company. Howard drove them on the primitive dirt road into the Kalahari region.

Late that afternoon they arrived in the village of Maun, which was located along the wide banks of the Thamalakane River. This was the last town of significant size before they reached Shakawe and would be the perfect place for an overnight stop. Maun was a rough town, not unlike the frontier towns of the Wild West in America. Goats and donkeys wandered freely about the streets, competing for right-of-way with pedestrians and vehicular traffic. Mike noticed the women in the village all wore very brightly colored clothing with distinctive designs.

Early the next morning, the group headed 50 miles to the southwest before turning to the north. This diversion was necessary to skirt the massive Okavango Delta, through which there were no passable roads or trails. The road north was dust-covered and rough, but the Land Rover negotiated the terrain with relative ease.

As the explorers traversed the Kalahari Basin, they were treated to spectacular views of African wildlife: zebras, ostriches, wildebeests, impalas, kudos, and warthogs. They stopped to view the extraordinary Tsodilo Hills. This outcrop of rock hills are a site of ancient and culturally significant rock paintings. The San people of the Kalahari were responsible for the crude paintings within these hills and considered the area to be a spiritual cathedral, as well as the site of creation.

By late afternoon the group arrived in Shakawe, a distance of over 400 dusty miles from Francistown. Shakawe is a small village in extreme northern Botswana, near the Caprivi Strip of Namibia (sometimes called the Okavango Panhandle). Its location on the Okavango River is convenient for anyone who wants to see wildlife. The town was populated by native fisherman and visiting hunters who stayed at the many lodges and camps along the river. This would be the first time anyone had come there to catch birds.

OKAVANGO RIVER

Once the group settled into to their base camp in Shakawe, they began to appreciate the beauty of their new surroundings. They were now in the middle of Africa, free from nearly every vestige of western civilization. A beautiful lawn sloped gracefully from their lodge to the Okavango River. The camp provided suitable accommodations and a staff to cook meals and handle other domestic chores. It was an arduous journey to Shakawe, but Mike had no complaints concerning the provisions of his base camp.

The Okavango River is a labyrinth of lagoons and channels that meander through vast open grasslands before expanding farther south into the alluvial fan of the Okavango Delta. Wetland areas extend out some distance from the river. Palms and other towering trees offer shade over crystal pools, known as "pans" in southern Africa. Waterfowl and other birds abound in these environs. Mike couldn't wait to find them.

Setting camp at Shakawe. Howard the guide standing on spare tire.

Mike: A swamp stretched for miles and miles along the Okavango River. The African Pygmy-geese were in and out of this area, but that wasn't the best place to catch them. The plan was to explore the waterholes just outside these swamp areas. Those pools are where the birds were more isolated, and it would be easier to set the nets to catch them.

    Some of the waterholes were too far away from the base camp, so we needed to take enough provisions to stay out 3 or 4 days, maybe more. We figured whenever we came across one, we'd evaluate it and decide whether or not to camp there and set up nets.

The next morning, the expedition party departed their base camp in the well-provisioned Land Rover, searching for suitable waterholes where they could catch birds. They drove through a little fishing village. Further down the narrow road, Mike found an intriguing chain of ponds only about 30 minutes outside of Shakawe.

From the Land Rover, Mike spotted White-faced Tree Ducks, Red-billed Pintails, Southern Pochard and a few Comb Ducks. He also saw Jacanas, Spur-winged Plovers, and Open-billed Storks. Unfortunately, Mike didn't see any African Pygmy-geese, possibly because there were only a few trees around this particular pan. Still, there were plenty of birds and a good place for them to make camp not far from the water.

Mike: I got really excited about this spot and asked the others set up camp so I could immediately go over to this water-hole and observe the birds. There were three or four ponds that joined into each other. The first one was small, the next two were bigger, and the last one was quite large. I watched to see where the birds were flying within this water system. Then I decided to put up nets between the smaller pans, because that's where the water narrowed down to a channel. The birds would usually fly along this channel.

Mike observed that the birds flew low between the ponds, and he expected to catch them there with three of the shorter nets he'd brought from New York. He waded into the ponds, which was about chest deep and drove the posts into the muddy bottom.

Mike: I designed the nets so that we could put them between tow-
        ers. The towers were made from a type of angle iron with
        holes in it. They can be easily assembled and driven into the
        ground and then tethered down in the water to get the net
        into a tight position.

        The nets could be set at any height. I also had pulleys
        to adjust the height of the net. If the birds saw the net in
        the daytime and flew over top of it, I could lower it to
        almost water level and pull hard to snag them as they flew
        between the towers. This worked quite well.

Setting three nets required several hours of standing in the water to
sink the towers into the bottom of the pan, and to set the stakes for the
guide ropes. Mike received only
minimal assistance from Sam and
the others in setting up the nets.
Late that afternoon, he walked the
short distance from the pans to
camp for some rest and to see what
the women had made for dinner.

As the light of day faded into
dusk, Mike took out his flashlight
and shined the powerful beam
toward the pond to see if any
birds were in the net. To his surprise, what he saw was the reflec-
tion from a great number of eyes
from every spot around the pond.

Crocodiles! They had been
lurking in the grass as he installed
the nets.

Mike with net pole.

Mike: I never considered the possibility crocs being there.
        Earlier in the day, some little kids came out from the vil-
        lage down the road to watch me put up the nets. They
        never mentioned crocodiles – not one of them.

        Even more frightening was when I remembered we
        didn't have a boat with us!

He did recall seeing dugouts when they passed through the little fishing village not far away. Mike and Sam went to the village and negotiated a trade for the use of one of their boats. The villagers brought the boat to their camp, dragging it behind a team of oxen. It was very heavy and difficult to maintain a balance when standing in the boat to work on the nets. Although falling from the dugout into the water was a real possibility, it was still better than wading in the water with all those crocodiles lurking.

The next morning, Mike awoke and looked out at the nets from the door of the tent. As dawn's light appeared, he could see the first net wobbling up and down. He thought there must be loads of birds in it.

Mike ran to the water's edge, jumped into the dugout, and paddled to the net.

Mike: I saw a Red-billed Pintail struggling in the net. I soon learned why the bird was in such a desperate panic. As I grabbed the bird by the back legs and pulled it out of the net, a big croc shot out of the water and bit it 'round the middle – chopped the bird right in half. I was left with two legs and blood dripping out the back part of it. At least I still had my fingers and hands! I looked down into the water just beneath the dugout. The croc was still splashing around. I thought, "Hmmm, this isn't any good!"

He decided he'd better get to shore. The croc followed the boat as he paddled furiously. Mike clobbered the croc in the head with the paddle, nearly tipping over the dugout and launching himself into the water.

The blunt strike stunned the croc long enough for Mike to reach the shore. He jumped out of the tiny boat and pulled it onto the bank. Before he could turn to run, the croc sprung halfway out of the water towards Mike with jaws open to strike. Joanna, who watched the scene unfold from the camp, screamed with fright as he nimbly side-stepped the lunging croc. Mike made a clean break of it and scrambled back to the campsite while the croc retreated into the water.

Sam and Gloria Weeks had not witnessed the attack since they were still sleeping in their tent. However, they'd been roused awake by

Joanna's scream. Mike, still breathing heavily from the ordeal, told everyone the entire alarming story of how he escaped the huge croc.

Mike: Now I have a dilemma. I have one of my nets down in the water; I have a dugout canoe in which I cannot safely standup. How am I going to get my net back? The croc had already made big holes in the net he attacked. The other nets he hadn't disturbed.

So I paddled over to it and got some birds out of one of the standing nets – a few White-faced Tree Ducks, Red-billed Pintails, and some Jacanas.

I made sure the nets were set a little higher off the water so the croc couldn't actually reach it. I was getting fed up with the crocodiles as they were a bit of a hazard.

There was still the issue of the net the crocodile attacked. It lay limp in the water – completely useless for catching birds. It couldn't be left there as the expedition would be severely crippled without it. It must be repaired.

Mike determined it would be best to retrieve the net during the heat of the day when the crocodiles seemed inactive. He courageously waded out in the water to get the net. He had the dugout, but trying to stand up in it had proved to be more trouble and less safe.

As he waded into the pond, he listened closely for any sound of a slap or splash, indicating a croc had entered the water. All the little pieces and parts of the net were collected without any interference from crocs. He breathed a sigh of relief and returned to camp where he attempted to repair his net. He had taken a pointless risk – the net was damaged beyond repair.

Even more dangerous than recovering the net ruined by the crocodile was the job of taking down the other two nets and the six towers. For this, Mike again had to wade into the water. The towers and guide ropes were anchored in the tall reeds that grew from the muddy ground where the crocs typically rested during the daytime hours. He wouldn't even have the benefit of hearing a splash before an impending attack.

Mike: I managed to retrieve the remaining two nets and all six towers, but nobody else volunteered to get in the water to assist me. Sam Weeks was not at all helpful. He complained of having terrible stomach problems, diarrhea, and everything else. He stayed behind the trees most of the time, doing whatever he was doing. He was supposed to be helping me care for the birds, especially the non-waterfowl like the Jacanas and the stilts we were catching for the National Zoo.

They broke camp at the croc-infested pan and went to other areas in search of birds. Not finding anything to Mike's liking, they returned to the base camp in Shakawe. Howard, the guide, provided some of his people to set up pens in the shade for the birds they had caught. Mike made sure the pens were constructed properly, food was available, and the overall care for the birds was satisfactory.

At this point in the expedition, they had collected Red-billed Pintails, Comb Ducks, and White-faced Tree Ducks. The African Pygmy-geese remained elusive, as did the African White-backed Ducks and Maccoa Ducks.

Mike contemplated what to do next. He thought they should go to an area which the guide said would be a good habitat for the birds they needed. It was almost to the border of Namibia. They drove for a very long time, but saw no birds. The water was all dried up.

When the pan areas dry up and there is no rain to refill them, the birds will not breed. Although the waterfowl had gone elsewhere, the drive through the bush afforded many opportunities to see elephants, giraffes, ostriches, and other animals typically associated with Africa. For Mike, it was a wonderfully inspiring sight, reminding him of his boyhood dreams.

After returning to base camp at Shakawe, Mike thought they should continue looking in the Okavango Swamp. He could see African Pygmy-geese in the trees from the camp in Shakawe, but could not find a place to catch them. They seemed to taunt him.

Meanwhile, the outlying pans were rapidly drying up from lack of rain. Mike was running out of options for finding birds. There was one last thing he could try.

THE BUSHMAN

Mike went to see his guide, Howard, to find out if he had any suggestions for finding birds. He offered no viable suggestions. Mike lamented his luck in coming to the Okavango during a drought. There must be somewhere the water wasn't totally dried up. That gave Howard an idea.

After speaking to some of the locals, Howard suggested that Mike visit the Bushmen who had recently set up a camp outside of Shakawe.

Mike: Howard said the Bushmen would welcome our party to
        their camp that evening, when they performed a
        ceremonial dance. He said we may be able to convince
        one of them to go into the bush with us. Howard had
        heard the chief Bushman could smell water. You can be
        in an area and he could tell you if there's water within
        forty miles. I wasn't sure about all this, but I thought it
        was worth a shot.

The Bushmen were originally nomadic social groups that traveled through the African bush as hunter-gatherers. The term "Bushmen" is considered disparaging by these people. They prefer to be called San People, or simply San. Since the 1950s, government-mandated modernization polices have gradually forced the San to switch from their traditional hunter-gathering lifestyle to farming.

The San at Shakawe that Mike Lubbock met may well have been the last of the tribes to maintain their nomadic way of life. They built little huts at each new camp. The huts were constructed of straw or other plant material. In front of each door they would build a small fire. The women tended the fires on a nearly constant basis. There was also a large fire in the middle of the circle of huts where the ceremonial dance took place.

It took a bit of coaxing to convince the other members of the exploration party to go along with Mike to the Bushmen's camp that night. Perhaps it was a far-fetched idea, but there were really no other options to consider at the time. It came down to this or nothing.

Mike: The Botswanan men that were on the expedition with us
        went along to the camp. They took a dim view of the

Bushmen and thought of them as a class of people beneath them. That was interesting, because the Bushmen could kill them in a flash if they so desired. You don't really want to mess with them. They're very peaceful unless you get them riled.

There were at least 30 members of this tribe. The women looked very old, though they probably weren't. But they lived with all that smoke and fire around and seemed overly tanned from the heat.

We sat down in the special seats they prepared for us. All the women came out and took seats around the main fire. Then the men, with seed pods around their ankles, would dance around the women, chanting in a "click language."

The chief had a big stick and he repeatedly hit the ground with it while the other men shook their feet. It was all very interesting. I actually recorded some of it on my tape recorder. The women were the ones making the music, chattering, and calling. The ceremony went on a long time. One woman dozed off. I saw her head bob and the chief came over and whacked her with his stick.

After the dance ceremony, Mike, with the assistance of some Shakawe locals, arranged for the chief of this band of Bushmen to go with him into the bush to search for water, and hopefully birds. He agreed to meet Mike and Sam the next morning in their camp. Bushmen don't keep time, so they arranged to meet as the first rays of light broke at dawn.

Mike: We were up and waiting at the appointed time, but we didn't see him. Then in a flash, he was right there with us. We didn't see or hear him arrive, but there he was, wearing no clothes – only a little thong, plus his bow and arrow, and poison darts.

We said among ourselves, "Well, he won't be able to travel in the vehicle that way; he'll burn himself sitting on the hot seats." The Land Rover wasn't the most comfortable of vehicles under good conditions. So we searched around and found some khaki shorts, which he put on, although he didn't want to.

The group packed up and was ready to roll. Mike took the passenger seat; one of the Botswanans was the driver. In the back seats were the Bushman and two other Botswanans. Neither Sam, Gloria nor Joanna wanted to go on this trip.

Mike, the Botswanans, and the Bushman chief, clad in khaki shorts, headed northwest in the Land Rover. He wasn't sure how long this trip into the desert would take.

Mike: The Bushman was sitting in his seat doing all right. After an hour or so, I took out my tape recorder. I wanted to get back to the place on the tape where I had recorded the Bushmen singing in their camp the night before. So I listened to that on playback. The Bushman went nuts! We had to stop the vehicle, get him out, and explain to him that his whole village was not in the box. We got him back in the vehicle after he calmed down and we were off again.

The plan was to go to areas where they could overlook the edges of the Kalahari Desert and then let the Bushman tell them if there was water in the pans. Mike knew where the pan areas were, but it was absurd to drive 50 miles to a place where there was no water and therefore no waterfowl. That would be a waste of time and gasoline, both of which were precious commodities.

They arrived at one of the overlook areas. The Bushman got out and indicated with a gesture that there was no water. After driving a considerable distance farther, Mike asked him to check again.

The Bushman stepped out of the Land Rover and faced the warm breeze of the Kalahari. He got excited and pointed to the area where good water would be found. The terrain they needed to transverse provided a rough ride.

Mike: It was fiercely hot as we rode into the desert. I decided we needed a drink. We had a cold box in the vehicle with a little ice in which we stored some bottles of Coca-Cola. I passed a bottle to everyone.

90

The Bushman took hold of his Coca-Cola. Immediately he exclaimed in fright and dropped the bottle with a look of shock on his face. He never in his life felt a cold drink or even the sensation of cold. He put the bottle to the side of his seat and periodically touched it until it had warmed up. Then he was ready to drink it.

I handed him the bottle opener (no screw caps in those days). He couldn't work that out either. We showed him how to remove the cap, and then the fizzy liquid caused him some additional concern. But once the foam subsided, he drank it and liked it.

These Bushmen were very intelligent. They just had very little experience in the world we know. In their world, they are extremely knowledgeable.

After what seemed an eternity, they arrived at the pan recommended by the Bushman. To Mike's surprise, there was water there. However, there were not many birds. It wouldn't be worth the effort to put up the nets and endure the desert heat any longer.

During the ride to the birdless waterhole, he had come up with a plan he thought would help him catch African Pygmy-geese. It was time to leave the Kalahari and get back to Shakawe as soon as possible.

Mike was glad he would be spending the night in the relative luxury of the lodge in Shakawe. The trip into the Kalahari Desert gained no birds. So far he had been chased off a lake by a crocodile and toured the desert with a Bushman. Furthermore, he'd caught no pygmy-geese, no maccoas, and no white-backed ducks. These birds comprised his reason for being in Botswana. The African dream was transforming into a nightmare.

NIGHT OF THE PYGMY-GOOSE

The only redeeming virtue of the desert trip was that since Mike wasn't actually catching birds, he had plenty of time to think about catching birds. Now back at the base camp in Shakawe, he began to implement a plan he devised while in the Kalahari with the Bushman. He had figured out how to net African Pygmy-geese.

Peter Becker had definitely suggested the right place for finding pygmy-geese. Since the day he'd arrived, Mike had seen scores of them in the trees around Shakawe. But getting a net on birds that sit in trees all day was going to be difficult. However, the birds had finally revealed their secret to the Waterfowl Man.

Mike: I figured out the African pygmy-geese were primarily nocturnal – they didn't move around in the daytime very much at all. After observing them for many hours, I knew this had to be the case. I noticed they rested in the trees all day long, right by our camp in Shakawe. I never saw them looking for food much in the daytime. But at night, suddenly they were everywhere.

Before leaving on the excursion to the Kalahari, Mike had noticed a small motor boat normally used to give visitors guided tours on the Okavango River. He talked to Howard about renting the boat. With a stable craft, rather than a top-heavy dugout, he could explore the swamps at night to find out where the pygmy-geese were feeding.

After acquiring a boat and motor, Mike set out on a night surveillance cruise on the small tributaries of the Okavango River. Some of the channels were very narrow, and he became concerned that hippos might overturn their small boat.

Mike: Before going out at night, we surveyed the area in the daytime. That's when we came across hippopotamuses under the water. In the narrow channels of the river, they could have easily come up and tipped over our boat. I didn't realize until much later that hippos leave the river at night to forage. So what we were doing at night wasn't dangerous with regards to hippos, even though I was worried about them at the time.

During the night survey, Mike used a flashlight to position the boat and locate the pygmy-geese. He discovered their primary feeding areas were among the lily pads. This was the final piece of the puzzle he needed to begin the hunt.

Mike: One of the reasons these ducks are colored the way they are is because they live amongst the lily pads. In the daytime, lily flowers are open, but at night the flower is closed like a fist. When you look at the colors and shape of a closed lily flower, it's very much like the head of an African pygmy-goose. They hide and feed in the lily pads at night.

With both day and night surveillance runs under their belt, Mike decided they were ready for the night hunt for pygmy-geese. He had mapped out where the birds would likely be and was confident his plan would bring African Pygmy-Geese to Duck Puddle Farm.

Mike: I figured if we motored very slowly into the lily pads at night with a light, we could get close to them and scoop them up with a net. That's why I wanted this boat. I had read where people had hunted birds with a glowing light and a net, though not a flashlight. A flashlight beam will move and the birds see that and know something's up.

While stuck out in the desert, Mike remembered something he had read about the way Persians would catch ducks. It was called the Gong and Flare Method. The hunters actually walk in line. The man in front has a glowing light. Another walks behind with a big net made out of bamboo. Behind him is a man with a gong that is softly struck at various levels of loudness, so the birds couldn't tell where it was coming from. The birds, confused by the light and sound, would remain perfectly still as the man with the net walked by and scooped them up.

Having brought no catching net on the trip, Mike constructed one out of materials he had with him or could scrounge from around the camp. He needed a net as wide as a butterfly net with a long handle. A piece of thick wire was bent into a hoop, to which a six-foot wooden pole was attached. The netting itself was cut from a section of the large net ripped apart by the crocodile at the first field camp. At least some good had come from the risk Mike took retrieving the damaged net.

Darkness shrouded the Shakawe marsh as the boat glided quietly through the narrow waterways. Sam steered the craft while Mike stood ready at the port side with his recycled net in hand. The chugging noise of the outboard motor supplied a sound effect similar to a bang-ing gong. In the bow of the boat, Mike hung a glowing kerosene lamp with tinfoil behind it, which reflected light, yet didn't cast a shadow.

Mike: The light shining without a shadow was important because the birds became mesmerized. The whole area was glowing and the birds couldn't focus on us approaching. Going through the lily pads you could see the pygmy-geese staying very still. They couldn't see me coming because they couldn't see through the glow. Then I could just scoop them up with a net as we trolled through the marsh.

The plan worked brilliantly. Mike's adaptation of the Gong and Flare hunting method resulted in procuring numerous pygmy-geese during the night.

Netting African Pygmy-geese using Gong & Flare method.

Mike: I caught them in pairs, which was important. I banded the pairs so I knew which ones had already pair bonded. When we eventually got them back to Duck Puddle Farm, those were the ones that bred. This plan worked much better than having a net across the water, because then you wouldn't know if you had any pairs.

However, prior to my decision to go on a night hunt, I did set a 100-foot long net across a small channel in the Okavango River. I caught only one pygmy-goose in it, although it was pretty neat to catch one in a net that long. That's when I knew I needed to get out on the water at night if I was ever going to catch more than a few.

Another interesting thing about the pygmy-geese is we put them in boxes as we caught them on the water. When we got back to camp, I noticed the boxes had small fishes in them from the ducks. So they weren't just eating seeds, they were also eating very small fishes amongst the lily pads. That was something no one had ever before reported seeing.

Now that Mike had caught his limit of pygmy-geese, he had to make sure they would safely make the journey back to Duck Puddle Farm. Overseeing the care of these and the other birds became the most important job for the next few days.

A hunt with a diffuse glowing light in the dark had turned the expedition from a nightmare to the brightest of achievements. Despite this success, Mike was about to make drastic changes in the team's personnel and location in Botswana.

THE GREAT WHITE HUNTER

Many pygmy-geese were now in hand along with the other birds he had caught, filling the pens at the Shakawe base camp. Mike had seen African White-backed Ducks among the trees in the swamp, but had not caught any. Trying to catch them was not worth spending any more of the two weeks he had left in Africa. The time had come to return to Francistown and figure out how to locate the next big prize – Maccoa Ducks.

Mike flew from the small airstrip in Shakawe to Francistown with the birds. The Botswanans, along with Howard, Sam, and the two women, made the journey in the Land Rover. The drive again included an overnight stay at the small hotel in Maun.

Mike was in immediate need of a place to safely keep his birds for the remainder of his time in Botswana. He knew of a fellow in Francistown, Jack Bousfield, who might have the proper facilities to house his birds. Jack owned Botswana Bird and Game, which was the only company in town that could legally catch animals and export them. He also had a small animal collection at his home.

Mike planned to visit Jack Bousfield right away, but first he had important business to take care of, something he'd considered during the flight from Shakawe.

Mike: Once in Francistown, I decided that Sam Weeks and his wife should go back to America. He wasn't really pulling his weight. I told him I would keep catching birds for the Smithsonian.

I also decided it would be best if Joanna visited friends in Kenya while I stayed in Botswana to search for waterfowl. I knew the moment I heard her scream as I was attacked by the crocodile, that I shouldn't be on adventures like this with my wife. I was concerned there might be times when I'd need to take swift action that she might consider dangerous, and I didn't want to second-guess myself at a critical moment.

With his cohorts preparing to leave Botswana, Mike took his birds to Jack Bousfield's compound to rest and feed while he made arrangements for the last leg of the expedition. He still didn't have a clue where he might go to find Maccoa Ducks. To his surprise, Jack told him where Maccoas could be located, as well as other species of waterfowl.

Mike: I went to see Jack Bousfield about keeping my birds with him. He said, "Look Mike, I know you've had your problems on this trip. I have to go out to catch young ostriches and other things. If you teach me how to catch waterfowl, you can go with me and use my guys on this trip."
It seemed like a good way to catch more birds, especially Maccoa Ducks.

A handshake partnership was struck between the two explorers. Jack would take Mike to the pans he knew Maccoa Ducks frequented and Mike would teach Jack how to set nets and catch waterfowl. Mike was eager to begin the wild ride into the Botswanan plains.

Early the next morning, two Land Rovers set off into the bush on a joint expedition. Mike drove one and Jack drove the other. The passengers included Jack's foreman from Kenya, plus the Botswanan helpers. Fourteen people were on the two-week trip.

The excitement was palpable as the caravan cruised through the bush. This was how Mike had always imagined an expedition to Africa – the roaring motors of the Land Rovers dashing across the open plains, a rush of wind blasting his face. How wonderfully different the adventure had become, now that he was on expedition with the prototypical African hunter.

Mike: Jack Bousfield came from Kenya originally. He was a larger-than-life character, though only about five feet, six inches tall. He had a handlebar moustache and smoked a pipe – like one of those guys in the book *Out of Africa*. He resembled the clichéd "great white hunter" and had all the stories to go with the image. I really enjoyed my time with him.

As we rode along the plains, we encountered a group of elephants. Instead of going around them, Jack drove straight through the middle of the herd. I didn't quite know what to think about that, but the herd divided and moved away. The guys that worked for him were terrified. They were hanging off the sides of the Land Rover screaming as we buzzed past the massive elephants, sometimes just missing them. It was all how I imagined it as a boy in England.

Eventually the expedition arrived in the pan areas of the Makgadikgadi region, nearly 100 miles west of Francistown. Here Mike hoped to catch waterfowl, especially Maccoa Ducks. Recent rains filled the pools with water, and lush vegetation had sprung up around them.

During the first week of exploration, they found numerous waterholes which attracted scores of birds. Mike collected six Spur-winged Geese and other waterfowl among these pans, but no Maccoa Ducks.

They camped beside the pans and set up nets. They had not taken into consideration the Cape buffalo that also come to the water's edge. These aggressive animals (called the widow-maker by the locals) not only presented a danger to the camp occupants, but also to the nets Mike deployed. The buffalo, surprised by the nets at the waterhole, would gather a whole net in their horns and disappear with it.

Evening meals in the camp with Jack and his crew provided interesting tales for Mike's enjoyment.

Mike: Jack loved curry. We started out on Monday with a curry and he'd add to it every day. It got stronger and stronger – he just kept pouring curry powder in it. My eyes watered up every time from the curry. But that's what he liked to eat, so that's what we had.

Occasionally we'd get a bird that died in the net. We'd give it to the Botswanans because that was good

meat to them, they loved that. They didn't even gut it.
The youngest guy plucked every single feather from
around its beak down to its legs. Then they cooked it
very quickly over the fire – turn it, turn it, turn it – and
that was about it.

How they would eat it is that the foreman would get
the first bite, and so on down the line, until the last guy
in the pecking order would be left to suck the bones.
They'd do that with a snake. They'd cook it in the fire
and eat it rather like corn on the cob. Rather strange.

Despite the enjoyable circumstances of being in the African bush
with the gregarious Jack Bousfield, a level of frustration was building
within Mike. Birds were plentiful in these pan areas of the savannah,
but not a single Maccoa Duck had been netted. The Maccoa Duck had
never been brought out of the wild. Mike intended to not only bring
this species home to Duck Puddle Farm, but also to be the first to
breed it as well. Time for finding the Maccoa Duck faded with each
pan he left empty-handed.

The Land Rovers arrived at another pond. Mike spotted Maccoa
Ducks flying in the area, but as was the case with the other pools, getting them in the net was the trick. Jack assured Mike there were no
crocodiles here, because this area was dry most of the year. Mike figured setting the nets close to the water would improve his chances.
With no crocs in the area, they could wade waist-deep in the water
safely while putting them up.

Unfortunately for Mike and the rest of the crew, it wasn't crocodiles they needed to avoid.

Mike: That evening, as it was getting dark, I could see a Red-
        billed Pintail caught in the net. I grabbed my binoculars
        and from the camp I could see the bird struggling, so I
        ran down to get the bird. Before I could get there, the
        poor thing was bled dry from leeches. It had been in the
        net probably less than half an hour, but there was noth-
        ing left of it.

        Suddenly, we realized that we all had leeches all over
        our legs from when we'd put up the nets. They all go to
        one place on the body and form a cluster. Each leech is
        an inch and a half long when they begin feeding, but

soon expand up to six inches – full of blood. The worst thing you could do is break one off, because it would keep draining blood out of your leg.

Jack and his foreman, plus two of his crewmen, had numerous leeches in very sensitive and private places on the mid-section of their bodies. The only way to treat such a bad case was to go back to Francistown and be hospitalized. Due to Mike's tall stature, the water never came up to his waist, so the leeches couldn't attach above his legs. Unfortunately for the much shorter Jack Bousfield, the pond water came above his legs, causing major problems for him.

The expedition had only just started the second week of a two-week trip in the bush. Mike felt bad for Jack, yet he couldn't help but think his opportunity to catch and breed Maccoa Ducks had slipped through his grasp. The birds were there – he could see them!

The Land Rover taking Jack and his two leech-infested crew members to Francistown was about to depart. Mike assumed he would follow in the other vehicle once he got the camp packed and loaded. Jack signaled to Mike to come over to the vehicle. He told Mike he wanted him to stay out here with the remainder of his crew and catch the birds he wanted.

It was a wonderful gesture, yet at the same time Mike was dismayed at the prospect of being a green 25-year-old in charge of Botswanans ranging from 14-year-old boys to 35-year-old men, most of whom did not speak English. He did not know if he could handle the state of affairs this would present.

One big problem for Mike was that the foreman was going back to Francistown with Jack Bousfield. The Kenyan, a black man, had been with Jack for many years and was crucial to deflecting disputes and complaints among the Botswanans. The foreman could not only speak the various native dialects, but also Swahili, which Jack also spoke fluently. They could speak confidentially together in Swahili, even within earshot of the crew.

Before he left, Jack gave Mike instructions on how to deal with the situation of overseeing his crew, but it would still be a real learning experience.

Mike: I heard Jack's advice in one ear, but I could also hear my father's stories of the difficulties he had with his South African crews in the other. I couldn't be sure what they might do once Jack and his head guy were gone. It was scary to be in the bush under those circumstances.

Fortunately, I had an ally in one of the Botswanans. He wasn't one of the older guys, but he spoke good English and helped keep any problems to a minimum. He was very supportive.

Since Mike was now within a week of leaving Africa, he decided he might find Maccoa Duck eggs easier than catching adult birds in nets. He had a portable incubator with him that could charge from the battery of the Land Rover. Besides, birds raised from eggs hatched at Duck Puddle Farm would be less difficult to breed than wild-caught birds.

Mike stopped at several ponds similar to the ones they had already explored. He and the men searched the ponds for nests, but found none. The crew still had thoughts of leeches in the back of their minds. They would reluctantly go into the water and quickly come back out saying, "No nests, Boss. No nests there."

Mike knew Maccoa Ducks were nesting because he spotted them in pairs and occasionally just the male. There had to be nests with eggs in the vegetation of those waterholes.

Mike: I smoked in those days and had cartons of Winston ciga-
         rettes. All of these guys liked to smoke, whether it was a
         butt or anything else. So I slapped down a pack of ciga-
         rettes on the hood of the Land Rover and said, "Look!
         The first person that brings me a Maccoa egg gets the
         packet of cigarettes." The guys went back into the water
         and brought out Maccoa eggs right and left.

The expedition was now a success in Mike's mind. He had the most important birds he came to collect. African Pygmy-geese were at Jack Bousfield's place in Francistown and Maccoa eggs were in his portable incubator.

The last two days of the trip in the bush yielded yet another unbelievable prize – Wattled Cranes.

Mike: I'd spotted Wattled Cranes flying around one of the
         ponds we were checking out. I decided to set a second
         net above another, effectively doubling the height. About

100

20 cranes eventually flew in over the top of my nets and landed at one end of the pond.

We quietly maneuvered behind them and then rushed at them, flailing our arms and yelling at the top of our lungs. The startled flock flew straight into the nets. Several were briefly caught, but managed to get loose. After all, the nets were designed for waterfowl, not cranes. But three of them got their feet tangled in the net.

Wattled Cranes were very rare, especially in America, and they are still today. I was thrilled to have found those cranes!

Mike steered the Land Rover packed with nine Botswanans toward Francistown. The expedition was rapidly coming to an end and the birds needed some rest at Jack's facility before being shipped to the United States. He had African Pygmy-geese and Maccoa Duck eggs, and the unexpected bonus of Wattled Cranes. The only thing missing from his pre-trip wish list were the African White-backed Ducks.

While driving through the bush, a tire went flat. The crew changed to the spare and they carried on. Just as they reached the paved road into Francistown, yet another tire went down. They couldn't travel on only three good tires and a flat. Mike decided to take the birds out of the Land Rover and put them in the shade. He managed to flag down one of the cars that would occasionally pass by on this stretch of road, a distance of 30 or 40 miles from Francistown.

Mike left the Botswanans with the birds while he hitched a ride to town to get the tire mended. He asked them to just wait there for three or four hours. Ultimately, it was five hours before he got back to the disabled Land Rover with the repaired tire.

Mike: When I returned, I found my guys on the bank of the road, all lying flat out fast asleep – feathers everywhere! I thought, "Oh my God, what's happened?"

They had killed and eaten my three Wattled Cranes. They didn't eat something more common – they had to kill the rarest birds.

"Why did you do that?" I exclaimed. "Well, Boss, we got hungry and you didn't leave us with supplies. We had to eat."

My assistant had tried to stop them, but they wouldn't listen to him. You can imagine when I got back into Francistown, I wasn't pleased. I still had the other birds, but the cranes were my pride and joy.

THE LONG WAY HOME

After the stunning loss of the Wattled Cranes, Mike regrouped a few days at Jack Bousfield's place in Francistown. There his focus was strictly on caring for the birds in preparation for their long flight to New York. He could not just get on a plane and leave with wild-caught birds. They would need at least three or four days to settle and for Mike to make sure they were doing well. Then they would be strong enough to survive the long flight and quarantine period required to get into the United States.

However, there was one more errand Mike needed to do before he himself could rest up at Jack's compound.

Mike: I had a Polaroid camera with me on the trip. The young man who helped me so much in the bush had asked if I'd take a picture of him and his family once we returned to Francistown. I went to his home and enjoyed spending some time with him and left several photographs, plus my safari clothes and hat.

A little down time with Jack Bousfield and his wife was just what Mike needed. The hospitality of his new friend allowed the tension from the trip to melt away. He also enjoyed visiting the little zoo Jack had on his property. Being around animals, especially birds, always brought him peace of mind and clarity of thought.

During his stay, a film crew came to Jack's place. His collection was well known by people who wanted to film or photograph animals. He had a number of wild animals there, including some that were more like pets. This film crew belonged to Marlin Perkins, who had an interest in Jack's pet leopard.

Marlin Perkins had come to Botswana to film an episode for his Mutual of Omaha series, *Wild Kingdom*. This was a popular TV series in America from 1963 to 1985. He wanted to film a scene in which he encountered a leopard.

Mike: Marlin seemed a nice enough sort of guy. He and his crew were only there long enough to film a scene where the leopard jumped over the top of him, from a rock or ledge. When I got back to America, I actually happened to see that episode. The scene was so funny. Perkins was standing beside a rock, supposedly in the wilds of Africa, and then suddenly this leopard leaps right over the top of him. Marlin reacts to the cat in utter fear. I saw this scene filmed at Jack's zoo. The leopard came from around the corner after the shot and licked his hand.

Marlin Perkins provided some much needed comic relief. Not that Mike didn't appreciate a program designed to present the world of animals to the public, but he preferred shows like Peter Scott's and David Attenborough's. Those documentaries provided real-life adventures of animals and where they lived in the world – not fake scenes with pet leopards.

The time had come to get to the business of shipping his birds to New York. Because of Newcastle's Disease, Mike could not go into Europe with waterfowl. In order to enter the United States he had to first go back into South Africa. From there he could get to Nairobi, Kenya, and then catch a Pan Am flight to JFK airport in New York.

Jack's people made crates for the birds while Mike prepared the incubators that would carry the precious Maccoa Duck eggs. Once the remainder of his gear was packed, he said good-bye to the Bousfields and began the journey home.

Mike arrived in Nairobi, Kenya, and had a 12-hour layover. The flight continued on to Rome, but he couldn't go because the birds were not allowed to land anywhere in Europe. Instead, he waited for a direct flight to New York.

His friend Jeff Lewis met him at the airport. Jeff managed the safari park outside of Nairobi. Jeff said, "Let's go see your birds." Mike thought they should move the birds into something like a quarantine area and make sure they had water and everything they needed. When they arrived at the airport cargo claim, there were no birds!

Mike: The plane had taken off for Rome with my birds on board. This was technically illegal. So I panicked and got on the phone to the airline authorities and said, "Send those birds back immediately!" Once in Rome, they got them off the plane and onto another flight back to Nairobi. They arrived that evening, about eight hours later.

The birds were taken to the Livestock Holding Station at the Nairobi Airport, where Mike could take them out of the crates, put them into pens, and make sure they were all right. Unfortunately, a few of the birds did not survive the ordeal, including one of the Spur-winged Geese. They were under too much stress.

Jeff said, "You can't leave tomorrow. These birds need time to recover. We need to keep them in Nairobi a couple of days or more."

Mike feared the success of the expedition might be in jeopardy. Jeff was right about the need to stay in Nairobi longer for the sake of the birds, but he also had to consider the eggs in the incubator. How much longer could it provide constant heat? Soon the eggs would start hatching. There was still such a long distance to go before the birds and eggs would reach Duck Puddle Farm, and it seemed they had already traveled halfway around the world.

Mike was distressed after these events. He took time to clear his thoughts to avoid being overwhelmed. Instead, he began to reassess his situation: the facilities at the airport were good; the birds seemed to be calm and eating well; the incubator gave no evidence of failing. This positive reassessment made him feel much better about the prospects of success. And he was about to receive a bonus.

Mike: Jeff had a pond in front of where he lived, and occasionally wild waterfowl would land on it. I went out there one day and saw African White-backed Ducks on the pond. I said, "Jeff! I still have my permits for white-backs!" We waded into his pond and caught up some of them. So I added the African White-backed Ducks to the trip home.

Mike stayed in Nairobi three days to allow the birds to rest. He packed up the birds again and flew back to New York without further incident, except for an aggravating itch that made him uncomfortable during the long flight. Mike's curator, Robin Clifford, met the flight early in the morning and got the birds to quarantine.

Relief was the only word that described his arrival at Duck Puddle Farm.

Mike: From those birds, we received a World's First Breeding Award for African Pygmy-geese. The reason for this, I believe, is I caught them in pairs and banded them as such, so they were already pair-bonded when they arrived at Duck Puddle. We also hatched Maccoa Ducks and raised them. That was an important achievement and another World's First Breeding Award.

Africa was a tough trip. I thought we'd just go over there and come back with a few birds and that would be that. But it wasn't easy. It was my first major expedition, although I'd been to Iceland, Alaska, and the Canadian Arctic before. This was the first time I felt I was in another world.

I guess I did a lot of growing up on that trip – and very quickly. It was a matter of learning to endure in the wild. That put me in good stead for literally surviving a future trip to South America.

It was a rough trip indeed, but soon Mike would be forced to make one of the most difficult decisions of his career.

CHAPTER FIVE

In Her Majesty's Service

Coming home to Duck Puddle Farm afforded Mike a much-needed respite after the demands of the African expedition. He could finally address the severe itch that made him agonizingly uncomfortable during the flight from Nairobi. It had gotten even worse since he had gotten back to New York.

The doctors in New York diagnosed him with schistosomiasis, a parasitic disease caused by the blood fluke bilharzia, named after the German pathologist who discovered its eggs.

Mike: On the flight back I had "swimmers itch" as they call it –
it was terrible. I must have picked it up from standing in
Jeff Lewis's pond catching the African White-backed
Ducks. Snails will lay eggs in the tissue, which hatch and
enter the bloodstream. After two or three years, it will kill
you, if not treated properly.

The treatment they proposed was to take his blood out, filter it through a sieve, and then put it back into his veins. Mike wasn't convinced this afforded him the best route to recovery, so he called his stepfather, who was a physician in London.

Mike: England was much more advanced with these types of
tropical illnesses, due to the country's involvement in
India, Africa, and other places. My stepfather's father was
an important originator of the Tropical Disease Hospital
in London.

I told my stepfather what the American doctors wanted to do. He said, "Hold on! Don't even go there! Get on
a plane and come home."

Mike immediately flew to London, where he underwent a week of specialized treatment at the Tropical Disease Hospital. He impatiently counted the days before being released from the hospital and on his way back to New York. As a distraction from the agonizing bilharzia treatments, he began working his mind on new breeding projects and adventures for when he returned to Duck Puddle Farm.

Mike's innovations had made Duck Puddle Farm the most technically advanced avicultural operation in the world. There would be much more to come as soon as he could get out of the hospital. However, as he lay in his bed thinking he would soon be on a flight back to America, an unexpected visitor approached, who would once again change the direction of his career.

"Hello, Mike," a man said as he entered the hospital ward. A bit startled, Mike looked up from his bed to see a familiar figure. It was Sir Peter Scott.

BACK HOME AGAIN

At first it seemed Sir Peter had driven the long distance from the Wildfowl Trust in Slimbridge only to pay a visit to a friend and colleague in the hospital. The initial conversation centered on Mike's trip to Africa and the resulting disease. Eventually, it became evident he had another reason for his trip to London.

"Mike, quite honestly, the collection at Slimbridge is deteriorating. I know since you've been in America you have pioneered new techniques in aviculture, and now we really need you to come back to the Wildfowl Trust."

The notion stirred Mike's thoughts. Only moments before his mind had dwelled exclusively on the challenges at Duck Puddle Farm. Now Peter Scott presented him with an entirely unexpected request which would be nearly impossible to refuse.

Leaving Duck Puddle Farm would not be an easy decision. In the time they had lived in New York, he and Joanna had established many friends and acquaintances. He had much more freedom to experiment with his ideas on improving aviculture. Winston was also willing to fund trips to wild, exotic places every year to increase the size of the collection – something the Wildfowl Trust was unlikely to finance. Was it really best to leave such splendid advantages?

Mike had always maintained a sense of gratitude toward Peter Scott. Not only was he a childhood hero, he had become a mentor and advisor regarding his career, and to some extent, his personal life. Peter had encouraged Mike to take the job in America to expand his knowledge of aviculture and perhaps one day return to apply his expertise at Slimbridge. It seemed that day had arrived.

Mike: It turned out that Tommy Johnstone was retiring as the curator of the Wildfowl Trust. Peter Scott came to the hospital and asked me if I'd consider coming back to Slimbridge as the new curator of aviculture.

    I felt I owed something to Slimbridge. Early on I had hoped one day to become the curator, and now suddenly the opportunity was presenting itself. I wasn't sure, but I had a feeling that Winston's interest in his collection was waning. He had been talking about moving to Florida.

    I was leaning toward coming back to Slimbridge. But there was one caveat. I first wanted to go down to the Wildfowl Trust and see why Peter Scott was so eager to get me back. I needed to see what I was getting myself into.

After being released from the hospital in London, Mike went back to New York to discuss the offer to relocate to Slimbridge with Joanna and Winston. He then flew back to England to speak further with Peter Scott and inspect the operation at the Wildfowl Trust.

Mike: I looked around and decided the entire breeding area needed to be re-engineered. I suggested they tear the whole thing out. I would provide the design to rebuild it.

    This is what I wanted before I would agree to come back, and they did it. They completely rebuilt all the duckeries according to the plans I laid out. I guess they were anxious to get me back. I became the curator of the Wildfowl Trust in 1973, just a few months after my return from Africa.

By the time Mike left the United States, he had become a recognized authority in the field of aviculture. During his four years in New York, he attended numerous conferences of the International Wild Waterfowl Association (IWWA), American Waterfowl Association, and the American Federation of Aviculture, as well as other meetings. He was in demand as a speaker at these events. People wanted to know more about Mike Lubbock, who had achieved so many first breeding awards. He was returning triumphantly to England and bringing many new ideas with him.

Despite having made an inspection of Slimbridge before agreeing to come back, Mike's arrival as curator soon revealed a surprise.

Mike: When I finally got there, I found the avicultural program had badly deteriorated. The ratio of males to females was sorely unbalanced, and the Wildfowl Trust's reputation for breeding birds had declined significantly. I didn't know this was happening while I worked in America. I kept in contact with people in England, but this caught me unaware.

I had many problems to work through with the birds. The White-fronted Geese, for example, consisted of 21 males and one female – a breeding

Mike at the Wildfowl & Wedlands Trust.

program just won't work with numbers like that.

Before I had left, the Trust had 14 pairs of White-headed Ducks, which is one of the species I'm credited for breeding first, but upon my return there were only three pairs. They had not bred them since I'd left. There were lots of cases like that all around the grounds.

No stranger to hard work, Mike got the breeding program back into shape in about a year.

He was successful in getting the White-headed Ducks to breed within that first year, based on what he observed in Africa. The nesting habits of the Maccoa Duck, which is a stiff-tail like the White-headed Duck, provided him with an idea for getting better results with White-headed Ducks. In Africa, he noticed the Maccoa Duck does not build a nest, but rather waits for a coot to finish nesting and then uses the old nest. Mike went to the local gravel pit and picked up all abandoned coots nests and put them in the White-headed Duck pens. Lo and behold, they bred very quickly.

Mike: It was satisfying to build that collection up from nothing to getting noticed again. We were getting more first breeding awards and people were once again interested in what was happening at Slimbridge. Peter Scott was happy with the progress on the White-winged Wood Duck project, an extremely endangered species. We also got all the flamingo species breeding prolifically.

Mike garnered nine more World's First Breeding Awards after his return to England. These were birds that collectors wanted to breed and zoos wanted for their displays. Bird curators and waterfowl breeders in North America all knew who Mike Lubbock was, and now those in England recognized him as well.

Mike: I wanted the English aviculturalists to be able to attend conferences like we held in America. I thought this would be a good thing to do in England. There were people breeding birds and some good collections in England, but they never got together. Nobody knew who was even breeding birds, except maybe by telephone.
        I decided to put a conference together. We met the first time at Blakney in Norfolk. I invited 50 people. It was a great success. Those meetings went on for many years before eventually merging with the International Wild Waterfowl Association (IWWA).
        The IWWA served to bring private collectors closer to the Wildfowl Trust. Before this, the Trust had been a bit aloof. Private aviculturists have a lot to offer the field of avian husbandry. One person may find that a specific

technique works well, but no one else may have even thought of it. The IWWA presented a forum to share ideas that worked.

Mike's second stint at Slimbridge had certainly advanced his avicultural career. However, his personal life would soon begin a roller coaster of emotions.

ALONG COMES ALI

Domestic tranquility was never an abundant commodity in the Lubbock household. Long hours at the breeding center and Mike's intense travel schedule certainly contributed to a strained marriage over time.

Joanna and Mike were married only one year before the fragile family roots were disrupted by the sudden decision to move to New York. Problems began almost immediately after the relocation.

Mike: In those days, America was wide open. We both developed
        separate friends and acquaintances while we were there.
        Joanna and I had multiple problems with our relationship.
            Our marriage was already heavily strained when I
        agreed to become curator of the Wildfowl Trust. I had a
        great challenge to turn things around, and we drifted
        apart even more after moving to the curator's cottage
        at Slimbridge.

Differences became irreconcilable soon after Mike returned from one of his international expeditions. Events came to a boil very quickly and the couple decided it would be best if Joanna moved back to New York immediately, after which they would seek a divorce.

Mike: It was the best move for Joanna's life at the time. I drove
        her to the airport and helped her board a plane to
        America. That made it very difficult to get a divorce
        decree, since she was in the United States and I was in
        England. The long and the short of it is that she stayed in
        America, but we did get a divorce eventually.

After Joanna moved back to America, a young female volunteer started work with the Wildfowl Trust's Scientific Department. Alisonjane Stewart from Edgemere, Scotland, had a desire to study waterfowl and found her way to Slimbridge. Ali, as she was called, began working in the Scientific Department with Professor Jeffrey Mathews. Before long, Ali encountered the imposing curator, Mike Lubbock.

Mike: Professor Mathews sent her out to the grounds to observe the Bewick's Swans, which were nesting for the first time. A guy at the Scientific Department had a bicycle, so she asked if she could ride it down to where the Bewick's Swans were kept. She rode this bicycle, unaware that I didn't allow bicycles on the grounds.

As I saw her come by, I yelled at her to stop. I asked, "Who gave you permission to ride a bike on grounds?" I may have said this a little too gruffly.

"Professor Mathews," she answered incredulously.

"He has no right to tell you to bring a bike in here!" I said.

Then we engaged in one of those shouting matches that crescendo throughout the duration. The whole performance was witnessed by a group of startled visitors.

To make matters worse, she had borrowed the type of bicycle that had two locking mechanisms you twist so it will fold up and fit into the trunk of a car. Once she had grudgingly agreed to get off the bike and walk to her destination, it immediately collapsed, dropping her and the bicycle to the ground. She felt so humiliated with me having shouted at her in public and then awkwardly trying to recoup from the fall.

That's how we met. Ali didn't like me very much then, to put it mildly. She hated me, actually.

After a bitter first impression, Ali vowed to do all within her power to avoid the cantankerous Mike Lubbock. For a significant period of time, that's exactly what she did. However, as time passed, she began to appreciate Mike's other qualities more than she had perceived during their turbulent introduction.

Mike also came to notice Ali had the same drive and passion for waterfowl and their preservation as he did. She eventually accepted a position as Mike's assistant, handling his travel schedule, making his appointments, and keeping track of his work in the breeding programs.

The partnership continued to blossom, and in a few years, Ali became Mike's permanent assistant

Ali with little Brent, Mike with "Mrs. Wiggins" at the curator's cottage.

in life. During a visit to the United States, they were married in Las Vegas, Nevada. A few years later they had a son, Brent.

Ali would be that "one in a million" who was willing to invest all of her life and effort into the dream Mike Lubbock chased around the world. Ali not only provided support to their family, but also in Mike's desire to be the world's best aviculturalist. Together they would strive to reach the pinnacle of waterfowl preservation, doing all in their power to save endangered species from extinction.

IN HER MAJESTY'S SERVICE

During Mike Lubbock's time as curator of the Wildfowl Trust, he was occasionally asked to contribute his avicultural talents to the service of the Crown. His encounters with the Royals have long been told and retold, most frequently to dinner guests and interns who visit the Lubbocks' home in Scotland Neck.

THE ROYAL GOOSER

Her Majesty the Queen enjoyed birds and had been a patron of the Wildfowl & Wetlands Trust for many years. She had also visited the grounds at Slimbridge, during which time Sir Peter Scott gave her the grand tour. As a thank-you for her patronage to the Trust, Peter donated four pairs of Red-breasted Geese to Buckingham Palace.

Buckingham Palace has vast lawns, beautiful gardens, and a big island with a moat around it. Wild Tufted Ducks fly in and breed on the island. The palace walls that encircle the grounds provide protection from both people and predators. It's a great place to have waterfowl.

But the Queen had a problem. Despite all the wonderful attributes the palace grounds provided for the natural breeding of waterfowl, the Red-breasted Geese she'd received from Slimbridge had never multiplied. For the several years she had them, the geese preferred to hang around the island, eating the succulent grass rather than engaging in amorous activities.

Frustrated by her unromantic geese, Her Majesty called Sir Peter Scott on the phone for advice. "I have had these Red-breasted Geese for several years and they have never bred. It would be nice if we can get them to breed."

Peter Scott replied, "Well, that's very interesting. My curator, Mike Lubbock, would be the ideal person to come up and take a look at the situation and advise you on what can be done."

Mike: I think it was in 1975 that I drove to Buckingham Palace in the Wildfowl Trust's little green Leyland van. I remember stopping at the side gate of the palace. There was a policeman there and I said, "I have an appointment with Her Majesty at eleven o'clock."

He looked me over a bit, and I began to wonder if he was going to let me in.

Finally the policeman said, "Yes, Mr. Lubbock, we've been expecting you. Drive right through to that gate on the other side of the courtyard." He opened the gate and allowed me through.

Buckingham Palace had, as usual, a throng of visitors outside the gate looking through into the courtyard. Any activity within the courtyard can be seen by the public and will always cause curiosity as to what might be going on. As Mike steered the little green van slowly along driveway, he could feel all those eyes upon him, as if to say, "Who is he and what's he doing? Is he delivering something to the Queen in that silly-looking green van?"

Mike: I got to the second gate, and a man there opened it up and asked me to wait. So I waited there for some time before an old boy came out of the palace wearing something that looked like carpet slippers on his feet. It was a chap named Sir Bonham-Carter. He was the Queen's

115

personal attendant and a retired admiral in the Royal Navy.

The admiral said, "Ah, Mr. Lubbock, what you should do is look around the grounds and see the birds; yes, and come back in a half hour and then I'll show you to the Queen."

I left my van behind the gate and walked around, inspecting the grounds. I met up with a gardener, called Mr. Nutbeam, a really nice old boy. He was the head gardener at Buckingham Palace. We walked around the gardens and went out on an island in the middle of a pond and saw the Red-breasted Geese.

I said to him, "What are you feeding them?"
He said, "Well, we give them a bit of corn."

I continued my inquiry of Nutbeam: "When the helicopters come to the palace, where do they land?"
He said, "They land very close to the water here."
I said, "Well, I hear there are a lot of dogs around."

Nutbeam replied, "The Queen has eleven dogs – her corgis and some mutts. They come out every morning and they run everywhere. But they don't go on the island."

I said, "Well, the other thing I hear is that the garden parties occur in June, when the birds breed."

"Yes, that's right. People move all around the island – even way in the back there. Sometimes there are three thousand people at these parties, plus lots of tents and tables."
That could be causing problems, I thought.

My tour of the grounds was completed. All the things I discussed with Nutbeam the gardener were in my mind as I walked back to the door to meet up again with Sir Bonham-Carter.

He said, "Well, Mr. Lubbock, have you got some ideas for getting the geese to breed?"
"I think so, yes."

The Admiral opened the door and led Mike inside the palace and down a long corridor into a room. From there, they proceeded up the stairs and stopped outside a door with an official-looking man standing in front of it. After a quick knock, the Admiral opened the door and took Mike inside a room where the Queen was sitting at a desk. She beckoned him to sit down in a chair in front of her.

Sir Bonham-Carter backed out of the room and disappeared. (Protocol dictates that you never turn your back on the Queen.) The man who was standing outside the door was now standing inside the door and remained there during the interview.

Mike: I was very nervous, as you can imagine. I had been walking around the grounds, and now I noticed that my shoes were getting mud on the exquisite carpet. But she immediately made me feel very much at ease.
"How are we going to get the geese to breed, Mr. Lubbock?" the Queen asked.
I said, "We need to change the feed, for starters. They're getting corn, and they should have a more nutritious pellet. But they are eating some good grass on the island. Is it possible we can get the helicopters to land further from the moat?"
She said, "I think we could arrange that."
"Another problem is the dogs," I continued. "Could they be kept away from the geese, especially in June when they breed?"
I forget her exact wording, but clearly it was difficult to train the page boys to look after the dogs, as she indicated they went through more page boys than dirty linen in the palace. However, she seemed to believe the situation with the dogs could be improved.
"One other thing," I said. "Is it possible to stop the garden party guests from going all the way back to the moat and island areas? The parties often occur during nesting season, and so many people walking nearby can greatly disturb the birds."
"That might be difficult," said the Queen. "We've held garden parties this way for three hundred years. It's become a tradition."
We talked about a few other things, such as Slimbridge and the birds there. With that, she thanked

me and the interview was over. It all lasted about fifteen minutes. I got up, bowed, and backed out of the room.

Mike was escorted back to his little green van. He drove across the courtyard again, pulled out of the palace gate, and sighed in great relief.

He didn't go back to check on the geese, although he stayed in touch with Mr. Nutbeam, who reported that he had changed the feed as Mike had suggested. Still, he was worried about not having received any word about the birds nesting.

Mike: Really, I was concerned the geese might not have bred and the Queen's people were keeping quiet about it. I began to wonder if my intervention had failed.

Later that summer, Ali and I were invited to a garden party at Buckingham Palace. As we drove our little Volkswagen on the highway to London, several people driving Rolls-Royces passed us sporting the special Palace Parking Pass in the window. Each time, Ali held up our pass to show them we had the same one!

We strolled into the party and I had a look around. A military band played music. There were people everywhere, but to my surprise, they had cordoned off the island and no one could get back to where the geese were, just as I had suggested to the Queen. There was no way I could see how the birds were doing on the island and I certainly wasn't going to jump the rope to find out.

For Ali it was a very special occasion, attending this party. I was more worried about the Red-breasted Geese.

"THE QUEEN IS ON THE PHONE"

One Sunday not long after the garden party, Mike was surveying the grounds at Slimbridge when a member of his staff hurriedly came up to him and gasped, "The Queen is on the phone! She wants to talk to you!"

Mike reacted calmly to the message because he'd been told that the Queen rarely spoke to anyone on the telephone, so it couldn't be her. He surmised it was either a prank or Sir Bonham-Carter wanting to speak to him about something.

Mike: I hurried back to my office and picked up the phone, still a little out of breath. Sure enough, it was the Admiral. "Hello, Mr. Lubbock. I'm glad I got up with you. Her Majesty would like to have a word with you."

"Oh, shoot!" I thought. "It is her! What should I do – stand up? Sit down?"

She told me how absolutely delighted she was because three of the four pairs of Red-breasted Geese had laid eggs. She was over the moon!

"Mr. Lubbock," she said, "you've been so good with those birds, we're thinking of having more at Sandringham. Do you think you could come and advise us there, too?"

Mike rowing at Buckingham Palace with Sir Max Williams, President of the Law Society.

With the Queen's new excitement for breeding waterfowl, Mike started going to Buckingham Palace about three times per year. She became more interested in birds because of the success she had with the geese. His friends even joked that Mike was the Queen's Royal Gooser, a title he hasn't been able to shake even to this day.

Mike: I even got flamingos for her. I didn't see the Queen every time I went up there, but one time I saw her on the grounds riding her horse. She pulled the horse to a stop and said, "Hello, Mr. Lubbock." She even remembered my name. That was really nice.

The only other time I was actually inside the palace was for a World Wildlife Fund fundraiser with the Queen and the Duke of Edinburgh.
I was on a diving holiday in the south of France and had to fly back for it. I don't remember what year it was. I was on the grounds six or seven times. I'd always drive to a side gate near where Mr. Nutbeam had a cottage.

My mother came to the palace with me once and got along very well with Mr. Nutbeam, who gave her cuttings from the grounds. She was very green-fingered and kept a garden at her house in Oxfordshire. It was called The Old Manor in Shilton, built in the 10th century as a monastery. She planted all those starts from Mr. Nutbeam inside the garden wall and told her friends it was her "Buck Garden."

THE RAVENS AT THE TOWER OF LONDON

Mike Lubbock has a place in British legend as a result of his passion for keeping pets – in this case, ravens. Although his participation is not well known, it is significant, assuming you believe the premise of the tradition regarding the Tower of London.

Mike: All my life I had pets; that's just how I lived my life. I'd always liked ravens and all the birds in the crow family – jackdaws, also. But ravens always fascinated me. They are large and intelligent.

I had tame ravens in those days. I used to get them from Wales, which wasn't too far away – a three- or four-hour drive from Slimbridge. There was a place near Abergavenny. I would explore the area to find raven nests. It was much like the other collecting challenges I've had over the years. It's what keeps me going.

Ravens nest very early in the season, around February or March. I'd try to time these trips when the sheep start to lamb, because ravens will eat dead lambs. They always seemed to nest in the trees that were the most challenging to climb.

The ravens in the Tower of London play an important part in British history. For many centuries, the Tower has always maintained six ravens. According to legend, if for any reason the number of ravens should fall below six, London's "White Tower" will collapse and a terrible catastrophe shall befall England.

The legend of the ravens in the Tower of London was originated in medieval times by a chronicler named Geoffrey of Monmouth, who authenticated many of the Welsh Celtic myths and legends. Monmouth wrote a book in 1136, called *Historia Regum Britanniae* (History of the Kings of Britain) in which he refers to a British king of the Dark Ages called King Bran Hen of Bryneich. An interesting note is that "Bran" is the Welsh word for raven. King Bran Hen declared that should he be killed in battle, his head should be buried on Gwynfryn (the "White Mount") where the Tower of London stands today. The king, who indeed fell in battle, believed his burial there would serve as a sort of lucky charm against any future invasion of England.

King Charles II is believed to have decreed that at least six ravens should be kept at the Tower at all times to avoid a national calamity. To this day ravens are considered essential residents of the Tower of London. At minimum six "charmed" ravens inhabit the Tower of London, along with a Ravenmaster, who has the specific duty to care and feed them.

Mike: I was awakened in the middle of the night by a call from the Ravenmaster at the Tower of London.

"We have a problem. We desperately need two ravens. Can you get them up here before we open to the public at nine o'clock tomorrow morning?" he said with a real sense of alarm in his voice.

I told him, "I do have two ravens, actually, but I've already promised them to a wildlife park."

"But you see, Mr. Lubbock, this is a national emergency," the Ravenmaster replied.

I don't know how the Ravenmaster knew I had ravens. I never publicized the fact that I kept them.

Slimbridge is at least a three-hour drive from Central London. The Ravenmaster bent my arm a little bit, but I ended up dashing off to London with my birds. I met with the Ravenmaster at the Tower, where he took them on and my two ravens became part of the six.

The only special favor I asked was regarding the history of my ravens in the Tower. Background information of the Tower's birds is available to the public. I asked that these two be listed as coming from Wales and that my name not be associated with them.

When one goes to the Tower these days you can see the history of the birds. These records only go back to the '40s or '50s, even though they've had these birds much, much longer. One can see my two birds listed as coming from Wales. My birds were bred at the Tower, although I believe they both have died now. Ravens will live 30 or 40 years.

They did pay me for those birds. But that's the story. The Tower of London would have fallen if I hadn't gotten those ravens up there in time. [Mike chuckles.]

THE QUEEN AT SLIMBRIDGE

Every spring the Queen and all of her family would attend the Badminton Horse Trials, which is held at the Duke of Beaufort's estate in Gloucestershire – about a half an hour's drive from Slimbridge.

One Sunday morning at 9:00 o'clock, Mike received a call from the Duke of Beaufort's secretary informing him that rain had cancelled the trials at Badminton.

"The Queen wants to come down for a visit," said the secretary.

Mike: The Queen wanted something to do since the trials were cancelled. As she's a Wildfowl Trust patron, she thought she'd come to see the birds. Also coming were the Duke of Edinburgh [Prince Philip], Princess Margaret and [her daughter] Sarah, all the other Beauforts, plus a whole list of people.

Mike said to the secretary, "I've already opened the grounds to the public."

He said, "Well, don't worry about that. We'll be there at 10:30."

"Oookaay," Mike responded to the news.

He immediately called Jeffrey Mathews, who had the

day off. "You need to get out of bed. Come down here and help me out. I've got the Queen and her whole entourage coming. Beauforts – all of them! They'll be here at 10:30."

Mathews swore, hung up, and grudgingly made his way to the Wildfowl Trust.

Mike: I decided the best tour for the Queen and her party would be to go around the grounds backwards, instead of the usual way that visitors are directed. That way the public would see her and be surprised, but then we'd move on and that would be a good way of doing it. Otherwise there might be those who'd attempt to tour along with the Queen.

As Her Majesty's arrival time approached, I started to get nervous. I went over the details with my staff about opening gates and all that. I tried to organize it as best I could on such short notice.

Mike knew the tropical house might be difficult to negotiate since the entryway had two sets of doors to keep the warm, moist air from escaping outside. So Mike asked one of the volunteers if he could manage holding two sets of doors for open for the Queen and her party.

"Oh yes, sure. No problem at all," he chortled confidently.

Then it all started to happen. Looking out at the entry road, Mike saw a fleet of cars arriving. The caravan seemed to go on forever.

The Queen got out of her car, along with the Duke of Edinburgh. Jeffrey Mathews and Mike stepped forward to greet them.

Mike: She was very easy to talk to. Of course, I'd already met her several times at Buckingham Palace and she knew who I was.

When we started the tour, I had a basket with some bread in it so they could feed the birds. Mathews was in charge of escorting the Queen, while I was with the Duke of Edinburgh. However, by making the tour in the reverse direction, Mathews got confused as to which birds they were looking at. So I had to explain which birds we were seeing to both the Duke of Edinburgh and the Queen. Eventually, Mathews dropped behind altogether

Mike with the Queen.

to escort other members of the Queen's party. From that point on, I escorted the Queen and the Duke.

It was a long ways around, about a half-mile walk in all. The funny thing was whenever she'd stop to look at a particular bird, the entire column of Royals suddenly jammed up and came to an abrupt halt.

The public turned out to be no problem at all. They had no idea the Queen was coming that morning. It was quite fun to watch their faces when they unexpectedly came nearly face to face with her. The expressions of surprise and delight were most amusing.

The tour arrived at the tropical house. The trusty volunteer stretched himself beyond normal human limits, attempting to keep the two sets of doors open while the Queen's elongated line of followers strolled slowly into the exhibit.

Mike: During the tour I talked to her about breeding the birds, since that was a large part of what we did at the Wildfowl Trust.

"Where does this bird breeding take place?" she asked me.

"At the breeding center ," I replied.

"I'd like to see that if it's possible," said the Queen.

"Well, that certainly is available, if you'd like," I said.

This was a real twist to the plans Mike had made. He barely had time to get things ready for the Royals' visit, and now they were about to abort the planned tour and make a behind-the-scenes excursion. Nothing had been done to clean up the breeding facility. The Queen was very interested in the birds and how they were bred, and she wanted details.

Mike: We got to the egg room, but it was too small to have the whole party in there. So I took in the Queen, the Duke of Edinburgh, Sarah, I think the Beauforts, plus myself. There were so many people milling around. All I know was the Queen was the only one I was worried about. I directed all my comments to her. I don't really know for sure who else was in that tiny room.

I went inside the incubators and brought out some eggs. She said, "I would like to see inside the incubator. Could I watch you candle the eggs?"

I said, "Why, sure."

I got out a candler [flashlight and tube]. I think I had one of my staff in there with me, because I said to him, "Can you turn out the lights?"

And that's when all hell broke loose. (Whenever you host the Queen, she has bodyguards with her. They blend in, but they're always nearby and ready to step in immediately if necessary.)

I had put the Queen in a small, dark room! The bodyguards were in a panic outside. But she had asked me to show her how the whole operation worked. It was her idea to candle the eggs. You had to turn off the lights to do that.

After that, I took her to the duckeries, where she enjoyed holding the ducklings and goslings.

Mike was with the Queen for over two hours. The Queen's party were all invited to stay for lunch, but other plans had already been made.

Mike: Later on, I was talking to the chief of security. I told him what I did in the egg room.
"You turned off the lights in the incubator room? Oh, you shouldn't have done that! That's not the protocol!" he retorted.
"What was I supposed to do?" I said. "Refuse a request from the Queen?"
I never really got any trouble from it. I think she enjoyed the experience. None of that other stuff seemed to bother her.

BACK TO THE WILD

Returning to England did not curtail the number of egg-collecting expeditions Mike conducted, some of them financed by his old boss, Winston Guest. These included trips to Argentina, the Falkland Islands, and Chile, and yielded many new birds – the Black-headed Duck, Torrent Duck, Falkland Island Steamer Duck, and Argentine Ruddy Duck. None of these birds had been bred before or even kept in a collection until the Wildfowl Trust acquired them.

Mike also journeyed to Australia to bring the Pink-eared Duck to the Wildfowl Trust and made numerous trips to Spain as part of the mission to save the endangered White-headed Duck. Those two expeditions were to become Mike's most successful missions of his career.

CHAPTER SIX

Search for the Pink-eared Duck

Wildfowl Trust, Slimbridge, England
April 1979

Rain pelted the ground, which was already saturated from three days of unrelenting spring showers. The inclement weather had Mike Lubbock holed up in his office, which had become extensively muddied from his trudging in and out during the downpour. Mike detested administrative work with the same fervor as he loved breeding waterfowl. Since the rain forced him to be inside, at least he could call and check in with his contact in Australia.

He slowly twisted in his desk chair, holding the receiver to his ear and beginning to doubt that Tom Spence, director of the Perth Zoo, would ever come to the phone. The assistant who answered the call assured him that Tom was in the office and would pick up soon. Mike reluctantly decided to wait another minute or two and stared out his office window, watching as the puddles along the visitor pathway quickly grew into small ponds. "This is ironic," he thought. "Why couldn't it be raining like this in Australia?"

For the past three years, Mike had endeavored to explore for waterfowl in the land of the Swan River Colony, as the area around Perth in Western Australia was originally named by the British in the days of Captains Stirling and Freemantle. Twice Mike had to cancel the expedition due to a severe drought in the region. The birds in Australia won't nest unless there's a rainy season.

Now for the third spring in as many years, he called Tom to find out if waterfowl were breeding on the lakes around Perth. It would be pointless to go halfway around the world if they weren't. Mike was hoping the weather would not force him to abandon his campaign for the third year in a row. He was concerned that the window of opportunity for him to explore for eggs in Australia would soon close.

No one outside Australia had ever been permitted to take water-fowl eggs out of the country, but Mike had authorization from Wildlife Headquarters, the government's wildlife agency, to be the first to do so. It was the opportunity of a lifetime. For this, he owed a huge debt of gratitude to his longtime friend, Bill Makins.

Bill had a collection of birds at Pensthorpe Wildfowl Park in Fakenham, Norfolk, England. He and Mike had made many trips together. It was through Bill that Mike received permits to collect eggs in Australia. Mike's work with the Wildfowl Trust and his contacts with the Australian wildlife agency were helpful; however, Bill's brother-in-law worked for a company in Australia, and that relationship opened the door for Mike to collect eggs there. This would be a one-time occurrence, so Mike couldn't afford to waste this opportunity if the multi-year drought prevented the birds from breeding yet again.

Mike tapped his pencil on the desk impatiently and was about to hang up the phone when at last he heard Tom's booming voice: "Hello, Mike!"

He listened intently as Tom responded to his question about whether there was enough rainfall for the waterfowl to breed this season. The report was mixture of good and bad news. There had been a little rain in Western Australia, but not a significant amount. Tom couldn't really say if it would be worth his while to come down. Mike would have to make that judgment himself.

Mike hung up the phone and leaned back in his chair. He sighed loudly as he ran his hands slowly back through his salt and pepper hair, considering his options. He was concerned the window of access might be closing, and he was anxious to take advantage of the opportunity before it vanished.

Two breeding seasons had been lost because of the drought. Was this sparse rain enough to warrant going down there? He didn't know how much longer he could wait.

Once more he turned to view the rainfall outside. Was this an indication that he should move ahead on his plans to go now? Mike knew it wasn't logical, but the deluge outside inspired him. Perhaps he should go, despite the uncertain report from Tom.

With a deep breath, the decision was made. He exhaled, picked up the phone and dialed Bill Makins at Pensthorpe. "Bill! It's Mike. I just talked with Tom Spence. Let's make this Aussie trip happen."

Australia exclusively held several waterfowl species Mike hoped to collect, but the Pink-eared Duck and the Freckled Duck were his most important objectives.

The Pink-eared Duck is sometimes called the Zebra Duck, perhaps a more fitting name since the black-and-white stripes on its flanks are far more noticeable than the small pink "ear" patches that are scarcely visible except at close range. The odd-looking duck is a very unusual species of waterfowl, due primarily to the manner in which it feeds. Their large bill has fleshy flaps near the tip, allowing them to more efficiently filter algae and plankton (their primary food source) from the water.

Their atypical feeding routine makes them extraordinarily difficult to breed in managed populations, which is why no Pink-eared Ducks had been successfully raised outside the wild at the time of Mike's Australian trip in 1979. This was one reason Mike was keen to bring them to the Wildfowl Trust.

The Freckled Duck is camouflaged exactly as its name suggests – with thousands of alternating light and dark tiny spots uniformly spread over all feathered areas. Unfortunately, it is one of the least numerous of native Australian ducks. Their habitat continues to shrink due to wetland clearing and drainage. Although the Freckled Duck had already been bred outside the wild, Mike desperately wanted to take eggs back to England as part of a breeding program to insure their survival.

PORTABLE INCUBATOR ADVANCEMENT

Mike is proud of his pioneering use of portable incubators on long-distance flights to bring eggs to avian breeding facilities such as the Wildfowl Trust. This development revolutionized modern aviculture and gave relevancy to survival breeding programs as a means of conserving endangered species.

Mike: We had asked the Australian government if I could collect eggs of several species of waterfowl native to Australia. They agreed, especially since it was requested by the Wildfowl Trust, which had a lot of influence in these matters.

Because I wanted eggs and not adult birds, the success of the trip would require the use of an advanced portable incubator I had been developing. I was going to collect eggs around Perth in Western Australia.

Mike knew that collecting eggs on an expedition was the best way to bring birds in from the wild. The main advantage would be that he could hatch and rear them back in England without their having much wild instinct. This causes them to breed much more quickly than wild-caught birds. Even more importantly, he would not lose any birds from transporting them over long distances.

Mike: Another plus was getting permits in other countries. I could tell them I just wanted to take a couple of eggs from each clutch, and then the parent birds could hatch the rest of the clutch and rear them. Then I'd explain to them that a female may lay eight to ten eggs in a clutch, on average; however, she'll only raise four of those in the wild. So taking two eggs from a clutch wouldn't disturb the wild population.
The only disadvantage is you can't sex the eggs. So there's a possibility if you brought ten eggs back you might have ten males. But it was still a far better gamble than catching wild birds.

As battery technology was advancing, Mike thought there should be an incubator developed that could operate in a car or on an airplane over long distances. That way he could candle the eggs in the field, collect them if they were three weeks set, or mark the nest and come back for them at a later time. Eggs that are well-set travel better and the hatchability rate is higher.

Mike: I discussed the development of a portable incubator with my friend and fellow aviculturalist Bill Makins. Bill knew a chap named Anderson Brown, who built traditional incubators for hatching eggs, the kind that plugged into an electrical outlet. I remember Anderson came to lunch one day at Bill's place and I asked if he could build a portable incubator.

It had to be designed to fit under a typical passenger seat in an airplane, and the battery would need to be easily changed.

Anderson Brown worked with Mike's specifications for the first portable egg incubator in 1974. The first version was made out of plywood with insulation and used two six-volt dry cell batteries and had a forced-air fan inside.

Mike's portable incubator design was a crucial element for his trip to Australia to collect Pink-eared Duck eggs. It was also helpful later during his 1981 trip to Chile for Torrent Duck eggs and when he worked with SeaWorld San Diego to bring back penguin eggs from sub-Antarctica.

SAN DIEGO
September 5, 1979

The months of preparation had finally come to an end. After an eleven-hour British Airways flight from London to Los Angeles, Mike arrived in San Diego, the first leg of his long journey to Australia. He had timed his travel to include giving a lecture on flamingos at the American Federation of Aviculture conference while in the city.

He was met at the airport by his good friend and colleague, Frank Todd, the curator of birds at SeaWorld San Diego. They went to Frank's home, where Mike would stay for the next several days. The two had dinner, a few drinks, and many laughs reliving old times, after which Mike got some much-needed sleep.

Mike: In those days, I would come out to SeaWorld twice a year to help Frank with a variety of avian husbandry tasks. Frank would also visit me at Slimbridge, especially when he was working on his book, *Waterfowl: Ducks, Geese and Swans of the World*. I helped him with the egg data tables in the appendix of his book. He's a waterfowl expert and aviculturalist. When he was at SeaWorld in San Diego, they had one of the largest waterfowl collections in the country.

After a refreshing night's sleep, Mike spent the next morning tying up some loose ends on his lecture and handling bird issues back in Slimbridge before going to lunch with two friends in town for the AFA conference.

He returned to SeaWorld later that afternoon and found the staff in a panic. Frank took him to see some birds that appeared to be lethargic and unstable.

Mike: Frank brought in some birds that afternoon that were dying from botulism. I helped out the best I could.

Botulism in birds was something I had experienced before, as I dealt with it in New York at Duck Puddle Farm. I had kept in contact with Winston Guest in case they had any problems after I moved back to England, which was one of the conditions of my return to Slimbridge. One time I flew over on a weekend to help him with a botulism outbreak.

We had managed to save a lot of those birds, so I was sure I could help them out at SeaWorld. We worked on Frank's birds and got a few healthy. Still, that didn't put and end to it; botulism will stay around a little while.

Over the next two days Mike split his time between the AFA convention, where he presented his lecture on flamingos, and dealing with the botulism outbreak at SeaWorld. He and the staff were able to save numerous birds before he had to fly back to Los Angeles, where he began his long overnight flight to Australia.

SYDNEY
September 12, 1979

The view of Sydney Harbour from the Taronga Zoo was stunning, especially on such a sunny day. Mike attempted to focus on the leopard seal exhibit; however, the allure of the sparkling blue-green water, the resplendent Sydney Opera House, and the iconic Harbour Bridge on the horizon enticed him to continually look away from the massive animal.

He had arrived in Sydney nearly 24 hours earlier, but the long flight, which stopped only briefly in Hawaii and New Zealand, caused him to essentially "lose" a day, along with a great deal of his memory of the day before. A shower and a long night of sleep revived him enough to tour the Taronga Zoo, where his good acquaintance and host, John De Jose, worked as curator of birds.

Mike: This is the same John De Jose whom I found hanging around the 7-11 convenience store back in New York. After I returned to England, John helped Robin Clifford manage the collection at Duck Puddle Farm. He had gone back to college and gotten his Bachelors Degree while he was still working with the birds.

In 1973, when I made a trip to Argentina and the Falkland Islands, John De Jose accompanied me on the Falkland Islands leg of that trip. Robin Clifford did the first half with me in Argentina. They were both working at Duck Puddle at the time.

A few years later, Winston and Helen sold the estate on Long Island and moved to Florida. John De Jose was looking for a job in zoology. Kerry Muller, whom I'd gone to Alaska with when he was at the National Zoo, had moved to Taronga Zoo in Sydney. He eventually had an opening on staff, so I put John in touch with Kerry and he got the job of curator of birds at Taronga Zoo.

Mike was a guest at the home of John and his wife Mary during his time in Sydney. Before Mike's plane touched down in Sydney, John had been called away on an animal rescue mission. An oil spill threatened the lives of seabirds in the harbor.

John had returned to the zoo and was alternating between cleaning birds and speaking to the news media about the environmental disaster, but finally he had time to give Mike a proper tour.

The zoo's waterfowl collection commanded Mike's interest. He watched as a Musk Duck chased a Canada Goose. The Musk Duck is a highly aggressive species, and one of the birds he wanted to collect in Australia. He saw the White-quilled Pygmy-geese (colloquial name for Cotton Teal) and Blue-billed Ducks, a type of stiff-tail, which Mike also hoped to collect.

Mike was amazed by the number of birds and the wide variety of aviaries. One of the most impressive exhibits was a swallow martin breeding aviary. He got some good pictures of the rare Green Pygmy-geese – the first he had ever seen.

They made their way to the duck-billed platypus exhibit. Mike was intrigued by this strange egg-laying mammal, which he had never before seen. John also took him on a return visit to the leopard seal exhibit, taking him inside the enclosure. They stood upon a rock ledge over the pool. The fearsome predator came out of the water toward them. Mike left with great respect for this 1,000 pound seal-killing machine.

The next morning Mike met some of the Taronga Zoo staff and rode with them to the construction site of a dam. The rainforest surrounding the area was scheduled to be clear-cut, but the Taronga staff was allowed to remove any biologically significant plant life they wanted – eucalyptus trees, orchids, and enormous bird's nest ferns.

While the others were busy collecting plants, Mike searched for birds. He saw a flock of Maned Geese (currently called Maned Ducks), a duck species with a goose-like bill, which were grazing in open country. He headed into the forest, but did not see as many birds as he'd hoped. Little birds darted through the trees, but identifying them was difficult. There were quite a few species he had never seen before, and he heard numerous strange bird calls that were difficult to recognize.

Mike: This area reminded me of Sheldgeese country in South America. I came across a wombat that was not a bit disturbed by my presence. I got right up to it, but it still did not run away. Instead it grunted and made a fake charge. They're funny animals that live in big burrows they dig out. One has to be careful walking by their holes, as the ground near them is liable to cave in.

Mike hiked into an area where the machinery and saws had already been at work. It was evident how quickly any rainforest could be completely obliterated, just leaving sand, stumps, and bare rock. He continued bird-watching and made his way back to the open country to see the Maned Geese more closely.

Mike: When going through the forest, there were leeches on the leaves of plants. Anytime I would brush against the leaves, the leeches jumped on my neck. Once I got out of the forest, I had to pick the blasted things off. I'd already had my fill of leeches in Africa.

The zoo trucks came out of the forest and picked up Mike late in the afternoon. They vacated the area just before the construction company started blasting. Mike wondered what would become of all the wild creatures he had observed during his day in the rainforest. At least some of the plants had been saved.

The next two days were reserved for Mike to spend time diving on the Great Barrier Reef, something he had longed to do since he first trained to scuba dive. After this wonderful excursion, he paid his farewells to John and Mary De Jose and boarded a plane for a flight that would first take him to Melbourne and then west to Perth. Soon the endeavor of finding Pink-eared Duck, Musk Duck, and Freckled Duck eggs would begin.

PERTH
September 15, 1979

Warm rain showers greeted Mike's plane as it descended over the Swan River estuary and touched down in Perth. Tom Spence met him at the airport terminal. He had known Tom many years ago when he worked for a zoo in Scotland, and now he was director of the Perth Zoo.

Mike gathered his gear at the baggage claim and piled into the Jeep Wagoneer, and the two men headed for Tom's country house about a hundred miles outside of Perth. It was Saturday morning, and Mike only had to get through the weekend before he could immerse himself in the outback of Western Australia. He had wanted to explore this part of the world so long that he could hardly stand the relatively short wait.

Along the route to Tom's weekend home they stopped at several ponds to look for waterfowl. Before long, Mike had spotted Grey Teal, Black Ducks, Black Swans, and Blue-billed Ducks. They stopped at several more ponds before eating lunch near a large lake with lots of rush – very much like what Mike had seen in Argentina.

Scanning among the various duck species with his binoculars, or "binnies" as he called them, he spotted a large number of Australian White-eyed Ducks and 12 Freckled Ducks! Only an hour off the plane and 20 miles outside of Perth, Mike had already glimpsed the endangered Freckled Duck!

Tom was very surprised, since he had not seen that many Freckled Ducks during his entire twelve years in Australia. "You must have brought luck with you," he said.

Mike took many photographs of the rare ducks and began to think that he had come to Western Australia at the right time after all.

Mike: I had a good look at them. They are a very strange duck, indeed; they reminded me of the Pink-headed Duck [an extinct species from eastern India, Myanmar, and Bangladesh].

They traveled on to Tom's country home at the edge of an estuary. It was a lovely little house built on stilts overlooking the water. From the porch, Mike watched pelicans and followed the flight of a Black Duck as it landed with a soft splash in the marsh. They reminisced over a few beers before grilling some steaks for dinner. Mike retired at ten o'clock Perth time, listening to bullfrogs echoing all around outside the house.

Early Sunday morning Tom cooked breakfast while Mike watched birds out the window. Black Ducks came again into the marsh and Twenty-eight Parrots mingled around in the trees. (Twenty-eight parrot is the name of the bird. "Twenty-eight, Twenty-eight" is the call they make as they fly through the trees.)

After breakfast they drove further south to look for waterfowl along the coast, stopping at various lakes not far from Tom's house. Mike saw four emus. One was by the roadside, trying to get through the wire fence.

They arrived at a salt lake called Lake Clifton, where they saw nearly a hundred Musk Ducks, mostly males. Some of them were displaying vigorously, although very few females were around to witness it.

About 150 kilometers south of Perth, they came to an area called Benger Swamp, which is a controlled-flooding area. Mike saw hundreds of Black Swans, many with broods two or three weeks old. Altogether, they counted over twenty pairs with their young.

They stopped again at the lake where Mike had seen Freckled Ducks the day before. The birds were exactly where he'd seen them yesterday.

Mike: We drove back to Perth Zoo. I met a couple of the keepers and looked at their waterfowl enclosures. I thought they were quite good — even better than those at Taronga Zoo. Perth Zoo had good numbers of Blue-billed Ducks, Musk Ducks, and Australian Sheldgeese.

Late Sunday afternoon Tom Spence dropped him off at a hotel in Perth that was just down the road from the zoo. Mike went for a walk to get his bearings. As evening light faded, Mike relished the peaceful sight of pelicans flying in rigid formation over the water that divided the city. Western Australia had quickly caught his heart as a place of penetrating natural beauty and diverse wildlife.

Mike had enjoyed spending the weekend with Tom and getting a sense of the magnificent birdlife on this unique continent. The next day, he would begin the serious business of finding the Pink-eared Duck. He already knew where he could find the rare Freckled Duck.

In the Outback

Jim Lane arrived at the hotel early the next morning and drove Mike to Wildlife Headquarters in Wanneroo, on the outskirts of Perth. Wildlife Headquarters is the official name of the fisheries & wildlife department in Australia.

Mike: Jim Lane was my contact at Wildlife Headquarters. He suggested certain lakes where I might find waterfowl nests on my trip to the outback.

We discussed plans for the week on the way. It appeared Wildlife Headquarters would give me all the assistance possible. However, he said my collection list had to be presented before the State Wildlife Headquarters in Adelaide. Even worse, I had to assure them I would not collect Freckled Ducks.

That was quite a blow, because I knew I could catch Freckled Ducks in the lake near Perth. Jim also informed me that it was a very bad year for waterfowl breeding, as the rains just never came. At this point, I didn't feel very hopeful for the outcome of my expedition.

Before leaving England, Mike had been given preliminary permission to collect the species he wanted during the expedition. Now the combination of government red tape and the drought could potentially deal a crushing blow to his expedition before he even stepped foot in the bush. Despite these setbacks, however, Mike determined to press on with the mission as planned.

In the first phase of the expedition, Mike would explore lakes for nests with eggs and mark the locations. In the second phase, he would return to gather the eggs just before he was scheduled to leave Australia. This would provide a window of opportunity to get the eggs back to the Wildfowl Trust in the portable incubators, where the chicks would hatch and be reared.

At the Perth Wildlife Headquarters, Mike met Don Monroe, another one of his Australian contacts, and Grant Pierce, both of whom reported to Jim Lane. Don and Grant were willing to be guides as well as assist Mike in the field.

Mike: Don was about 40 years old and quite a character. He was easy to get along with. I jumped into Don's big Ford truck, which had a small aluminum boat and a canoe strapped to the roof. We drove a short distance to Troll Lake, got the boat down, and put the 6-horsepower Evinrude motor on the back.

Once on the lake, Don had problems restarting the motor every time they stopped to search for nests. They saw a number of Musk Ducks and a couple of Blue-billed Ducks, but only one Pink-eared Duck (or "Pink-ears," as Mike often called them).

They returned to Wildlife Headquarters to drop off the outboard motor for repairs before the next day's outing. Troll Lake was a mere trial run before venturing deeper in the areas they thought would hold nesting waterfowl.

The next morning Don and Mike headed out in the bush to Lake Chandala, about 40 miles north of Perth. They paddled the canoe out to a large stand of Australian paperbark trees in the middle of the lake. These trees have bark that peels off like a birch and often have hollows in them where Pink-ears nests can be found. Paperbark trees also form root masses above ground in which Black Swans or Musk Ducks build nests.

They paddled into an enormous colony of Straw-necked Ibis, but saw only a few waterfowl, so they decided to move to another lake.

Once the gear was packed on the truck, they drove off-road to other lakes near Lake Chandala. Some of the lakes had salt in the water and the trees had all died. No birds would be found in these lifeless salt pools, so they continued on. The terrain became much more difficult to transverse, often requiring the Ford truck to plow through deep water which covered the tire ruts in the bush. Eventually they arrived at Lake Bambun.

Mike: This lake was more open with only a thin covering of paper-bark trees around the edge. I could see and hear a Musk Duck. There were lots of Black Ducks, Grey Teal, some Pink-eared Ducks, and a few Blue-billed Ducks. I decided it might be worth searching the trees around the edge.

Don and Mike took the aluminum boat off the truck and fitted it with the motor. They had cruised only a short distance before the shear pin broke. Don put a new one on the prop and they continued around the lake searching for nests.

Mike: We got up to the north side of the lake where most of the ducks were congregating. I spied Freckled Ducks – at least 12 took wing and circled above us. One female was in molt, so she was flightless and had to stay on the water. We followed her for a while so I could get some pictures. She kept diving just in front of the boat. Later we found six more flightless Freckled Ducks. I could have easily caught them. So near, yet so far.

Early the next morning after breakfast, Mike and Don packed the truck and drove to a place with easier access to the water of Lake Wannanah. The weather had turned cloudy and windy.

They got the boat down, fixed the motor to the transom, and set out for the south end of the lake. Here they found dense scrub in the water, encircled by paperbark trees. Don stayed in the boat, as it was difficult to anchor it in the rough water.

Mike: The vegetation was too dense for the boat, so I had to get out and wade in the water. The best nesting areas seemed to be in the paperbark trees in the deeper water.

Don came by on the other side to pick me up with the boat, as the water became too deep for wading. We

Mike holding down while inspecting Pink-eared nest.

carried on the search and soon found the first Pink-ear nest in a small hole of a paperbark tree, about six feet above the water level. There were six eggs, ten days set.

The Pink-ears pull a lot of down onto the nest, but I'm not sure why they need to do this. It's possible they leave the nest for a long time since Pink-ears take longer to feed because they sift food with their special bill.

The extra down keeps the eggs warm while they're gone. The down itself was thick and oily.

As soon as I picked up a Pink-ear egg, I knew it was different than any other waterfowl egg I had ever handled. The texture was much different than a Ringed Teal or anything else. It had a greasy feel, which probably came from the down.

Mike soon found three other Pink-eared Duck nests and marked them by attaching tape on the trees. He would come back for the eggs later on as he was about to leave for England.

A thorough search for Musk Duck eggs continued until they had examined every coot-type nest on the far side of the lake. They searched another two hundred nests without finding even one Musk Duck egg. As they made their way back to the truck, Mike spotted a male Musk Duck coming out of some thick vegetation, making quite a stir with a mating display.

Standing up in the boat with his binoculars, he could make out a coot's nest with a lot of down. On closer inspection, he found one Musk Duck egg at 14 days incubation. Among the twisted tree branches, he found also another Pink-eared Duck nest in the crook of a paperbark tree.

Camp setup in bush.

Mike: On these expeditions, I always had with me a black cloth
       and flash light. I would candle any eggs I found by plac-
       ing the cloth over my head and shoulders like a hood.
       Then I'd place the flash light, which has a cardboard cone
       attached, against the back of the egg. This allows me to
       see the vein structure and other indicators within the egg
       which tells me about when it should hatch.

The search of Lake Wannanah had taken over four hours. A weary
duo loaded the boat onto the truck and brewed a cup of tea before setting off over the railway line again and onto the dirt road.

The two men remained in the outback two more days, searching
numerous other lakes for nests as they slowly made their way back to
Perth. They continued checking the inland lakes, but found no nesting birds on them.

Mike could easily observe the terrible toll the multiyear drought
had extracted from the natural environment of the southwestern
Australian outback. Most of the lakes were surrounded by dead trees,
dried out, or had lowered water levels. Campfires were easy to make
because of the abundance of dead wood around. Old Black Swan nests
were found five feet up in the trees where the water level had once been.

It would be fruitless to continue searching for eggs on the inland
lakes, so they decided to drive to the coast. Here the situation was only
modestly better. The salty coastal lakes had some water, but no viable
nesting habitat. The last two days of their excursion in the outback
yielded no egg locations.

THE METROPOLITAN LAKES

Mike and Don arrived at Wildlife Headquarters in Wanneroo late on Friday afternoon and met with Jim Lane and Grant Pierce. They needed to discuss the week-long outback journey and make some decisions on how to proceed.

Mike: Once I got back to town, I had to rethink where next to search for eggs. We had found a few Pink-ears nests. Some of the eggs were ready to collect, but I still hadn't found enough other species to consider gathering them yet. So at the weekend I just stayed around town, waiting until Monday when Don or Grant could help me again.

I couldn't do a lot on my own without Don giving me a hand. I had to rely on what time the fisheries people would give him to help me.

Over the weekend, Mike debated when to book a British Airways flight back to London. All he could do was estimate where and when he might locate more eggs. Hopefully, it would be the following week. He decided the flight home would be on October 3, leaving him just nine days to complete the mission.

On Monday, Don and Mike loaded up the truck and headed off to the metropolitan lakes. These were lakes within the city limits of Perth or just outside in the bush. After using the boat to search Lake Joondalup and finding nothing of importance, they carried on to Lake Claremont. There was an abundance of dead trees, which Mike searched and found several Pink-eared Duck nests. In fact, he found three fresh eggs in among deserted Black Duck eggs.

Mike: I also found fresh eggs among spoiled eggs from a previous nest of Pink-ears that only just finished hatching. This is only the second lake on which we found Pink-ears eggs. And this was a city lake, just outside Perth – very surprising.

They returned to Wildlife Headquarters. Mike called Ali to check on things at home. He also arranged for incubators to be brought to Wildlife Headquarters in preparation for collecting eggs in a few days.

He returned with Don to his house, where he would be staying for the remainder of his time in Australia.

September 25, Tuesday

The next day, Grant joined Mike to search for eggs on Bibra Lake, near the town of Fremont. Before they even got the boat in the water, Mike spotted Musk Ducks, Blue-billed Ducks, Freckled Ducks, and Australian White-eye Ducks.

Mike: Bibra is a big lake with lots of reeds and rushes around the edge. We decided that wading would make for a better search. The water was only a couple of feet deep in most places but occasionally came up to my chest. Searching in this manner was very tiring as the bottom was mud, which sucked my feet down with each step.

The lake took all day to search. There was one partic-ular plant called aldarium rush. It grows in isolated thick clumps in deep water. It was deadly stuff to search in, as the ends were sharp as needles. My face, arms, and hands soon became raw as I moved it aside to check for eggs. Much of it was so thick that you could stand on top of it.

Mike collecting Pink-earred Duck eggs.

Some of the Musk Duck nests were found in the middle of these clumps. How the birds got in, I'll never know. I never did catch one on a nest. They always had left in time to cover the eggs before disappearing out of sight. The female would go to deeper water and watch.

143

The circumference of the lake must have been at least eight miles. We found ten Musk Duck nest sites, seven with eggs. A Black Duck was sitting on two Musk Duck eggs, plus her own. Sometimes two nests would be very close to each other. These clumps of rush would be in a certain area and it could be a half a mile before you'd find another clump. Because of the scarcity of nesting sites, birds built nests next door to each other.

Both men were relieved when they finished searching Bibra Lake at four o'clock. Grant dropped Mike off at Don's house where he showered and pulled spikes of caldarium rush out of his hands and arms. It was an extremely tiring day, walking the better part of eight miles around a muddy-bottom lake, in chest-deep water. However, it did yield a lot more Musk Duck eggs.

"BOMBAY DUCK"
October 1, Monday

The Musk Duck eggs discovered on Bibra Lake were exactly the treasure Mike needed to enable him to move from the searching phase of the expedition to the collecting phase. He now had nest locations marked for Pink-eared Ducks and Musk Ducks. However, Mike had only three days to relocate and collect the eggs from the nests he had marked throughout a wide area of Western Australian territory.

After breakfast, Don and Mike drove to Wildlife Headquarters. Mike arrived, only to be met with the disappointing news that the State Wildlife Headquarters in Adelaide had denied his request to collect Freckled Duck eggs. Mike had hoped to collect eggs of this rare species, in addition to Pink-eared Ducks, Blue-billed Ducks, and Musk Ducks, all of which had been approved by the agency.

There was no time to dwell on the Freckled Duck situation – there were eggs all across Western Australia Mike needed to collect. He placed the portable incubator in the truck and made the short drive with Don Monroe and Jim Lane to Bibra Lake to recover the Musk Duck eggs he knew were there.

Mike: While going to the first nest we'd marked, I searched a
        nearby clump of reeds, and lo and behold, I found eight

Blue-bill Duck eggs that certainly had not been there on the 25th. I could hardly believe my eyes!

We carried on around the lake and collected the Musk Duck eggs we had previously located. Unfortunately, one nest had hatched; however, we found another nest with two eggs. We also collected two Musk Duck eggs we found in a Black Duck's nest, though one small egg was infertile. We got very wet when the sky opened up and poured rain while we were only half way through collecting. We also got more nasty scratches from the caldarium rush, with some near misses to the eyes.

Mike was back at Wildlife Headquarters early the next morning to check the temperature of the incubator holding his newly acquired Musk and Blue-billed Duck eggs. He and Jim made the long journey out to Lake Wannanah.

They reached the remote lake at about ten o'clock and collected Musk Duck and Pink-eared Duck eggs. They finished by one o'clock and headed back to Wanneroo, where the eggs were placed in the incubator.

The next morning was the last Mike would spend in Australia. His flight to England left that night. Mike and Jim traveled north to Lake Nowergup to collect the two Musk Duck eggs from a nest they had marked and then into Perth to Lake Claremont for Pink-ear eggs. Unfortunately, most of the eggs in the nests they had found previously had hatched and one was chipping. However, there were still several freshly incubated eggs which were perfect for collecting.

Mike: I had to climb a rotten tree for one nest. As I lifted the eggs out of the nest, the limb snapped, sending me and the branch crashing into the boat. Yet I managed to cushion the eggs in my hand so they didn't break. That was a close call!

He had now collected the 40 Pink-eared Duck eggs he was permitted to take out of Australia.

Mike went back to Wildlife Headquarters where he packed the eggs into the portable incubator at about five o'clock in the afternoon, before going to Don and Kay Monroe's to pack and have a celebratory supper. As soon as the meal concluded, Don gave Mike a ride to Perth Airport to start the long flight back to England.

Mike: I got through Customs easily, having all the necessary papers. I then had to go through special security, due to the portable incubators I was carrying.

Mr. Frick, the British Airways agent, took me to my seat before any other passengers boarded. The big incubator had to go sideways into a space on the floor.

It was a long haul back from Australia, about a 22-hour flight. The batteries on my incubator would only last 11 hours, so I had to have an extra set in order to make it home. The airline was very good about it. They allowed me to have the incubator right next to me on the flight, so I could change batteries and keep an eye on the eggs.

Mike was pleased to be heading home, even though it was a brutally long flight. However, as his plane approached Bombay, India, there were reports of a fire at the airport. His plan had been to use the layover in Bombay to thoroughly check the eggs, but now he would not be allowed off the plane. Mike took a quick peek inside the incubator.

Mike: The airport at Bombay was on fire – I had no idea what was going on there other than that. We were on the ground over three hours and couldn't get off the plane. One of the Musk Duck eggs hatched during the delay. I decided he wasn't allowed to hatch just yet. I didn't have permits for birds, only eggs. So I got some tape and stuck him back in the egg! That way I got him through Customs. We called him "Bombay Duck," since that's where he secretly hatched.

SUCCESS AT SLIMBRIDGE

During his time in Perth, Mike and his Australian companions explored more than 200 lakes and ponds, searching for eggs of the continent's most treasured waterfowl. Mike was overjoyed with the result. He had found his limit of 40 Pink-eared Duck eggs, along with 14 Musk Duck eggs and a surprise find of 8 Blue-billed Duck eggs. After arriving home in Slimbridge, Mike delivered half of the Pink-eared eggs to Bill Makins at Pensthorpe Wildfowl Park. Ultimately, between the Wildfowl Trust and Pensthorpe, 20 Pink-eared Ducks were reared to adulthood.

Mike: Within nine months of coming back from Australia, one pair of Pink-ears at the Wildfowl Trust hatched young birds. That was quite an achievement, for which I received a World's First Breeding Award.

   Regarding the Musk Ducks, Bill Makins raised a few and I reared four or five. They were devils, those birds. The males would try to kill any bird near them, including their own species. We couldn't even rear them together; they had to be kept separately in quarantine.

   The call of a baby Musk Duck is like that of a mammal. It didn't sound like a duck at all. Weird noises they'd make. Each male on every lake has a different call. It's also the only duck that will mimic. I heard one of them mimic the voice of a keeper at Slimbridge. Sometimes they'd mimic a sound of a screeching owl or creaking sound – just a weird bird. The Latin name for the bird means bizarre (*Biziura lobata*). The scientists got that one right.

Of the many expeditions made by Mike Lubbock, he considers Australia to be the most significant. The primary reason for that belief is bringing the Pink-eared Duck to Slimbridge, and eventually to other breeding facilities around the world. Mike considers every waterfowl species equally important; however, the Pink-eared Duck may be the planet's most unique living duck. It's Australia's waterfowl equivalent of the Duck-billed Platypus. Yet, outside of Australia, very few people have ever seen one or even know of its existence.

Mike: The Pink-eared Ducks were the real success from that trip. All 40 eggs transported from Australia to England hatched. Pink-ears are difficult to rear because they feed so differently than other ducks. They have a shoveler-type attachment to their bill that they use to sift food.

Any of the Pink-eared Ducks in zoos or collections today, including those at Sylvan Heights, came from those birds I brought into England. None have been exported out of Australia since.

EPILOGUE

Today, there are a handful of Pink-eared Ducks in avian breeding centers around the world. Sylvan Heights Waterfowl Breeding Center has three pairs, but the species still remains very difficult to breed. Mike and his curator of aviculture Nick Hill are working diligently to raise more Pink-ears. They have used their powers of avian observation to improve their husbandry techniques. Mike and Nick are confident that enough of these unique Australian birds will be bred that Pink-eared Ducks will one day be on display for visitors to enjoy at Sylvan Heights Bird Park.

Even though Mike did not receive a permit to collect Freckled Ducks on his 1979 Australia trip, he did ultimately acquire some at Slimbridge. Approximately 15 years ago, the Australian Wildlife Headquarters reversed their decision to not allow them out of the country. The Wildfowl & Wetlands Trust became the recipient of Freckled Ducks. The agency also gave permission for five pairs of birds to be sent from the Trust to Mike, who by that time was at Sylvan Heights Waterfowl Center in North Carolina.

Visitors to Sylvan Heights Bird Park have benefited from Australia's change of heart. Unlike the Pink-ear, the Freckled Duck is relatively easy to breed and can be seen on display in the Australian and Multinational Exhibits.

Mike: I am forever grateful to the people of Australia for allowing me to be the only aviculturalist to export native waterfowl eggs from their wonderful country.

     Also, I'm very thankful for all the assistance I received from Jim Lane, Don Monroe, and the staff at the Wildlife Headquarters in Perth. Without their help, I could never have accomplished this important mission.

A few years after Mike's expedition to Australia, Tom Spence decided to retire as director of the Perth Zoo. His replacement was John De Jose, Mike's acquaintance from the 7-11 store in Oyster, New York, and bird curator of Taronga Zoo. Inspired by his love for birds and with a little help from Mike Lubbock, John went from being an out-of-work hippie to director of the Perth Zoo.

CHAPTER SEVEN

The White-headed Ducks of Tablas de Daimiel

Spain, February 1982

The Land Rover droned effortlessly along the rutted trail. The flat grassland terrain proved to be no challenge for the massive vehicle as Beltran De Ceballos easily maneuvered past a great pool of briny water that attempted to overflow onto the narrow passageway. A short distance ahead stood a tower which prominently marked his destination.

Beltran's four passengers, which included Mike Lubbock, maintained a constant vigil for waterfowl upon the Tablas de Daimiel, a massive floodplain formed by the confluence of the Gigüela and Guadiana rivers. These bountiful waters in the arid La Mancha plain of south-central Spain continually grant an oasis for tens of thousands of migratory birds in need of either a refreshing pause along their journey or a winter breeding grounds.

The metallic squeal of worn brakes pierced the pristine silence as the Land Rover came to a halt near the base of the tower. One by one, the core contributors to the White-headed Duck Restoration Project climbed out from the muddied truck. The team had designated Tablas de Daimiel National Park as ground-zero in the battle to save the rapidly disappearing White-headed Duck, a bird of great pride to the people of Spain.

Beltran led the group to a ladder rising to a viewing platform atop the tower. Trained at the Wildfowl & Wetlands Trust in England, Beltran had been hand-picked by Mike Lubbock to become proficient in the husbandry of the rare duck. Beltran, a Spaniard, was responsible to hatch the precious eggs and rear the offspring at the nearby breeding facility. Ultimately, he would give the birds their release into the wild of the Tablas de Daimiel.

Bill Makins, an Englishman and waterfowl breeder, followed behind Beltran and climbed up to the viewing platform. It was Bill who alerted Mike Lubbock to the problems occurring in Spain with the White-headed Duck and paid for Mike's trips from England to observe the situation. Mike considered Bill an authority on birds as well as a close companion.

Pedro Molina contributed a vital function as director of Tablas de Daimiel National Park. He became enthusiastic with Mike's plan on how to revive the Spanish population of the White-headed Duck. Pedro's support and his guidance through the administrative channels of Spanish conservation groups and government agencies helped Mike establish a restoration program that appealed to a diverse group of participants.

Also with the team was Tom Gullick, a wildlife guide who provided birding expeditions to the natural areas of Spain. English by birth, he now lived permanently in Spain. As a result of his detailed knowledge of Spanish birds and natural habitat, it was Tom who first noticed the White-headed Duck's dramatic decline in numbers and sounded the alarm.

Mike Lubbock was the last of the group to ascend the tower. His interest in the White-headed Duck began years before this trip to Spain. While at the Wildfowl Trust in England, Mike had discovered the breakthrough factor of breeding the White-headed Duck in captivity. This bird, and others in the stiff-tail family, had very strict requirements for nesting. To unravel the mystery, Mike drew upon his observations of another stiff-tail duck, the Maccoa Duck, while on his African expedition. His insight proved to be the key to successful husbandry, which he eventually parlayed into World's First Breeding Awards for both the Maccoa and White-headed Ducks.

All five men reached the elevated position of the viewing platform. From this advantageous perch, they surveyed the entirety of the Tablas de Daimiel. The view stretched across the alternating areas of grassland and wetland, all the way to the distant hills which loomed above the table-like plain. Sparsely dotted among the reeds and grasses they noted the Tamarisk, one of the few kinds of trees that manage to thrive in the unique soil of the Tablas.

The view of the area's terrestrial features was enthralling, but the real stars of these environs were the birds. The seasoned wildlife explorers audibly gasped in near disbelief as they absorbed the sight of thousands upon thousands of waterbirds dabbling in chains of pooled water as far as the eye could see, while others, by the hundreds, flew regally across the sky. Flocks of teal, shovelers, gadwall, pintails, widgeons, pochards, and mallards all made an eventual appearance to the scene. The observers had an unhindered view of cranes flying high above the wetlands, while shore birds such as the Black-winged Stilt and the Grey Heron dotted the edges of the lakes.

Despite how deeply this display of avian wonder thrilled the hearts of these men, they all knew the panorama was incomplete. There was an element missing from nature's handiwork. Not seen among the multitude of birds this day was the White-headed Duck. In spite of the team's four-year effort to re-establish the unfortunate bird into its natural habitat, it was still insufficient in numbers to make even a minor appearance in the team's encompassing view of the Tablas de Daimiel.

However, for these determined conservationists, the fight for the bird's survival was not over. Progress had been made, and this temporary disappointment would serve only to motivate them toward their ultimate goal – to one day return to this platform, look out over the Tablas, and observe the White-headed Duck among the species diving in the ponds and taking flight in the sky.

AVIAN RESCUE: The Mission Begins

April 1, 1978

Mike Lubbock scurried among the throng of travelers who had converged on London's Gatwick Airport. At last he spotted the familiar face of his friend and colleague, Bill Makins, founder of the Pensthorpe Wildlife Park. Together they boarded a plane for Madrid. Although happy to see one another, the mission they had taken on was extremely grim. Their conversation during the flight centered on the death of thousands of wild birds in Spain and how they could possibly put a stop to the carnage.

An extended drought was partially responsible for a severe outbreak of botulism in several of the most important waterfowl preserves of the Spanish peninsula. Avian botulism is a paralytic, often fatal, disease of birds that results when they ingest toxin produced by the bacterium, *Clostridium botulinum*. While attempting to save infected birds was the most urgent part of their task in Spain, Mike and Bill would also investigate the critical threat to the survival of the Spanish population of the White-headed Duck.

The men were met in Madrid by Tom Gullick, an Englishman now living in Spain, who drove them south to his home in Villanueva de los Infantes.

Mike: Tom Gullick was very knowledgeable on birds, but his main thing was organizing partridge shoots. That's how Bill knew him. He sponsored similar pheasant shoots in Norfolk, and Tom would come over for the events.

But Tom also took people on birding trips. He knew all the raptors, waterfowl, and shore birds. He would take folks from the north of Spain all the way down to the coast in a Range Rover, camping along the way. He guaranteed they'd see many species of birds.

The next morning the trio drove to the Tablas de Daimiel National Park to observe the botulism crisis first hand. The Tablas de Daimiel is a large wetland area that had only opened to the public the year before. There had already been 50,000 visitors to the park, which had the primary function to preserve habitat for wild birds, especially waterfowl. This mission was being severely compromised by the botulism plague.

Mike had already sent birds to the park from Slimbridge to become part of a display area to entertain and educate the public on European species of waterfowl. He had also assisted in designing the aviaries so that the birds could thrive and be healthy.

Mike and Bill met Pedro Molina at the park. Pedro was chief administrator of Tablas de Daimiel. Mike first wanted to know how the birds were doing in the public display area. Pedro assured him they were healthy, due to having large amounts of fresh water available to them, a critical feature of Mike's aviary design. However, this was not the case for the wild birds in the wetlands, which was severely dried up because of the ongoing drought.

A jeep tour of the park's wetlands quickly confirmed the state of conditions. Each place Pedro stopped to view the shoreline was littered with hundreds of dead or dying birds. It was a heartbreaking sight for anyone, but especially for Mike and Bill, who had spent their lives saving waterfowl for future generations to enjoy.

Mike: You know they have botulism when the birds get "rub-ber-necked" and just fall around. I had dealt with other botulism outbreaks, once in New York and again at SeaWorld San Diego. We were able to save most of the infected birds in those cases, but this was beyond any-thing I'd seen in my career.

Mike immediately cut the tour short and had Pedro drive them back to the park headquarters; there was no time to waste. The staff was gath-ered and Mike trained them how to treat the birds that were still alive. Within a short time, Mike, Bill, Pedro, and his entire staff immersed themselves in the dire scene and began the rescue.

Mike: With a botulism outbreak, you've got to get the dead birds away from the edges of the lakes. If maggots get into the carcasses it spreads much faster. There were a lot of carcasses around, so Pedro had his staff and volunteers go around and pick up all the dead birds. The ones that could still hold their necks up a little were brought to Bill and me for the water treatment.

At one time there was a vaccine available to treat the birds, but they stopped manufacturing it because it was too expensive. The other treatment is to flush the birds with fresh water.

A tube is inserted down the infected bird's throat. Holding the bird tightly, water is pumped through the tube and into the stomach. Then while standing with the feet spread apart, the bird is forcefully swung downward between the legs so that the head ends up pointed toward the ground. This expels the water before the bird chokes or drowns. The water removes the poison out of the bird's stomach. After this procedure, the birds can be put in an area with fresh water. This process must be repeated the next day.

I trained Pedro's staff how to perform the treatment. That gave us a team that we took around to all the lakes in Spain that had sick birds. It was hard, messy work and it was terrible to see all these dead and dying birds around the lakes – Greylag Geese, Red-crested Pochards and other ducks, coots, even a Marsh Harrier, which had apparently eaten a dead bird and caught it that way. Fortunately, we did not find any White-headed Ducks with botulism. That could have wiped out the whole population.

On this trip we treated over 3,000 birds. We were able to revive maybe 60 percent of the affected birds, which I thought was very good, because some of them were nearly dead when we got to them.

Coot Nests and a Plan

After lending their assistance to quash the botulism epidemic at the Tablas de Daimiel, Mike and Bill moved on to the next important phase of the trip – how to save the White-headed Duck.

Prior to this trip to Spain, Mike was already aware of the difficulties related to breeding White-headed Ducks and disturbed by their tenuous predicament in the wilds of Spain.

Mike: Before I left Slimbridge for America, we had 14 pairs of White-headed Ducks that came to us from Pakistan. We placed them in various breeding areas, but they never bred. One reason for that was that they were all wild birds. Wild-caught birds are always difficult because they have a migratory instinct in them which prevents them from settling down to breed. They just want to fly to their natural breeding grounds.

When I came back to Slimbridge in 1973, there were only three pairs of White-headed Ducks left. The others had died, but the survivors still wouldn't breed. In the meantime, I'd been to Africa, where I collected Maccoa eggs. The Maccoa Duck is in the stiff-tail family of waterfowl, same as the White-headed Duck.

I'd observed while in Botswana that the Maccoa Duck relied solely on coots for nesting, meaning that the coot would take all the nesting material into the rushes, build a nest, hatch their young and then the Maccoa would immediately take over the abandoned coot's nest.

156

When I came back to Slimbridge, I figured that if a coot's nest was good for the Maccoa, it would be good for the White-headed Duck. So we made three platforms in the European Pen where these birds were kept. Not far from Slimbridge at Frampton on Severn, a good friend of ours had old gravel pit lakes on which coots were nesting. I asked if I could get some of the abandoned nests. We put these nests on platforms out in the middle of our ponds along with some reeds over the top.

The long and the short of it was that it worked, and all three pairs of White-headed Ducks bred that year, which was a World's First Breeding for us. We found that the offspring would breed even more prolifically since they weren't from the wild. The younger ones would nest in all kinds of places, including low-lying nest boxes.

Mike's success in breeding the White-headed Duck using a coot's nest was a major breakthrough in aviculture and would prove to be an important first step for saving the White-headed Duck in Spain.

Tom Gullick was the first to become aware of the decline of the Spanish White-headed Duck population. His previous work to save bustards along with his bird watching trips put him in position to observe the species' significant decline in numbers each year. He also conducted a census in 1979, in which he estimated there were only 45 White-headed Ducks in Spain – frightfully low numbers. Lake Zóñar, near the area of Tablas de Daimiel, held 75 percent of the species' population.

Mike: Tom could see the problem. Many of the lakes and lagoons where the White-headed Ducks bred had water diverted by olive growers for their crops. As the water receded, the reeds and rushes dried out and died, so the ducks had no materials to build their nests. If any did nest, the rats moved in and ate the duck eggs.

The White-headed Ducks used coot nests in those areas the same as they did at Slimbridge. The birds would actually re-nest again, lose their eggs to rats and re-nest again. It was reported that that one pair re-nested three times and lost all their eggs.

Mike, Bill and Tom's thoughts were focused on the White-headed Duck's dire situation as they drove south from Tablas de Daimiel National Park to ICONA headquarters in Coto Doñana National Park. Here on the Atlantic coast south of Seville, they would meet with local conservationists to work out a long range plan to save the bird that was so important to the Spanish people.

Mike: The Spanish are proud of their birds and their heritage. We could be advisers, but the decisions would have to come from them. Three Englishmen coming in and telling them they should be doing this or that wouldn't have gone down too well.

Coto Doñana National Park is one of Europe's most important wetland reserves and a major site for migrating birds. The park encompasses an immense area and is known for its enormous variety of bird species. Besides the many permanent residents, the park hosted winter visitors from northern Europe, as well as summer visitors from Africa, including numerous geese and flamingoes. It also held the last remaining pairs of the rare and endangered Imperial Eagle.

Soon after arriving, they met Raymond Corrinado, who was in charge of the operations in Coto Doñana. Raymond took his English guests on a tour of the park, which was teeming with a variety of birds. He told them that the lagoons once had White-headed Ducks, but now there were none at all. Mike carefully assessed the habitat to determine if it was suitable for a possible re-introduction of White-headed Ducks.

The White-headed Duck preservation planning meeting was held the next day at ICONA headquarters. ICONA is the national conservation organization for Spanish territories in Europe, Central America and South America. Based on his observations at Tablas de Daimiel and Coto Doñana National Parks, Mike suggested at the meeting that a breed and release program using birds raised at the Wildfowl Trust in England might well restore the numbers of White-headed Ducks in Spain. Because funds were limited, he recommended Tablas de Daimiel as the initial release site because they already had built aviaries and facilities for rearing waterfowl.

Another topic discussed was how to negotiate with the olive growers and other farmers the need to use less water for irrigation. The water was being diverted from the duck's nesting habitat, causing the reeds to dry up and die. Eventually the nests were overrun by rats and other predators.

In addition, Mike suggested that someone from Spain be selected to come to Slimbridge for advanced avicultural training. That person would then be in charge of the breeding program in Tablas de Daimiel or any other place the ducks may be released in the future.

Raymond also voiced his concerned about the botulism epidemic in the Tablas de Daimiel. Mike informed him that he thought Pedro Molina and his staff were already making progress and that many birds had been saved. If there was any way more water could get into the lakes, the botulism would go away on its own.

Mike: Another really good thing came out of that meeting. The group was distraught that the Marbled Teal had disappeared almost completely from Coto Doñana. We said that would be an easy problem to fix. We would send birds from England which could then be bred and released into the park. This would be much easier than the proposed breed and release program for the White-headed Duck, because they are really no problem to breed.

They were quite pleased that we could help with the Marbled Teal. Bill Makins later sent some of his birds to them and we sent some from Slimbridge. They released them in the park and you can see Marbled Teal there today, some probably related to those birds we raised in England.

Mike, Bill, and Tom spent the day after the meeting driving all around the area outside Seville to evaluate different lakes and lagoons for possible White-headed Duck habitat. They went to the small port of St. Marina to see flamingos, but also looked for habitat on the way there. Mike noted plenty of lagoons, but they were almost dry.

They were invited to dinner by Marrito Gonzales, owner of a major sherry company. He owned part of Las Marisma, an important estuary adjacent to the Coto Doñana National Park. He was interested in what Mike and ICONA were doing to preserve White-headed Ducks and Marbled Teal. It was here Mike first met Beltran De Ceballos, who ultimately was chosen to receive avicultural training at

Slimbridge and oversee the White-headed Duck breeding program at Tablas de Daimiel.

Mike: We drove to a big lake called Medina, where the water was also low. A lot of birds there had been affected by botulism. We picked up carcasses and buried them. Not many live birds were seen. I went back to England a few days later after looking at more lakes and lagoons.

Fortunately rain was right around the corner. I remember it poured rain less than a week after we left Spain. It filled up the lakes and the botulism menace was over.

I thought the meetings had gone well. From those meetings we planned the foundations of the mission – training Beltran in avian husbandry and building the White-headed Duck breeding facility in the Tablas.

The botulism rescue demonstrated to ICONA that I had more in me than just talk. I came over and worked side-by-side with them. After that, they were ready to listen to my ideas about saving the White-headed Duck. I'm not sure this would have been the case had I not helped them with the botulism outbreak. I believe those birds would have died had I not gone over there. It was written up in the Spanish papers at the time and I was given a lot of credit for it.

My first trip was a good start for the project.

In the years following his initial trip to Spain in 1978, Mike worked diligently on getting funding for the White-headed Duck Project. They needed incubators, special tanks and ponds to raise the ducklings, as well as funds to train Beltran. Based on his request, the International Wild Waterfowl Association provided significant funding for the project.

Tom Gullick had spent $1,500 of his own money to pay keepers to trap rats at Lake Zóñar, which was the area where wild White-headed Ducks were nesting. Mike convinced ICONA to fund the keepers going forward.

Mike made several trips each year from 1979 to 1981 to check on the breeding program Beltran conducted at Tablas de Daimiel and to monitor the progress on ducks breeding in the wild.

Mike: It was vitally important to set up breeding pens at Tablas de Daimiel. We needed to be ready for the 1982 breeding season, because we lost time with each year that went by and the birds declined in numbers.

We had already talked to the olive growers and farmers about not taking so much water for irrigation. Most of them were fairly amenable with that, so water levels weren't dropping as badly as in the past. But rats eating the eggs were still a problem.

RETURN TO THE TABLAS

Mike flew into to Madrid in February 1982, again with Bill Makins as his companion. While progress had been made on the White-headed Duck Restoration Project, there were still many things that needed to be done.

Tom Gullick drove them to his home in Infantes, stopping at various lakes along the way. They saw large flocks of waterfowl. One lake had 1,500 shovelers, 500 pochards, plus scores of teal and coots. The lake had lots of reeds surrounding a large area of water. It looked to Mike like a good area for White-headed Ducks to be released.

This area was privately owned by Jose Mario Blanca. His land near Madrid was very well protected from both hunters and predators. However, it was "shot over," meaning it was used for partridge shooting. The shot remains on the ground and can be harmful to birds if ingested. Fortunately, no shooting took place on the lakes. Even the King of Spain shot partridge on this land with Jose.

The previous September, Tom had invited Jose to meet Mike at the Wildfowl Trust, where he made a spectacular arrival in a helicopter. The discussions resulted in Jose offering any help he could to the project, including the use of his property as a potential breed and release site.

Mike and Bill had a dinner at Tom Gullick's home along with Beltran and two others who worked with Jose Mario Blanca. The conversation over dinner was focused on how to save the White-headed Duck.

Mike checked his notes and listed several questions he had for Pedro Molina, whom he would see the next day at Tablas de Daimiel. The aviaries had already been built and some of the birds, eggs, and equipment from the Wildfowl Trust had already arrived at the park. But the staff didn't have everything needed to complete the breeding facility. They still needed broody bantams, cages, incubators, a candler, and fen traps (a type of trap for catching rats, invented in the fens of England). It was decided that Bill Makins would return to Spain in June, bringing the eggs with him.

The next morning, Mike, Bill, and Tom arrived at Tablas de Daimiel National Park at 8:30 and met up with everyone from the previous night's dinner party. Pedro Molina arrived soon after.

After coffee, they went down to the new duck enclosure, which had been built to house the ducks from England, most of them from Bill Makins' preserve. Reeds surrounded the water and hid the fencing. Observation slats had been installed to allow public viewing.

Mike: This pen was designed for more common European waterfowl that would attract the public and build interest for saving the White-headed Duck and Marbled Teal. Although there were a few of those species set up for breeding in the aviary, the special White-headed Duck aviary was built the next year, in 1983, I believe.

There were a lot of visitors that day and they all seemed delighted with the ducks.

We then went in the Land Rover to the tower which had a great view of the Tablas. From the top of that tower, I could foresee a day when we would once again view wild White-headed Ducks at Tablas de Daimiel and many other lakes and wetland areas throughout Spain.

EPILOGUE

Mike Lubbock invested the greater part of five years in the White-headed Duck Restoration Project. During this period of time, he also maintained extensive avian breeding programs at Slimbridge along with his other duties as the assistant director of the Wildfowl Trust. In addition, he made epic egg collection journeys to Australia in 1979 and Chile in 1981.

His last official trip to Spain was the one in February 1982. However, as the year progressed, major changes in Mike's career surfaced and he was no longer in a position to make further advisory visits to Spain. At that point he was happy with the progress the team had made on the project, though he was concerned that the breeding facility would not be operational in time for the spring '82 breeding season.

Nonetheless, all the components for a successful breed-and-release program were in place by the end of 1982. In addition, Mike had worked closely with Tom Gullick and ICONA in restoring wild White-headed Duck nesting habitat.

When Mike and other members of the team climbed the tower to observe the wild birds at Tablas de Daimiel in February 1982, to a man, they were disappointed that no White-headed Ducks were to be seen that day. In October of 2005, Mike Lubbock returned to Tablas de Daimiel National Park. He climbed the very same tower and viewed the marshlands stretching out for miles. This time however, his eyes were rewarded by the sight of an entire flock of White-headed Ducks on the waters below. He also observed a sizeable number of the endangered Marbled Teal, which the Spaniards were keen to restore to the wetlands of the Tablas. It was a magnificent and a greatly satisfying moment in Mike's life as a waterfowl conservationist.

The White-headed Duck Restoration Project demonstrated what could be accomplished by combining a cooperative habitat restoration along with a well-managed breed-and-release effort. On any lagoon in Spain you can now see White-headed Ducks.

The conservationists in Spain have gone on to do similar projects. Mike and Bill Makins' initial work in providing Marbled Teal from England into Spain aided the ultimate restoration of that endangered species. Beltran has also worked on protecting the Imperial Eagle in Coto Doñana National Park. Although it is still vulnerable, the population of the Imperial Eagle is increasing.

Mike: In a project like the White-headed Duck, it's not just about the ability to breed and release birds back to the wild. Habitat protection is required. If there's no protected habitat for them to live and reproduce, there's no hope of restoring them in the wild. We need to do better in protecting habitat.

The White-headed Duck is one of the species for which I've been very proud to say, "In Spain, we saved that bird."

CHAPTER EIGHT

The Teno River

Andes Mountains, Chile
October 15, 1981

"Down a little...down a little more – it's just below you!" Bill's voice squeaked and crackled over the radio.

Suspended 200 feet above the Teno River, Mike Lubbock belayed the rope to slow his descent. Had he the inclination to glance downward, he could have witnessed a spectacular view of the waters rushing angrily through the gorge far beneath him. Instead he listened intently to Bill Makins' instructions coming from the CB radio tied around his neck.

"Stop right there!" Bill commanded, observing from his position across the gorge as Mike rappelled down the cliff face.

"I think the ledge is a bit farther down," replied Mike, his free hand fumbling to press the radio's talk button.

Bill's perspective was not nearly as distorted by the angle of the cliff as Mike's. All the same, Mike trusted his own judgment and lowered himself another 12 inches. He halted when he heard a soft "phhitt" sound from the ledge. The extra drop landed his boot square upon a Torrent Duck egg, now squashed by his miscalculation.

Somewhat disturbed with the blunder, he refocused his effort and managed to stand securely on the ledge. He saw there were three other eggs in the nest. This was typical for Torrent Ducks, which on average laid a clutch of only four eggs. He took two of the three eggs and placed them gently inside the wicker fishing creel lined with a thick layer of goose down.

Mike took a moment to survey his lofty surroundings and then tugged the life rope to signal Ian Mitchell waiting at the top of the cliff that he was ready to ascend. He began the arduous climb up the cliff as Ian made sure the rope tied around the tree remained secure.

Once on solid ground, Mike needed a plan to pass the eggs across

165

the gorge to Bill Makins, who had the portable incubator in the four-wheel-drive Peugeot 405 they had rented for the expedition. Even though they were within a hundred yards of one another, the gorge was virtually impossible to cross. It would require a two-hour ride on horseback before Mike could get back to the bridge downstream that spanned the river. He doubted the eggs would survive the jostling they were sure to get, despite the precautions he took to pack them in down. He needed to deliver them over the chasm to Bill.

While standing upon the ledge, he had noticed a spot where the cliff came down to a narrow point in the canyon. He figured if he could scale down there, he could throw a rope across to Bill on which he could transfer the eggs.

Mike and Ian climbed down a steep bank through bamboo, thorn bushes, and pines to the overhang at the chasm's narrow point.

Mike had a weighted disc which he'd had much practice throwing during this trip to the Andes. He attached a small line to a thicker line and tied them both to the disc. With Bill already in position on the opposite side of the river, Mike gave the disc a mighty heave. The disc travelled on a high arc trajectory with the ropes trailing behind. Ian held tight to his end of the line as the disc landed with a heavy thud on the bank of the river. Bill retrieved the lines and began to form a loop.

A double-line loop was completed across the river between Bill and Mike. They tightened the loop as much as they could. Then Mike attached the creel with the eggs on the rope and pulled it as Bill did the same on his side. The eggs were slowly propelled across the river on the crudely designed pulley system. Bill took the eggs from the creel and placed them in the incubator.

Mike and Ian hauled the climbing gear back up the slope to the trail, where their guide Eduardo waited with the horses. Eduardo was a young Chilean familiar with the birds and rivers throughout this mountainous region. He tied the equipment onto the saddles, and the trio set off on horseback for the two-hour ride back to the bridge.

An Intriguing Proposition

On horseback along the narrow trail, often just a few feet from a precipitous drop into the canyon, Mike attempted to enjoy the beautiful scenic views afforded by the Chilean landscape – the verdant forest, the raging Teno River, and the rugged snow-capped peaks of the

Andes Mountains. However, his appreciation for the awe-inspiring wilderness was interrupted by Eduardo's incessant pitch to extend the expedition by another ten days.

Mike: Eduardo talked to me about going to the Patagonian area of southern Chile to collect Magellanic Steamerduck and Kelp Goose eggs. Because the breeding season came early that year, the birds would still be laying and sitting on eggs. Eduardo said he had spent considerable time down there and his contacts could help us find eggs. He said it shouldn't be too expensive, as we could get there by train and boat, and we could do the trip in ten days easy.

Mike mulled over Eduardo's plan, but his attention reverted to the view of the Teno River bashing the rocks below. She was indeed a force to be reckoned with, and Mike and his team of explorers had already spent over a week chasing Torrent Ducks up and down this rugged gorge, as well as the Claro River in the higher elevations.

Locating their nests among the rocks and high cliffs had proven to be an enormous challenge, even for Mike, who normally was unparalleled when it came to finding nests. It required many hours of observation and detective work. Torrent Ducks in these remote rivers are not easy to follow along the white-water streams where they live and nest.

Mike: We got up early every day, just after dawn. We knew the females come off the nest to feed twice a day – in the morning early and in the late afternoon. The only time we could pinpoint the nest location was when the female returned to the nest with the male after feeding – and that could be up to an hour and a half. That's why we would watch a pair all the time while they were feeding and

Male (left) and female Torent Ducks.

167

then watch the female go back to the nest.

We knew the basic area the nest was in, but unless we knew exactly where it was, there was no way we could get the eggs. The rivers were too fast for wading. Boats would be swept downstream and crashed into boulders. The eggs were extremely difficult not only to find, but also to reach.

The ducks seemed to be cognizant of the fact that humans could not cross the river, and they cunningly built their nests in the rocks opposite the side of the river from the road. However, Mike had found the one rickety bridge that crossed the river. He also befriended some local homesteaders who lent them horses to get in position to climb to the nest they'd spotted from the other side of the river.

But so far their exhausting efforts had netted only a few Torrent Duck eggs. Perhaps this is why he became strangely intrigued by Eduardo's idea to extend his expedition and travel to southern Chile. He was especially keen on collecting Magellanic Steamerduck eggs, since that bird had never been bred outside the wild. It was true he had the time and the money to cover the trip, but now was not the time to decide. He still had more Torrent Duck eggs to collect.

HUNT FOR TORRENT DUCK EGGS

In between the trips made to Spain as part of the White-headed Duck Restoration Team, Mike worked intently on a return expedition to South America. On this trip to northern Chile, his goal was to bring to the Wildfowl Trust one of the world's few species of high altitude nesting waterfowl – the Torrent Duck.

This spectacular water bird is found only along the rapid mountain streams of the Andes Mountains, ranging from southern Chile north to Venezuela. Biologists were still learning about these unique waterfowl, and Mike Lubbock wanted to bring eggs to the Wildfowl Trust so they could be studied. He also hoped to be the first to breed them outside the wild, and in so doing learn much more about the unusual behavior of this bird.

Accompanying him on the expedition was his trusted companion from Fakenham, England and founder of Pensthorpe Wildlife Park, Bill Makins.

Mike: Bill was much like me – a down-to-earth waterfowl guy. I'd known him a long time, and he was the only person I could really work with closely and who was enthusiastic enough to go on an expedition like this. He had a little bit of money to help finance the trip; otherwise, I couldn't have done it. The Wildfowl Trust didn't have the money to do anything on this scale.

Joining the Chilean expedition was Ian Mitchell, a naturalist and acquaintance of Bill Makins. Ian would aid in the exploration for Torrent Duck nests and other important tasks. Since he had spent a great deal of time in Spain, Ian would also be helpful as an interpreter. They all convened in Santiago, Chile, on September 30, 1981.

Mike and Bill had a contact in Chile, a young lad named Eduardo Castillo.

Mike: Eduardo had sent some birds to the Wildfowl Trust a couple of years before, such as Chiloé Widgeons and Chilean Pintails. So he was one of our contacts in Chile, but he didn't speak much English.

We had no idea if he could help us, but he said he was familiar with rivers outside of Santiago and up in the Andes Mountains where we would find Torrent Ducks.

After arriving in Chile, we talked with him and figured he was a nice enough guy. He seemed knowledgeable on waterfowl and we thought he would be helpful on our quest. He functioned as a guide, although he wasn't with us every day we were in the field.

Bill Makins waited in the car for Mike, Ian, and Eduardo to make it back to the tiny, dilapidated bridge. Mike dismounted from his horse and walked up to the Peugeot, finding Bill in the middle of his usual afternoon siesta. Mike woke him up with a laugh and a loud bang on the side of the car. He was anxious to inspect the eggs he so cleverly sent across the gorge on the rope pulley.

Mike took out his flashlight and the black hood he used for candling eggs from his backpack. He discovered on close inspection that both eggs he had intrepidly collected from the cliff that afternoon were infertile. This was another piece of evidence that agricultural rainwater

Mike (right) with horses used on mountain trek.

runoff of the pesticide known as DDT was dramatically affecting the hatch-rate of Torrent Duck eggs.

He realized that finding Torrent Duck eggs in this rugged territory wouldn't be easy. They had been here nearly three weeks and had little to show for it. So far the white-water ducks were winning the battle. And now the few eggs they had procured were infertile.

Eduardo traveled back to his home in Santiago while Mike, Bill, and Ian returned to their camp outside the village of Los Queñes. The weary explorers dined on beef stew before turning in for the night. Not long after they fell asleep, they were roused by a disconcerting and violent series of earth tremors. The shaking of the ground seemed to go on forever. They learned some days later that the earthquake caused heavy damage in the port city of Valparaiso, not far from Santiago.

After a tiring day and lack of sleep due to the earthquake, they slept in until eight o'clock the next morning. A breakfast of coffee and biscuits, and they were off to find more Torrent Duck nests.

They drove a short distance out of the village and down the stream where a nesting pair of Torrent Ducks had previously been located. The only way to get across the river was on a rusty platform that was suspended from a cable going across the river. The cable was nothing more than a nylon rope. The contraption was operated by a set of antiquated pulleys bolted to wooden pillars.

Mike: It was hard work pulling oneself across a very thin nylon rope. You could tell this rope had broken a few times, because there were knots in it at various intervals.

170

Ian and I went across with the equipment we needed and located the area of the nest. I had to climb down the cliff about 70 feet on a rope ladder. I made it down to the ledge and soon located the nest in a hole that went deep into the bank. It looked like a rabbit hole, though it probably wasn't. I reached into the hole as far as my arm could go, but I couldn't get to the nest.

I asked Ian to lower the folding camp shovel to me. I spent a good while digging to get to the nest. It wasn't hard dirt to dig out, but the nest was a long ways into the bank. I kept digging and digging.

I finally got to the nest. It had four eggs and they were all fertile.

Going on back across the river on the pulley was problematic. Mike decided that Ian Mitchell should go first with the eggs. The platform crossed the river at a downward angle and Mike held tension on the nylon rope as Ian eased across. Bill took the eggs once he reached the other side and put them into the incubator.

Mike: The problem was how I would get across. There would be no one at my end to help put tension on the rope. How would I control my downhill speed?

I decided to just go for it and hopefully I could get it stopped at the other end. What I did was to hook a short piece of rope around the nylon rope to act as a brake. That worked, except there were these bloody knots in the nylon rope. The rope I was using as a brake was ripped

Mike crossing river suspended on old cable.

apart by one of these knots. The platform picked up speed and I was really zipping along.

When I neared the opposite river bank, I put my feet up and used my boots to break my fall as the platform crashed into the wooden pillars at the end of the line. I thought I broke my ankles. I didn't, but it was a hard crash landing. It was a much faster trip back compared to the way over.

The team searched several other high mountain rivers for nests but did not find anything worth climbing to for a closer look. Mike and Bill decided to spend their last two days of the trip collecting eggs on the Maipo River, an area where Eduardo had scouted Torrent Ducks at the beginning of their stay in Chile. Mike had located fertile eggs there.

Mike: We didn't want to take those eggs when we first started the trip. We could have taken them and put them in an incubator, but then we'd have them with us all the time. Something could go wrong with the incubator or they could be damaged as we traveled the rough mountain roads. The nest was fairly easy to get to, so we decided to collect the eggs on our way back to Santiago.

The advantage of Torrent Duck eggs in this case is that they have a long incubation period, over 4o days – meaning that if you find one that's just starting out, you have 40 days before they hatch.

Ian tied the ropes around a big rock and dropped them over the cliff. The nest was under an overhanging rock, and was more difficult to reach than Mike remembered. The ledge was only 20 feet above the water; however, the river was fast and dangerous. He certainly did not want to fall in.

Mike lowered himself down the rock face and onto the ledge. The female was on the nest and wouldn't fly out. Mike stuck his arm in between the rocks where the nest was located. He managed to reach the eggs and place them into the wicker creel slung over his shoulder.

Mike threw over the weighted lines to Bill on the other side of the river, the same manner as he did on the Teno River, though the Maipo was not quite as wide. Mike and Bill successfully ran the creel across the river.

Upon inspection, Bill noticed that all the eggs from this nest had small cracks, probably caused by the female being frightened off the nest.

Mike: It was unfortunate that the female got really scared when she saw my big arm coming at her. She probably rolled the eggs into the rocks trying to get out in a hurry.

One item we didn't have with us was nail polish, which we used to strengthen cracked egg shells for such a predicament. The cracks weren't bad; just some hairline fractures. We put the eggs into the incubator, drove to the next village, and went into a little variety store. Ian spoke Spanish to the clerk, but it was very difficult to interpret "nail polish" into another language. Mostly, we just pointed at our nails. Eventually he got the message, although he must have thought we were nuts. We put the nail polish on the eggs and it did the trick. I know some of those eggs did actually hatch in England.

The trio met Eduardo for lunch and then drove to a nest site he had located during the past two days. It was in the open and the large amount of down gave the nest away. However, it was in a very clever spot – impossible to get at from above or below.

They went downstream to another location where Eduardo thought he had pinpointed the spot the female had the nest. Mike and Ian went to the other side and lowered the ropes after tying them to a tree.

Mike rappelled down the ropes. Before he reached the ledge, he heard a sharp crack and sickening crash from above. Mike looked up and saw Ian holding on to the tree for dear life. The tree he clung to was rotten and had broken and was now sliding toward the precipice. Ian barely managed to hold on to the tree without being dragged over the cliff. Mike made it safely to the ledge, but did not find any nests.

Bill dropped off Mike and Ian downstream to look for more pairs. They soon found one. The female was feeding while the male was watching and guarding. Mike was sure they were nesting. He watched them for some time before they went upstream to the opposite side of the river. They hoped to pinpoint the location by tomorrow.

THE PATAGONIAN PREDICAMENT
Monday, October 19

It was the final day in the field, and Mike hoped to find even more Torrent Duck eggs. They had an early breakfast at the hostel where they had stayed that night.

They returned to the territory of the pair they'd watched the previous night, but found no birds at all. They drove across the bridge and up

Torrent Duck eggs in Bill Makins' cap.

the other side to where the stream was located. Mike went to the rock where he saw the female disappear and walked 30 yards upstream from where the bird was last seen. He found the nest located under a big rock. The nest had three eggs.

Mike: It was pure luck to find that nest. We knew she went up the river, which was really a small stream, and there were no places up there except for this rock. The nest was almost at water level and just under the rock. It was the easiest nest we had found – didn't even have to climb or rappel. Amazing!

So we now had 17 viable Torrent Duck eggs and a permit for 20. We were feeling pretty good about the trip.

The weary group returned to Santiago. Bill boarded a British Caledonian flight to London. With him was the portable incubator containing 17 Torrent Duck eggs. All of the eggs would go to his wild-fowl park in Norfolk, England.

Mike was originally scheduled to be on the same flight with Bill. Had he boarded the flight to England that day, at least half of the eggs would have gone to the Wildfowl Trust in Slimbridge. Perhaps the Torrent Duck would have been established there had he continued the planned itinerary. Funds had already been procured to build a special Torrent Duck brooder at the Trust. Although Bill Makins did raise five of the fast-water ducks to maturity at Pensthorpe Wildfowl Park, due to various problems, they never became permanently established.

Years later, Mike admitted that his biggest disappointment with any of the trips he made was with Torrent Ducks, a species he really wanted to breed. Bill flew to England alone with the eggs because Mike had agreed to extend the trip and follow Eduardo to the Patagonia region of southern Chile. He was already physically and mentally exhausted from the weeks spent in the Andes Mountains. Unfortunately, he failed to remember a similar experience he wished never to repeat.

In 1973, Mike had planned an expedition that he later realized should have been separated into two trips. He'd organized an expedition to Argentina that focused on collecting Argentine Ruddy Ducks and Black-headed Ducks, as well as Red Shovelers, Silver Teal, Rosy-billed Ducks, and Crested Screamers. Since he was already going to be in South America, he ultimately decided to also go to the Falkland Islands, a series of islands off the coast of Argentina. There he spent a great deal of time trudging through the islands' tall, thick grasses, looking for eggs of Kelp Geese and Magellanic Geese. The length of the expedition caused him great fatigue. He vowed not to make such a long trip again.

Despite his vow eight years prior, Mike thought Eduardo's scheme seemed to be a logical extension of his Chilean expedition and a perfect opportunity to collect Magellanic Steamerduck eggs for the Wildfowl Trust.

However, the excursion would end in calamity and permanently alter the course of Mike Lubbock's career.

STUCK IN SANTIAGO

Mike dwelled at Eduardo's residence while he regrouped and prepared for the excursion to the southern coast of Chile. He Telexed a message to Ali letting her know his arrival home would be delayed. He also received a telephone call from Bill Makins in England, reporting that 16 of the 17 Torrent Duck eggs had survived the long trip to Norfolk, England. Mike was greatly relieved with the news.

For more than ten years, Mike had carefully planned each of his collecting itineraries, triple-checking even the minute details. To the best of his ability, he made sure nothing was left to chance. However, the travel and contact arrangements for this jaunt to Port Aguirre in Patagonia were primarily in the hands of the 20-year-old Eduardo Castillo.

175

From Mike's Journal:
> Trying to plan anything seems to take forever. We are still waiting for confirmation from Eduardo's friend in Port Aguirre that we can stay there. Every question is answered by "mañana, mañana" [tomorrow, tomorrow].

One aspect of the trip of which he had charge was retrieving the portable incubator Bill Makins took to England. He desperately needed the incubator before they left for Puerto Montt, the first leg of their journey to Port Aguirre.

Eduardo sensed Mike was becoming frustrated. He thought a change of scenery would be in order and suggested a trip to the mountains outside of Santiago.

From Mike's Journal:
> We drove higher and higher along a meandering dirt road. We must have reached 7,000 feet in altitude. I could feel the pressure in my ears. Eduardo told me that the land we entered was a protected area. We parked the car and decided to explore on foot. I heard two gunshots – so much for the protection.
>
> I saw a number of raptors, including Chilean Eagle, Goshawk, and Harris Hawk. I found a nest of Barn Owls in the rocks, and most exciting – a condor's nest which we climbed to.
>
> Later on the walk, I caught my foot in a rabbit snare. Also, I seem to be developing a cold.

Eduardo Castillo climbing to condors nest.

After several days of sleeping to recover from his cold, Mike received a call from Mr. Hendricks Pugaso, who was his main contact in Santiago. He was handling the import of the portable incubator, which had arrived at his office.

Still coughing and feeling ill, Mike took the train to Hendricks' office. His secretary told him the incubator was cleared by Customs, but Mr. Hendricks had to pay $300 duty. The whole trip relied on the incubator. However, a $300 out-of-pocket expense would severely constrain his budget. He asked the secretary if he could send the money once he returned to England. She said that it would be okay.

The incubator was shipped inside a rectangular Styrofoam box. Mike opened the box to inspect the incubator. It seemed to have survived two trans-Atlantic crossings in less than a week. Mike knew the whole trip relied on a properly operating incubator. Little did he realize that his life would rely on the Styrofoam shipping box.

Mike continued to need bed rest, which seemed to only frustrate him further. His impatience was escalating. It had been a week since Bill left Chile and Mike had moved into Eduardo's guest house. Plans for the trip advanced at a snail's pace, and Mike was powerless to help. He knew absolutely nothing about the area around Port Aguirre and had no contacts other than Eduardo.

Mike had now been in Chile for a month, including this past week spent cooling his heals in Santiago while he waited on Eduardo to confirm vital pieces of a trip to an unknown area – a place he had neither studied nor prepared to visit.

Already Mike was beginning to regret his decision to extend the expedition. Had he not learned anything from the debacle of 1973? That trip at least he had meticulously planned.

However, by the following day it appeared that the travel arrangements were finally in place. They were to board the train on the first leg of the trip to Puerto Montt the next evening.

From Mike's Journal:
> Let's hope we can at least do something tomorrow and
> get out of the city!

Before the end of this journey, he would pray to get back to Santiago alive.

CHAPTER NINE

Peril in Patagonia

October 28, 1981
Santiago, Chile

The ravaging effects of his cold had reduced Mike's already meager amount of patience to nonexistence. He had been abrupt and mostly intolerant with Eduardo. It seemed a host of obstacles stood in the way of his collecting Magellanic Steamerduck eggs. During the last 24 hours, he'd changed his mind several times as to whether or not he would proceed with the plans to follow Eduardo to Port Aguirre.

Inside his tiny guest room, an outbuilding of the Castillos' home, Mike strained to make out the names of the many islands on the map of Patagonia. He had trouble even locating the tiny isle where Eduardo planned for them to go. Port Aguirre might not even exist, for all he could tell. And yet Eduardo claimed he had lived there and swore that steamerduck eggs abounded on the nearby islands.

Steamerducks – they were the heart of the matter. They were why Mike discounted all the negatives, both real and potential, and finally decided to go to what appeared on the map to be the end of the earth.

The steamerduck is a marvel of waterfowl bioengineering. A large and sturdy seagoing duck with massive feet, they can swim at exceptionally high speeds, even against ocean currents and strong headwinds. Their odd name is supposedly derived from their ability to churn and spray water as they swim, resembling a paddlewheel steamboat.

Most steamerducks are flightless, although one species is capable of flight and is thus named the Flying Steamerduck. They all spend the majority of their life at sea, but during the breeding season they nest on the rocky cliffs and forests of Patagonia's numerous islands.

Mike: Steamerducks are very large and strong – their wings are also powerful. When people ask me what they're like, I always say, "They're basically a cross between a battleship and a pair of pliers" – because the beak is pretty powerful, too.

Mike had a strong passion for steamerducks. He held the World's First Breeding Award for the Falkland Islands Steamerduck, a bird he collected while exploring the Falkland Islands in 1973. The Magellanic Steamerduck had been bred before, though none were left in managed populations. He wanted very much to establish them at Slimbridge – enough to take the risk of going into the unknown region of Patagonia.

TRAIN TO PUERTO MONTT

The day had come to go south. Mike and Eduardo loaded their duffle bags and gear into the taxi, which delivered them to the Central Station in Santiago. The train platform was a beehive of activity as passengers, porters, and small boys looking for work carrying bags all scurried about in the moments prior to the train's scheduled departure.

They were fortunate to find room to stack their baggage in the overhead racks of the compartment, much to the disapproval of the carriage master, who insisted they had taken more than their share of precious luggage space. Eduardo shrugged his shoulders and exhibited a "what can we do?" expression. For his part, Mike merely indicated he did not understand what was said. The carriage master ranted awhile longer, before he gave up and left muttering what Mike assumed to be Spanish swear words. The explorers' travel companions did not complain about the situation, even though it required them to hold bundles on their laps.

In what seemed like a Chilean transportation miracle, the train left on time.

From Mike's Journal:

This is one of the bumpiest and most uncomfortable trains I think I have ever been on. Even the old steam trains I took to prep school were nicer than this. I've come to the conclusion that there would be no way any eggs could survive a train journey like this, so I will need to fly back to Santiago from Puerto Montt. I hope I will have enough money to buy an airline ticket when the time comes.

The majority of Chileans are quite small, so my being 6 foot 2 inches must make me seem like a giant to them.

Also, because I speak a different language, they stare at me for long periods of time, but I'm getting used to it.

The carriage lights went out at 11:30, leaving only a dim light. I tried to write my notes, but the motion of the train made it impossible, so I stuck my nose in an Agatha Christie novel I brought with me.

Mike managed to get some sleep, despite the frequent stops the train made throughout the night. After leaving each station, the old locomotive sputtered and gained speed in spurts that made the ride jarring.

He awoke to the morning's light streaming through the window blinds, opened little by little by fellow passengers as they stirred from their overnight respites. The new day doused rain on the Chilean countryside, which already appeared vastly different from the city sprawl of Santiago. The view showcased beautiful trees covered in red flowers and an abundance of gorse, bursting in yellow blooms. The gorse reminded Mike of Scotland, which stirred a sudden yearning to return to his home in Great Britain.

Soon after the excitement of spotting the sea from the train window, they arrived at the station in Puerto Montt shortly after noontime. Getting off the train with their luggage was almost as difficult as when they had boarded. People swarmed like bees to help or pilfer. Mike thought most of them looked very crafty.

They hailed a taxi to take them to the shipping office, where they intended to book passage further south to Port Aguirre. Riding through the narrow, grimy streets of Puerto Montt, Mike felt as though he had entered an alien world. He had travelled over a thousand kilometers south from Santiago, and many more remained between Puerto Montt and his destination. His doubts about making this journey were escalating.

The taxi driver dropped them off near the shipping office. Mike suspected he was greatly overcharged for such a short trip, though he felt powerless to argue. In these situations he relied almost totally on Eduardo, who merely shrugged his shoulders when Mike asked him if they paid too much.

The stewards at the shipping office informed Mike and Eduardo that there were not as many ships sailing to Port Aguirre as before. The schedule Eduardo had used for planning this part of the trip was not current. They were told a boat *might* be leaving for Port Aguirre on

Saturday, two days from then. If they came back after two o'clock, they could purchase a ticket for the possible voyage.

Since the taxi ride proved to be expensive, they decided to walk back through town and find a hotel room.

From Mike's Journal:

> We found a cheap, nasty, smelly hotel and booked a room for two nights. We had a bite of lunch in town on the way back to the shipping office. Being a fishing port, Puerto Montt stinks to high heavens. Even with my cold I can smell it.

They arrived back at the shipping office only to be told that there was in fact no boat to Port Aguirre on Saturday, but there would definitely be one on Thursday. Also the price had risen to 4,000 pesos per person.

From Mike's Journal:

> I am now getting very frustrated. Eduardo has not thought this trip through properly. I asked him if there was any other way around this dilemma we've gotten ourselves into.

Puerto Montt is the gateway to the Chiloé Archipelago, Chiloé Island and the many other smaller islands in the Sea of Chiloé. Mike wondered if there were any boats leaving south from ports on Chiloé Island, which was not very far from Puerto Montt. Eduardo had mentioned that he once took a boat from there to Port Aguirre.

They walked to the nearby telephone office and Eduardo rang the harbor office in Chiloé. They told him that there was a ship sailing to Port Aisén that night on the tide. According to Eduardo, Port Aisén was not far from Port Aguirre and boats went back and forth every day. All they needed to do was catch the last ferry from Puerto Montt to Chiloé Island.

From Mike's Journal:

> Our plans are changing again and we did not have much time to get to Chiloé Island to catch the boat to Port Aisén. We got hold of a cab and I told Eduardo to first ask how much the driver would charge to take us to the hotel and then to the ferry.

The taxi driver seemed much nicer than the last one and said he would charge 1,000 pesos per person, which did not seem too outlandish. We jumped into the cab, stopping first at the hotel. They seemed fine with us cancelling the rooms. I was pleased to be leaving there as they were cooking something that smelt disgusting, causing me to vomit.

Mike and Eduardo raced out of the hotel to the waiting taxi and quickly loaded their bags. As they approached the harbor, Mike could see that the ferry at the dock was nearly set to depart. The driver responded to Eduardo's admonishment in Spanish to "step on it." After swerving through traffic, the worn brakes reluctantly brought the taxi to halt a short distance from the gangway.

Mike hurriedly paid the driver the agreed upon amount, plus a bit extra for the speedy, though treacherous, service. Eduardo had already collected all but two bags and was running for the ferry. Mike snatched up the remaining bags and followed behind, his long strides gradually closing in on his younger, more heavily burdened cohort so that they both reached the ticket collector in unison. They breathed heavily as they strode aboard the aging ferry with only moments to spare.

Roundabout

Mike enjoyed the ferry's tranquil cruise past the wooded islands along the Chacao Strait. The idyllic panorama soothed his nerves and provided a welcome antidote to their frantic pace prior to boarding. Within a few hours, the plodding vessel entered the Gulf of Ancud and in time sailed through the circuitous series of peninsulas and channels leading to Castro, the primary town of Chiloé Island.

As the ferry entered the harbor, Mike was surprised at the beauty of this magnificent isle, especially since the smell and filth of Puerto Montt lingered in his memory. Looking up from the deck, he saw the elegant twin spires of the Church of San Francisco atop the plateau, which rose gracefully from the sea. In front of the ferry, an eye-catching row of quaint homes lined the harbor, all brightly painted in blue, red, or yellow, sitting on piers over the water.

Once the ship docked, Mike and Eduardo went to Customs and endured the terminally slow bureaucratic process of checking passports and visas. The officer could not speak a word of English, requiring Eduardo to intercede in Spanish on Mike's behalf. After a tense discussion, the weary travelers were given a tepid hand signal to pass through.

"What was it he asked you about me?" inquired Mike of Eduardo as they left the Customs Office.

"He wondered what the hell you're doing here!"

Mike didn't reply audibly, but at that point he was wondering the same thing.

Before leaving the docks, they sought information on the boat to Port Aisén. They were told the ship would come in to the dock with the tide at six o'clock. Mike could see her moored in the bay. He breathed a sigh of relief. They had made good time getting to Chiloé Island, thanks to the taxi driver, and now they only had to wait about an hour until they sailed to Port Aisén.

From Mike's Journal:

> At six o'clock, an official-looking person came around
> with a two-way radio and told us that the tide has not
> risen enough that evening, so the boat would not sail until
> the high tide tomorrow. This must be the Chilean way.

Because of the huge changes in tide levels along this part of the Chilean coast, boats in the bays are temporarily stranded on the mud-flats during low tide. On this evening, the lunar and solar positioning failed to influence the tide enough for Mike's ship to dock. Once again they would need to pay for overnight accommodations due to transportation difficulty. The purse was already getting light.

They made their way up the road to some houses Mike had spotted from the bay. From a distance, Castro appeared much cleaner than Puerto Montt, but upon closer inspection there seemed to be little improvement in the sanitary conditions. One house had a sign which claimed the residence was a hotel. For only 200 pesos each, Mike decided to take a chance. With a lack of funds, he had little choice.

From Mike's Journal:

> The Chiloé people are even smaller than those in
> Santiago – even the buildings are smaller. The hotel was
> like being in a very dirty, smelly dollhouse. I have to
> stoop all the time, especially going through doorways.

The bed had a straw mattress, and my feet hung over the end of the bed.

We ate downstairs in what they called the restaurant, where they served us bread and eggs with some kind of meat, which I could not work out what it was exactly. But we were very hungry and it wasn't too bad.

I turned in at about nine o'clock. Even the short bed felt good, as I had not slept horizontally since leaving Santiago, plus I was still trying to shake off my cold.

The next morning at breakfast, Mike met several crew members from the boat meant to sail to Port Aisén. They expected to sail no later than six o'clock that evening. Mike thought it best to take a wait-and-see approach.

With nearly a whole day to kill before departure, Mike and Eduardo went for a walk around the beach. There they saw their first pair of Magellanic Steamerducks. The massive birds became alarmed and swam speedily out to sea before Mike could get a picture. From the beach, he saw the boat to Port Aisén was high and dry in the harbor due to the low tide. Hopefully, the evening high tide would allow it to dock. Still, he was perplexed by the activity of the crew who were frantically heaving on a pulley, trying to get an anchor aboard. It seemed peculiar.

They walked back to town by way of the Customs Office to inquire about the boat and confirm that she would sail on the six o'clock tide. Mike was not shocked when they were told the ship had developed a problem and was beyond a timely repair. Not only would she not sail as scheduled, they didn't know when the next passage would occur.

From Mike's Journal:

> Who knows what may have happened. The crew probably dropped the anchor through the bottom of the boat! Eduardo made a call and confirmed that the ship we were originally told about was still on schedule to leave Puerto Montt Saturday for Port Aisén. It is difficult to believe anything anyone says, and of course I am hearing it all secondhand through Eduardo's interpretation. We have no choice but to backtrack to Puerto Montt.

The ferry ride back to Puerto Montt wasn't nearly as serene as the trip 24 hours earlier. The views were equally as scenic and the water still crystal clear, but the frustration of Chile's transportation system was exhausting Mike's patience and slowly eroding his confidence. No other expedition in his career had presented him with such an exasperating series of obstacles.

THE BOTTOM OF THE PLANET
Saturday, October 31

Of the few passengers aboard the ship steaming towards Port Aisén, two were Englishmen searching the world for gold. One had worked a claim in the United States and the other had done the same in New Guinea. The prospectors were traveling to Patagonia to try their luck.

Mike Lubbock enjoyed chatting with the quirky gentlemen and was intrigued by their quest. Their expeditions were not dramatically different from his. They were in pursuit of the precious yellow metal, while he sought rare and endangered waterfowl eggs. Both parties chose the same desolate part of the world to find their treasure.

The ship steered through the Moraleda Channel, far south of Chiloé Island. This waterway separates the Chonos Archipelago from the mainland. The Archipelago is a cluster of towering, forested islands, most of them uninhabited and unnamed.

Mike only half-listened to the chatter of his travel companions as island after island passed by and disappeared behind the ship's far-reaching wake. His mind was riveted on thoughts of home, Ali, and his young son, Brent. Despite the overpowering beauty of these islands against the backdrop of the glacier-clad Andes Mountains, he wished this ship was approaching the Royal Portbury Dock of Bristol rather than its actual destination of Port Aisén. Even while watching numerous pairs of his prized steamerducks from the deck, he wondered again what he was doing in this strange and extremely unsettling land near the bottom of the planet.

The seas swelled and roiled during the night, causing Mike to cling to the chair in his cabin. He had already been forced to move out of the bunk in an attempt to find a secure place to sleep. The morning brought only cloudy skies and intermittent cold rain. During the afternoon, the ship sailed past the tiny island of Port Aguirre, their ultimate destination. But she would not stop there. They must remain onboard until reaching Port Aisén late that night. Then they must figure out how to backtrack to this small island port that Eduardo had selected to begin the search for eggs.

The ship docked at Port Aisén at nine o'clock that evening. The travel-weary duo debarked and was promptly drenched in a heavy downpour of chilly Patagonian rain. If anything, Mike's cold had gotten worse.

Monday, November 2
Port Aisén

Arising from a restless sleep in yet another filthy, ill-suited hosteria, Mike and Eduardo sought coffee and a boat to Port Aguirre. For their morning caffeine they returned to the restaurant where last night's late dinner had been hastily choked down before any of the ingredients could be recognized by their taste buds. This was also where members of the ship's crew had dined, who had given them a lead on a boat called the *Elephantes* which was believed to be leaving for Port Aguirre that day.

The search for the *Elephantes* brought them to the ship's owner, Rodrigo, who would provide the needed transportation for 10,000 pesos. The fare could not be supported by Mike's rapidly dwindling purse.

For some odd reason, Rodrigo felt compelled to help the forlorn visitors and made a counter proposal. He would take them to Port Aguirre in his smaller boat for only 4,000 pesos and the cost of oil and gas. Mike cringed even at this reduced offer.

Rodrigo exhibited pity towards Mike's financial situation, as he conveniently recalled a Chilean traveler who also was in need of an economical fare to Port Aguirre. Perhaps he might be talked into contributing to the cost of passage.

After much time spent locating the Chilean fellow, followed by a lengthy negotiation, an agreement was reached in which the Chilean would pay 1,000 pesos as his share of the deal. It wasn't much, but at this stage, every bit of savings mattered.

Mike and Eduardo returned to the hosteria where they packed up their gear and happily checked out. Not spending another night in such a disgusting mess was itself worth the cost of hiring the boat.

Rodrigo's partner, Raul, pulled up outside the hotel and helped them load their equipment into the bed of his old pickup truck. It would be Raul who would pilot the boat to Port Aguirre. Before they reached the dock, the clouds opened up with another pounding rain, soaking the clothes in their duffle bags. The moment they reached the dock, the rain ceased.

Raul returned to town to get supplies for the trip while Mike, Eduardo, Rodrigo, and the Chilean traveler remained on the small craft now moored upriver from the docks. The river had once been navigable by larger boats until an earthquake turned the river into a deposit for silt. It was a blow to the tiny community that had already been dependent on a mere smattering of industry and travelers.

Mike viewed the horizon while they waited for Raul's return. Menacing clouds shrouded the mountaintops. The grand vistas he had enjoyed in previous days had disappeared. It seemed to Mike that the climatic conditions had changed permanently for the worse.

In due course Raul made it back to the boat with supplies and a telephone message for Rodrigo. It was from Hendricks Pugaso, Mike's contact in Santiago, reminding Rodrigo to be on the lookout for an Englishman and his young Chilean companion, and to help them in any way he could. Now Rodrigo understood why he thought these two men were important. Hendricks had informed him of their pending arrival a week or so earlier.

Rodrigo said his good-byes to the passengers and departed the cabin cruiser. At 5:30 that evening, the small boat made its way out of Port Aisén with Raul at the helm. Although the rain had stopped, they faced a strong frigid wind as the craft wound through the narrower channels. Mike felt uneasy with the fact that they were leaving without the benefit of a weather forecast. Rodrigo's small craft had a compass, but no radio. Raul would basically steer them to Port Aguirre by memory and sight.

Once they entered open water, the wind became fierce and the rain pelted them ruthlessly. The small cruiser tossed and bounced like a cork on the surface of the sea. By 8:30 that night, conditions worsened, and everyone was being thrown from one side of the boat to the other.

The passengers sought refuge below deck. The safest place for them seemed to be their bunks, where they were at least sheltered from the wind and could grab onto the rails. Above deck, the combination of rain and darkness conspired against Raul as he piloted the boat in near zero-visibility conditions.

At 9:30, the rain ceased, but the wind gained strength, though that would have seemed impossible only minutes earlier. The water boiled madly, and Mike feared the rough seas were now a serious threat to their safety.

From Mike's Journal:
> I could not stay in my bunk any longer. I was really beginning to wonder if Raul had any idea how to handle a boat in these weather conditions, let alone in the dark. I had boating experience and training from my time at Pangbourne Nautical College, so I went aloft to see if I could help.
> At 10 o'clock I spotted a sheltered bay and convinced Raul to head for it. From there we moved forward, hugging the shoreline so we could pass by small inlets and bays that were protected from the wind. It was not long before I found a suitable spot where we dropped anchor. It was a relief to finally be in calm water.

Everyone was chilled to the bone. Mike heated some canned soup on an old Primus stove he had brought. The hot soup was the perfect tonic on this cold night. Everyone turned in at eleven o'clock. There weren't enough bunks in the cabin for everyone, so the Chilean fellow volunteered to sleep on deck. He had, after all, paid less for his fare than Mike and Eduardo.

PORT OF GOOD SUCCESS
Tuesday, November 3

The appearance of the sun was a happy sight after the preceding night's tempest. The skies had cleared and the sea was calm as Raul weighed anchor and resumed the journey to the elusive Port Aguirre. By noon he was tying his boat at the weathered dock in the town's harbor.

Mike had seriously wondered if they would ever arrive at this secluded destination. It seemed ages ago that Bill Makins had boarded the British Caledonia flight to London with an incubator full of Torrent Duck eggs. Their arrival required six days of preparation in Santiago, plus a full week of arduous travel. They dealt with rural Chili's antiquated and mostly dysfunctional transportation system, endured filthy hotels and hostels with grossly substandard bathrooms, and consumed a string of quickly forgotten meals that often tested the limits of edibility. Added to this list of adversity was two weeks of suffering from a cold that lingered and continually drained Mike's strength. Despite the agony of the journey, he was overjoyed to be on this tiny speck of nearly inaccessible soil.

Beyond the dock lay the sleepy island port known as Aguirre, a name derived from the Fuegian word meaning "good success." Mike surmised that a good success was due him after such a daunting trip. Finally he could focus his attention on finding eggs of the vital waterfowl species that inhabited these climes. He was once again in his element.

Mike and Eduardo collected their soggy gear from the dock. They became aware that many of the townspeople had noticed their arrival and gathered on the hill to inspect the strangers that had succeeded in finding their island. They quickly recognized Eduardo from the time he'd lived there, but the tall Englishman incited a buzz among the villagers, most of whom were descendants of the Onah Indians.

Raul hurriedly turned his boat toward open water and a return to Port Aisén as Mike and Eduardo carried their baggage up the hill toward their new residence. Mike felt the denizens' prying eyes upon him. He thought they must consider him to be some kind of freak. Walking through the throng of diminutive Patagonian natives, he imagined being portrayed in a scene from Gulliver's Travels, surrounded by Lilliputians.

Eduardo had made arrangements for them to stay at the home of his friend Enrique and his family. They were met at the doorway by Enrique's wife, Marianna, who was at least aware that they were coming. Considering the loosely crafted plans Eduardo had put into place, Mike was relieved that they were expected. Enrique, however, was away on business in Port Montt.

From Mike's Journal:
> It was great to have a proper roof over our heads and a warm house that was fairly clean. We soon made ourselves at home, unpacking everything for the first time.

Mike inquired about the availability of electricity in the home. Marianna explained that power was only available during the five hours between 6 and 11 p.m. This was important to know, since that was when the incubator batteries would need to be recharged once eggs were collected.

Mike with mussel shells. Bivalves and crustaceans were staples in these islands.

Marianna was very friendly, though Eduardo had to interpret everything since she spoke no English. Mike borrowed a boat and some line and went fishing for the evening meal. He did not expect Enrique's family to provide food for them during their stay on the island. He was successful at catching six small fish, which Eduardo prepared with lemon and other ingredients he had brought from Santiago. The fact that Eduardo had once lived in Port Aguirre certainly was an advantage in that he knew to bring many of the things unavailable in this part of the world that was cut off from customary provisions.

They stayed up late and discussed plans for finding eggs in the coming days. Mike listened carefully to Eduardo and Marianna's conversations, attempting to decipher what they were saying. They had known each other previously, and he judged the stories must have been amusing from all the laughter they generated.

Enrique's small home was by far the nicest place he had stayed since leaving Santiago. He had already seen a number of steamerducks on the way to the island. Perhaps Eduardo's idea to come to Port Aguirre was a good one after all. "Good success" was the name of the place; he hoped it would be a successful stay.

Mike settled into bed. He had finally become excited about the adventure ahead.

Wednesday, November 4

After sleeping later than usual, Mike had a meeting with an Indian family Eduardo knew, who lived about three miles away in the other village on Port Aguirre. They came to Enrique's home in hopes of being hired to help the Englishman search for steamerduck eggs. The bargaining took two hours, but an agreement was reached. They would begin the exploring the local islands early the next morning.

Marianna gave Mike the keys to a shed and told him to look around and see if there was anything that would be useful for the hunt. He swung open the door and immediately saw a Yamaha 25-horsepower engine. It was an ancient model that would start up on a petrol-oil mix but once warmed up could be switched to kerosene.

Mike asked Marianna if she knew the history of the motor. She said it had fallen overboard about three weeks ago. Despite the fact that it had seized up, Mike was excited to have any motor at this point, as none of the Indians owned one. They rowed everywhere. Occasionally they'd hoist a sail if the wind was in the right direction, although none of their boats had any centerboards so proper sailing technique was impossible. They constructed all their boats out of the local cypress trees, which made them very heavy. These were clinker-built boats, where the planks overlap one another.

Mike spent the rest of the day stripping down the motor and testing it in a large barrel of water. He was pleased with his work and happy to have a motor to cruise through these waters in a heavy hand-built boat. Eduardo had not helped Mike work on the motor, claiming he knew nothing about engines, but Mike noticed he seemed unhappy for the first time since leaving Port Montt.

That evening, around six o'clock, there was a knock on the door. The Indian family Mike hired came by to say they were very concerned about the danger of crossing the rough water of the Moraleda Channel over to Melchor Island without a motor. Mike took them to the shed and showed them what he had worked on all day. The Indians actually smiled when they saw the operable Yamaha outboard engine.

Mike was still in need of a boat large enough to carry the Indian family. It was not yet dark, so with the assistance of the fisheries inspector he found a carpenter who had one of the bigger boats on the island. The only problem was it had two pointed ends and no transom on which to clamp the motor. The carpenter set about reconfiguring one of the ends, using his axe, hammer, extra boards, and six-inch nails. Before long, Mike had a 12-foot boat with a place to clamp the motor. As darkness approached, a successful test run was made with Mike, Eduardo, and two of the Indians as occupants in the craft.

Eduardo and Mike returned to the house and prepared for the morning exploration. They mixed oil and kerosene for the motor and readied the smaller of the two incubators. Mike lined the Styrofoam shipping box with a thick layer of down, which would be used as an egg carrier. In case they couldn't make it back by nightfall, they packed provisions, a tent, and sleeping bags. Everything was set for the next day's journey to the remote island of Melchor.

Long boat outfitted for exploration of the Patagonian islands with José (left) and Juan (right).

Thursday, November 5

The motor chugged and sputtered, moving the explorers' vessel slowly past small islands lying off the coast of the large isle of Melchor. Like most of the land mass in the archipelago, these rocky islets were heavily forested. Mike had already spotted steamerducks on the water and Kelp Geese on the shore banks. He was elated to finally be hunting for eggs after two weeks of planning and traveling. His concern at the moment was how much of the gasoline mixture had been burned on the trip across the Moraleda Channel. Would there be enough to get back to Aguirre? Fuel conservation would be needed from this point forward.

In the makeshift watercraft with Mike were two Onah Indians, Juan Hermon Nancupel, his teenage son José, and their two thick-bodied, short-legged mutts, which reminded Mike somewhat of the Queen's corgis that romped at Buckingham Palace. Also tagging along was Eduardo, who had little to offer on the trip other than his ability to interpret most of the Indians' strange dialect.

They tied up the boat at a deserted island with a dilapidated cabin. The structure certainly wasn't weatherproof, but Mike decided that it would make a nice base camp with many islands only a short distance away. The Indians unloaded all the equipment and made camp. He checked the gas and kerosene containers. There seemed to be plenty of kerosene, but he was worried about how little gas mixture remained. That afternoon they searched several islands. Since gas was needed to start the motor, and the longest trip would be the one back to Port Aguirre, Mike decided the Indians should earn their money and row to the various islands.

Their rowing technique was good, but choppy water made the task difficult. For once he was thankful he didn't understand their language, as he was sure they were swearing at him. After all the work of rowing from island to island, no viable waterfowl eggs were found. Since it was getting late in the day and the sea was getting rough, Mike decided to return to the base camp for the night.

Mike put up his tent, much to the amusement of Juan and José who opted for the dilapidated cabin. José went to the rocky beach with a three-pronged fork tied to a long stick. He came back in half an hour with eight enormous crabs and sea urchins. The sea urchins were eaten raw as a starter course, followed by the crabs, which were boiled on the campfire. Mike found the crabs to be full of meat and delicious.

After all had their fill of crabs and urchins, they went fishing in the boat, not very far from shore, using homemade hand lines. It was not long before they started to catch fish called "cabrilla," or sea bass, the largest being about two pounds. They returned to camp just before it got dark.

Juan prepared four fish, which he split down the middle, removed the guts, salted, and then placed skin-side-down on the fire. They were very good, and not too burnt for being roasted over a flame. They turned in not long after supper.

Friday, November 6

The wind howled and the rain poured throughout the night. Mike and Eduardo fared well in the tent, although it was tight quarters. Mike felt sorry for Juan and José in the leaky shack; however, they managed to come through unscathed and eager for the trip back to Port Aguirre.

They packed up camp and loaded the dogs and their backpacks into the boat. The sea was very rough, but Mike was confident they would make it back if the motor held up. Juan knew which direction to head.

The motor started up without a fight, and soon they were out to sea. With four people, the heavy boat cut through the waves sluggishly, taking on a significant amount of water. At first, Juan and José were efficient at bailing out the intruding sea water, but once they lost sight of land they hunkered down in the bottom of the boat, terrified. Mike had forgotten that none of the Indians in these islands knew how to swim. The water was too cold for them to learn and practice.

Eduardo was not much help either. As the journey progressed, his countenance soured and he entered a depressed state. The waves continued to splash over the gunnels. Mike was left to bail water as well as guiding the boat.

From Mike's Journal:

I had to concentrate very hard, hoping we were going in the right direction. It began to rain heavily, which made visibility even more difficult. The motor seemed to be behaving. It spluttered a few times, but kept running. Our gear got very wet, and at one time the incubator and Styrofoam box were floating on the bottom of the boat next to the bedraggled Indians. We passed near to a small island that I recognized from the trip out. So I felt we were headed the right way.

After two and a half hours of hell, I could see some houses on an approaching island, which I hoped to be Port Aguirre. The rain stopped as we approached the island. It protected us from the wind, and the sea became much calmer.

The Indians became alive again and got excited as they could see their house on the way in to port. Just then the motor spluttered and quit. I had used the last of the gasoline to start the engine for the trip over, so there was no way to restart it now. Juan and José rowed to the shore in front of their house. We all got out of the boat – four waterlogged people and two drenched dogs.

Eduardo and Mike decided to walk the three miles back to Enrique's house with only their backpacks. Juan and José would row the boat and the rest of their belongings back to the main dock later in the afternoon. Mike worried that the incubator might not work after floating so long inside the boat. As soon as he got back, Mike took a shower, which warmed him after his long exposure to the cold air and sea.

Mike sent Eduardo out to find kerosene and gasoline for the next adventure and then walked down to port. He was moderately surprised to see the *Elephantes* docked there. Eventually he found Rodrigo, whose small boat they had taken to Port Aguirre. After chatting in English for a while, Rodrigo said he might be able to help Mike find eggs. He invited him to dinner at a restaurant, which was actually someone's house in the village. Eduardo had successfully returned with fuel he had bought from the port captain, but was too depressed to go with Mike to dinner. Eduardo's state of mind really had Mike concerned.

During the meal, which featured boiled chicken and large quantities of Chiloé potatoes, the erratic weather turned foul once again. Rodrigo assured Mike the elements would improve by morning when they made their voyage to Inca Island.

Saturday, November 7

By early morning the *Elephantes* was furnished for the trip to Inca Island. Rodrigo was ready to leave, but Mike could not rouse Eduardo from his sleep. His depressed state had robbed him of any further enthusiasm for the trip. The only option was to leave him asleep at Enrique's house.

As Mike boarded the boat alone, Rodrigo made comments indicating that he didn't regard Eduardo highly. Mike figured it must be an unsettled dispute from Eduardo's time living at Port Aguirre. Mike was very pleased with the offer Rodrigo had made to introduce him to someone who would help him search for steamerducks.

The *Elephantes* quickly made the voyage to Inca Island, where Mike met Pedro, the caretaker of the island Rodrigo owned. Pedro knew locations of two steamerduck nests, a Kelp Goose nest, and the nest of an Ashy-headed Goose. Using his dogs for tracking, other nests might be located. They agreed to begin the search later that day.

The round-trip only took two hours. Back at Port Aguirre, it took Mike a while to pry the listless Eduardo out of bed. Mike told him that their luck had finally changed and how there were nests in an area they had yet to explore, which was not nearly as far as their journey the day before. The plan was for both of them to leave that afternoon for a return trip to Inca Island. Rodrigo would tow their boat from the back of the *Elephantes* and drop them off at Pedro's cabin. He then needed to return with the *Elephantes* to Port Aisén.

Eduardo continued to balk at the idea of sailing with Rodrigo, but Mike pressed him on the matter. Hesitantly, Eduardo told him that Rodrigo could not be trusted, but would not provide any details as to why he thought so. With nothing but suspicion to go on from Eduardo, Mike concluded on the basis of his positive interactions with Rodrigo that the trip must go forward. So far they had not collected a single egg. He needed Eduardo for assistance and as an interpreter. The whole trip was predicated on Eduardo's connections and understanding of this strange land and its people.

Cajoling an emotionally wrecked 20-year-old was not a strong suit for Mike Lubbock. However, using gentle persuasion and reassuring words, he convinced Eduardo to make the voyage to Inca.

By late morning, Mike and Eduardo arrived at the dock and loaded their gear aboard the *Elephantes*. The clinker-built boat was connected to a cleat by a long tow rope. They made way for Inca Island, arriving in less than an hour.

A cup of tea was the first order of business upon entering the little cabin of Pedro Vargas Pancupel. Mike was surprised at the cleanliness of the home, and actually enjoyed the smoky wood smell. Once all four men had tipped their cups for the final swig, Mike thanked Rodrigo for his kindness, said good-bye, and watched as the *Elephantes* disappeared into the distance.

Pedro loaded his dogs on board the small boat, while Eduardo and Mike boarded carrying the Styrofoam box for any eggs they might find. The motor started right up and they set off to a nearby island. Within seconds of stepping on the shore, Pedro and dogs disappeared into the dense, rocky forest. He returned within 30 minutes, carrying five Magellanic Steamerduck eggs. Mike was thrilled to finally have eggs to place into the down-filled Styrofoam box he had lugged around these islands.

They soon landed on a second island that was covered in cormorants and tussock grass near the peak. A female Ashy-headed Goose took off from the grass. They climbed up to the grass and soon found her nest. There were four eggs, which Mike packed in the down in the Styrofoam box.

Going ashore on another island, the three dogs immediately ran up a steep cliff. Mike heard the dogs barking and positioned himself to see them chasing a female flightless steamerduck that had gained forward momentum flapping her small wings. She plummeted over the cliff into the water, followed by one of the dogs that tumbled down onto the shore. The dog had a cut on his leg, but otherwise was unharmed. Mike climbed up and searched the area where the duck had been and found the nest with a clutch of eight eggs. He candled them with his flashlight and determined they were about a week set.

Mike found two Kelp Goose eggs on the same island. These were added to the growing number of eggs in the Styrofoam box.

From Mike's Journal:

> We carried on to another small island where the dogs managed to catch a female steamerduck. Pedro cut her throat, much to my disapproval. He replied that if I did not like this method of hunting eggs, he would stop using the dogs. Unfortunately, that would make our task impossible, as the female steamers go too deep into the forest to find a suitable nesting site. The nest might be 100 yards into thick vegetation. So I was forced to concede.

The manner in which the locals hunted for birds and eggs was disconcerting to Mike, but it was their way of life and a food source for them. He wondered how long the steamerduck species could survive in these areas if no other industry or methods of agriculture were implemented.

They sailed back to Inca Island. Mike was beginning to feel more confident about the potential success of the expedition. He had collected more eggs in one afternoon than he had the entire trip.

Back at the cabin, the eggs were quickly taken from the Styrofoam box and placed into the battery-operated portable incubator. Despite the earlier exposure to sea water, the incubator came up to temperature.

It was too late to cross the channel back to Port Aguirre. They needed to stay the night on Inca Island. Pedro prepared a meal of clams and fish, which Mike found to be delicious. Finally things were going his way. He had plenty of waterfowl eggs and could cease the island-hopping. Tomorrow morning he would return to Port Aguirre and start planning the long trip back to Santiago and then England.

Mike smiled at the prospect of soon being home with Ali as he slid into his sleeping bag around 11:30 that night. Even the sound of a strengthening wind failed to distract him from warm thoughts of their reunion.

Sunday, November 8

The wind howled and grew stronger through the night. Awakened from his sleep by the deafening sound of rain on the metal corrugated roof, Mike feared the entire house would be blown into the sea.

By morning the island was enveloped in a full-blown gale. Mike donned his rain gear and staggered against the wind to check on the boat. It was swamped with water. He was fortunate the boat was even there, as the relentless wind had chafed the anchor rope nearly clean though. Another fifteen minutes and their only means off the island could have been swept out to sea. After urgently bailing out the boat, he managed to move her to a sheltered part of the harbor. He was thankful he thought about the boat in time to avoid being marooned on a tiny island. That would be nothing short of misery.

From Mike's Journal:

It is now one o'clock in the afternoon and the storm is still very angry. No chance of getting back to Port Aguirre today. Even a big ship would be in trouble with this storm. We'll just have to sit it out and pray that it will end soon. Luckily we have a house here so we can at least keep dry.

I keep asking myself what the hell I am doing here. I miss my wife and son and cannot wait to get home. This trip must go down as one of the most frustrating I have ever been on. So much effort, discomfort, and exhaustion for a few duck and goose eggs.

Waiting for the storm to pass inside the dingy cabin tested Mike's patience. The only solution for his restlessness was to brave the weather and walk to the other end of the island where he thought they might find more nests. He gathered his binoculars and some fishing line to catch dinner for the evening meal. Pedro came along on the trek with his dogs, but Eduardo had gone back into a depression and opted to stay inside. Mike sensed he had lost all his enthusiasm for the very mission he had suggested and organized.

There were no paths for Mike and Pedro to follow through the dense temperate rainforest, overgrown with mosses and lichens. They navigated around a plethora of fallen, decaying trees that repeatedly blocked their route. Mike had hiked in thick wooded areas around the world, but this forest was truly eerie, the light literally blocked out for long stretches of time. More than once he fell through rotted trees into hidden crevices. Fortunately he had the flashlight he used for candling eggs; otherwise, finding their way would have been impossible.

The sea was never far from their route. On occasion the forest opened up and provided a view of the water, which remained stirred by the whistling wind. Mike saw several pairs of steamerducks but had no idea where their nests might be. The dogs had run far ahead of them, but as yet he had not heard the incessant barking that would indicate they'd found the nests.

Pedro became annoyed at his dogs' lack of results, telling Mike in a type of pidgin Spanish and hand signals that since the dogs had been fed recently, they would no longer hunt. Mike was revolted at the way Pedro treated his canines, often hurling rocks or sticks at them. The dogs knew to stay just outside Pedro's throwing range. Mike dismissed Pedro's theory about feeding them as the problem. He figured the windy, wet weather had covered the scent of the birds.

As they neared the far end of the island, the dogs found a Kelp Goose nest with three fresh eggs. Mike carefully placed them in his backpack and began the arduous journey back to the cabin, hoping not to fall and crush the valued cargo. There was no time for fishing. They would have to walk swiftly on the dank earth to make it back before dark, when travel through this forest would be beyond treacherous.

Mike was grateful to arrive at the cabin with the eggs intact. Eduardo had actually left the cabin to search for the nest of a pair of Chile Teals that Mike had spotted yesterday near the harbor. He had not found the nest, but Mike was encouraged he had tried. At least his day had not been totally wasted.

As darkness fell upon Inca Island, the storm raged without hint of ceasing. Pedro made clam soup, which was poured in the bowl over a large whole potato, and opened a tin of peaches.

From Mike's Journal:

> The rain leaks through numerous holes in the roof,
> and the sound of it lashing down on the corrugated roof

is getting on my nerves. There seems no end to the howling wind, which whistles through the many cracks in the walls. I am really getting the feeling I'm marooned on this island.

I wonder how long I can live on shellfish. Lack of vegetables is a problem. I suppose we could cook some seaweed. Decided to wash some socks and handkerchiefs, all of which have become very nasty. Will dry them around the fire.

Monday, November 9

Something strange appeared through one of the holes in the metal roof. Mike was still groggy from a fitful night's sleep, but what he saw appeared to be a narrow ray of morning sunlight. He rubbed his eyes and took another look to convince himself he was not hallucinating. Then he realized the din of the rain and wind had ceased.

He rushed outside only half-dressed to discover the storm had indeed passed. He ran to the harbor cove where he had stashed the boat for protection. The sea was still rough, but after a careful assessment, he believed passage back to Port Aguirre was possible, if he piloted the boat cautiously.

Convincing Eduardo it was safe to cross the channel was another matter. The young man wanted no part of any dangerous voyage in a small boat that was barely seaworthy. However, he did not relish the idea of remaining on Inca Island eating clams and seaweed while waiting for smooth water that might never appear. He grudgingly complied with Mike's desire to leave immediately.

Mike and Eduardo said good-bye to Pedro and loaded their gear and the incubator into the boat. Mike vigilantly steered the craft along the compass bearings he took on the outward-bound voyage aboard the *Elephantes*. The boat handled much better with just the two of them riding. In just over an hour they made the harbor of Port Aguirre.

They arrived at Enrique's house. Marianna was there to warmly greet them. Enrique had still not returned from his trip to Port Montt. Mike was not at all surprised, having himself been a victim of Chile's transportation system.

The incubator had continued to operate during the cruise, but because of the extended time on Inca Island, the internal battery was

201

on low and ready to give out. It was critical now to get it recharged. But the power would not be available until evening, and even then, five hours later it would automatically be cut off again. All the effort put into traveling here and collecting these eggs would be lost unless something could be done.

Mike took Eduardo with him to a hut occupied by Port Aguirre's detachment of Chilean Marines. Oddly enough, they controlled the electrical power for the island. Mike pleaded his case, via Eduardo's impassioned interpretation, to run an active power line directly to Enrique's house. This time Eduardo really came through in a pinch. The marines agreed to the request and immediately began rolling a power line downhill to Enrique's house, which had become the main point of interest for the entire community. Most of the townsfolk were puzzled as to why the eggs of Magellanic Steamerducks and Kelp Geese required such drastic measures, but they were all thrilled to witness the big event.

Once the incubator was connected to the local power station and fully recharged, Mike could finally begin planning his exit from Patagonia and his subsequent return to England. All he needed was confirmation that the boat to Port Montt was still scheduled to leave on Wednesday.

Upon inquiring with the Port Captain at the dock, he was told that due to the recent storm, the Wednesday boat had been rescheduled to leave Saturday.

From Mike's Journal:
> I guess I should have known. I don't think I am ever going to get out of here! My flight out of Santiago to London was on Saturday. So much for those plans – completely out of my control now!

Juan and José arrived at Enrique's house to find out what had happened to the intrepid explorers. Eduardo gave them all the details, greatly embellishing the conditions they'd endured during the furious storm.

Juan said he knew of some islands about an hour out of port that people from Aguirre never visited. He offered to guide them there, for a price, and promised they'd find more Kelp Goose and steamerduck eggs.

Mike mulled the idea over in his mind. If he didn't go, he would have to spend the next four days just waiting for the boat to Port

Montt. Mike never liked to wait. The weather seemed to be much better, and possibly because of that, his mood had improved and his enthusiasm had kicked in again. Plus the number of eggs they had collected to this point did not exceed the limits of the permits he had for each species.

He told Eduardo to tell Juan that if he came around tomorrow morning with his boat and his dogs, he would pay him as a guide. But it would just be Juan, not his son. Mike was giving back the long boat he had used to this point. He wanted only one other person, since it was proven how much better these heavy boats steered when they rode high in the water.

Mike knew without any explanation that Eduardo had no desire to be on this last trip. He wasn't interested in going anywhere except back to Santiago. Mike needed someone to monitor the incubator full of eggs at Enrique's home, and Eduardo was a good choice to do that. Mike would not have an interpreter to communicate with Juan, but his hand gestures and his newly acquired familiarity with certain Indian phrases would be enough to get by.

That afternoon Mike took the motor to Enrique's shed to inspect it thoroughly, clean the plugs, and adjust the carburetor. He returned the long boat to the carpenter, who wanted no payment for the use of it, or for his labor in modifying the transom to fit the motor.

Mike also washed his clothes, which smelled worse than nasty, then borrowed a fishing boat and caught several cabrilla for supper that night. Eduardo helped prepare the fish, which tasted superb. There was plenty for everyone, including Marianna.

Mike finished the one leftover fillet on the platter. It would be the last filling meal he would have for quite a while.

Tuesday, November 10

Juan arrived at 7:30 in the morning with two of his dogs and his small rowboat. The weather was beautiful, but always unpredictable. Eduardo seemed happy that Mike was leaving him in charge of the incubators. He would also be free to sleep a lot more with Mike gone.

Mike secured the motor to the transom and loaded his backpack, provisions, and the all-important Styrofoam box for the eggs. As the boat cleared the harbor, Juan made a grand pointing gesture to indicate the direction he wanted Mike to take.

They came to a group of smaller islands, but Juan shook his head as they cruised by each one. He was not interested in searching them, and Mike did not see any birds near them anyway. Soon a bigger island appeared where he saw steamerducks swimming offshore.

Mike beached the boat at an inlet and Juan let his dogs go on the hunt. It was not long before they came back, sharing the burden of carrying a female steamerduck which they had caught. Juan, like the other Indians would do, cut her throat. Mike was incensed by this type of barbaric treatment of waterfowl, but he had no power to prevent it.

They followed the dogs' lead and found the nest of eight eggs. Mike candled them and they all appeared to be fresh. Back at the boat, he placed the eggs in the Styrofoam box, while Juan hung the slaughtered steamerduck by her neck on the gunnels of the boat.

They moved on to another island, where a male Kelp Goose stood guard at the edge of the tussock grass. Upon landing, the dogs were released, flushing the female Kelp Goose off her nest, which in her rush to escape the dogs, sent all five eggs flying onto the rocks. Every one of them was ruined – badly cracked or broken.

Back in the boat and onto another island. The dogs caught another steamerduck. The nest held five eggs, which Mike also placed in the box.

Juan sets tattered sail on his boat in rough seas.

As the day wore on, the weather was gradually changing from sunny to threatening. A strong wind came up very quickly, turning the sea from calm to violent. Then the rain came.

Mike gave a signal to Juan that they had better head home. He quickly discovered that to get to Port Aguirre he had to head across the wind and waves at a severe angle, instead of into the wind. He slowed the motor as much as possible to prevent the waves from breaking over the gunnels. Mike found it difficult to steer the boat while holding the throttle open simultaneously. The boat was positioned between two deserted islands as the storm grew even stronger.

In a moment that haunts his dreams to this day, a massive wave came over the stern of the boat. Mike did his best to counter the action of the rogue wave, but the motor sputtered from the direct hit and stopped. Mike vigorously tried to start it again, without success. The craft had no steerage – they were sitting ducks for the next big wave that might come along.

Mike barked orders in English and furiously employed hand signals, beckoning Juan to man the oars and try to keep the boat headed into the wind. Juan nervously took hold of the oars and commenced the Herculean task he had been assigned. Based on their current course, Mike figured the boat might be carried near one of the islands, where they could at least gain some protection from the wind and waves while riding out the storm.

Juan signaled Mike to take over the rowing while he hoisted a homemade sail. Mike felt the wind was too strong for such a tactic, but thought Juan may have been in this type of situation before. It might give them more control of the crippled vessel. Juan managed to hoist the sail despite the enormous pitch and yaw action of the boat that threatened to toss him overboard. Unfortunately, the sail had rotted from years of exposure to the elements and was torn to shreds by the first big gust of wind.

Juan resumed rowing the boat. Mike's attention was riveted on the island and how close they could get to it, but a sloshing sound around his feet forced him to look down and notice the boat was filling up with water. The trim of the boat was decidedly lopsided. Mike kept his focus on the island while he reached down, desperately sloshing his hands in the water, searching for something he could use to bail out the boat. The island was getting closer; perhaps they were going to make it to the calmer water.

The next incident happened quickly, but for Mike it seemed to last a painfully long time. He saw it coming from the corner of his eye. The wave was huge, possibly appearing even bigger by the fact that the boat was already low in the water. A torrent of water crashed upon the helpless vessel, allowing sea water to rush inside and completely swamp it. She resisted sinking, but only the top of the gunnels remained above water. Some of their gear had already washed overboard and had sunk or was beyond reach. The outcome was undeniable – they would not make it to the island unless they could swim there.

Mike had his backpack strapped over his shoulders and instinctively grabbed the Styrofoam box containing the eggs before it floated away. The box served as an effective buoy, and he began swimming towards the island. He had not witnessed what happened to Juan after the wave hit, but the man had disappeared from sight. His two dogs were right beside Mike, padding for all they were worth.

As he swam towards shore, he looked back, barely able to see beyond the height of the waves. There was not even a glimpse of the boat or any other living or inanimate object. He remembered that none of the local Indians were able to swim.

From Mike's Journal:

It was difficult to say how far ahead the island was, maybe two or three hundred yards. Making even modest progress toward the shore seemed to take a long time and I began to wonder if I could make it. However the egg box was what probably saved me, as it was very buoyant. I used it to keep afloat whenever I stopped swimming to rest, which was numerous times on this epic swim.

I thought back to my days at Pangbourne Nautical College when we were made to swim a mile in the Thames River, wearing a boiler suit [coveralls or jumpsuit] and leather boots. I wondered at the time if I would ever be in such a predicament that I'd need to swim that far. I guess the training was useful after all.

It was such a relief when the dogs and I reached the island. I was very weak, wet, and cold. I pulled myself out of the water and made my way to the edge of the forest. I stationed myself behind some rocks that were big enough to protect me from the wind and rain. Also there were some ferns to sit on. I stayed there for a good half hour, shivering and stunned at what had just happened.

I knew Juan had drowned. I kept thinking to myself, "Could I have saved him?" This played on my mind.

I had to get myself together – assess my situation. I am marooned on an uninhabited island. All I have is my backpack containing my binoculars, a soggy camera, a lightweight jacket and a felt cap. In a side pocket there was a small Swiss Army knife. I had forgotten to bring the fishing line. I had no means of making a fire.

My boots were still swimming with water, so I took them off, shook out as much water as I could. I then took my waterlogged handkerchief, wrung it out, and mopped inside of my boots. I took my socks off and wrung them out as well. Slowly I went through all my clothes, getting out as much water as possible before putting everything back on, including the jacket that was in the backpack. Nothing was dry, but just having everything damp instead of soaked actually felt warmer.

I thought sitting down at this point was not good, so I got up and ran to the other end of the beach and back. This certainly got my circulation going and warmed me up. The dogs in the meantime had gone exploring into the thick, damp forest. I knew the island was not very large, as we had actually stopped on the other side earlier in the day looking for eggs. My watch was waterproof. It was 1:30 in the afternoon. The storm subsided, but there was no sign of any sun, which I was really hoping for.

I felt I should stay on the beach, since there was a good possibility that the boat would drift in on the wind and current. I scanned the sea with my binnies, but could not see her. The waves were still high, so it was hard to tell if the boat was drifting in or had gone to the bottom.

I looked around for a source of water. There were a good number of very large plants like overgrown rhubarb [Chilean Rhubarb (Gunnera tinctoria)]. At Slimbridge we had grown them as cover for waterfowl. The stems were four or five inches in diameter. One had to be careful handling them, as they had fur-like bristles on the stems that if you brushed up against them would give you a nasty rash, like stinging nettles did. But I remembered when we cut the stems they were filled with liquid, which was basically water. So I cut down one of these plants with my Swiss Army knife, carefully peeling the bristly skin away, and then squeezing the juice into my mouth.
It almost had a citrus flavor – quite good.

The next thing to think about is food. I know I can eat the mussels raw and also the barnacles, and at least I had a knife to open them up. The best time to collect the mussels and barnacles was at low tide, but the tide was coming in and would be at its high point in a couple of hours. The water was already covering most of the mussels and barnacles. However I still managed to get a couple of big mussels. I took them back to my rocks, opened them up with the knife and swallowed both. It would have been better with lemon.

Mike demonstrating how he drank from stalk of a rhubarb plant. This photo was taken after the shipwreck in Port Aguirre.

I figured I had three hours before it got dark, so the best thing to do was make a shelter. I thought I could make a roof by placing logs across the top of the rocks. There were quite a few that had drifted in on previous tides. I gathered up suitable logs from the beach and placed them next to each other on the rocks. This formed a base on which I could place big leaves, then place some smaller logs on top of the leaves to hold them down. The building of the roof took a couple of hours. I collected more ferns for the floor, so it was relatively soft to lie on.

It started to get dark, so I crawled into my new house. It had stopped raining a while ago, so I did not know how waterproof my roof would be. It was not that bad and I was completely protected from the wind. Just as it was getting very dark the dogs arrived back and came in and lay next to me. The dogs were not very big, about the size of a corgi with smooth coat. There was just enough room for all three of us, and though they were a little wet, they kept me warm.

I slept on and off through the night, my mind going through all kinds of scenarios. Will they send out a search party? Of course not – not even Eduardo knows where we went. Even with the storm, they must have presumed we took shelter on an island. Eduardo probably never gave it another thought that we'd lose the boat. So it seems I have got myself in quite a predicament. Losing Juan played heavily on my mind.

Wednesday, November 11

From Mike's Journal:

Crawled out of my abode at first light, still damp and very stiff. It was around 7 o'clock. The tide was high again, but starting to go out.

I looked up and down the beach. At the far end I could make out what looked like the boat. I ran to where the object was, and sure enough, she had come in on the tide, though not all the way onto shore. She was tilted on her side and full of water. The motor was still attached, but it was holding the boat on some of the rocks.

I thought the best thing to do was to wade out to the boat, tilt the motor, and try and drag her off the rocks onto a safer part of the beach. There was still a rope attached to the bow. Once I had tilted the motor, I man-aged to pull her slowly onto the beach. The tide was going out, so if I could secure the boat, she would be high and dry when the tide went out. I could then get the water out and make her seaworthy again. There was no sign of the oars. The only thing that was still on the boat other than the rope and motor was the dead steam-erduck Juan had hung on the gunnel. I thought the dogs might be able to get something off the carcass. I certainly did not fancy raw steamerduck!

The dogs were very excited to have the steamerduck remains and devoured them quickly. I secured the boat on the beach. She was now resting only on her side and there was still a lot of the water to bail out. I did not have any cups or anything that would make the job easier. I decided to go back to my base to retrieve my English cap and a couple of empty mussel shells, then come back to bail out the boat.

The bailing procedure took a long time, but it worked. By the time I had finished, the tide had gone out quite a ways. My hat had stretched so much it would never again fit on my head!

The boat was now looking a lot better. I placed another smaller log under, which kept her in an upright position. What I have now is a boat, with no workable motor and no oars.

The sun had come out. It felt so good to get some natural warmth. There was nothing more I could do with the boat for now. So I went back to the rock house to dry my clothes in the sun whilst I waited for the tide to go out and collect more mussels. I doubt if the temperature ever got above 60 degrees, but it was certainly better than the cold rain.

I tried to keep my mind busy by working out ways to catch food. As I was watched the tide go out, I noticed it left small pools in the rocks where I might be able to catch small fish or crabs. I suddenly thought about the steamerduck I had fed to the dogs. I should have kept some for crab bait. I went down the beach to where I had fed the dogs. There was little left of the duck except the two small wings, but they still had a bit of meat on them.

I then went to the boat and inspected the rope on the bow. It was too thick for a fishing line, but it was easy to unravel a single strand from it. I tied one duck wing to the end of the 15-foot-long line, then found a suitable small rock that I tied about six inches from the end. I waded out a little ways in my underpants and jacket, slung the line with the rock and wing out in front of me. I held the rope, occasionally pulling it slightly to feel if there was any resistance from a crab.

It was not long before I felt a tug, so I pulled the line to me very carefully. As it got closer, I could see the crab was not letting go of the wing. Just as I got it close enough to grab, it fell off. I thought if I could fish from the shore I could pull the crab onto dry land and then pounce on him before he could get back to the water. This method worked, but the only problem was that my enthusiasm in jumping on the crab resulted in a nasty nip on my thumb from one of his claws – but I still had dinner.

I had never eaten raw crab before. I broke the claws with rocks and then sucked out the mostly liquid meat. It tasted okay, but there was not much of it. I decided it would be more satisfying if I hunted for mussels, barnacles, and clams.

The tide was out but would be on its way in soon, as I had worked out that low tide was around one o'clock, with high around seven. I found a few big mussels, and barnacles that were big enough to eat, as well as several clam types. I brought these all back to my shelter. I opened up some mussels and clams with the knife and ate them. The clams were very chewy, but tasty.

As it had not rained since my first few hours on the island, there was no fresh water in the rocks. So I set about to find another rhubarb stem and sucked the water out of it. I noticed that my lips were getting a little bit sore. I figured it was from the bristles on the plant, but I did not mind putting up with a little soreness if I could get water.

There had been small fish swimming in the shallow pools in the rocks left by the outgoing tide. I went into the forest and found a stick with three prongs, which I sharpened with my knife, making a spear for catching fish. I ended up with quite a lethal-looking weapon. I really wanted to try it out, but unfortunately it had taken a long time to create my masterpiece and the tide was already halfway in, and all the little pools where I had seen fish were now part of the sea.

The sun had gone behind the clouds and it was cooling off. I decided to do some beachcombing to find some pieces of glass I could use as a magnifying glass to light a fire. I had some dry toilet paper in my backpack which would be ideal as starter fuel. I also hoped to find the oars from the boat. I went for a very long walk, the dogs came with me. We went way past where the boat was and around the end of the island, which was about quarter of a mile wide and several miles long.

It was getting dark, so I turned around, not having found the oars or any glass. The dogs chose to follow me back to base camp, where I ate more of the mussels and clams from my stash. It was about 9:30 at night. At least I was a lot dryer and warmer now. I had stuffed my backpack with tussock grass, which made a fairly comfortable pillow. The dogs did not spend much time in the shelter tonight. They went off hunting, as I am sure they were getting hungry. I slept on and off through the night, not nearly as worried as the previous night. I knew somehow I would be able to get back to Port Aguirre.

Thursday, November 12

From Mike's Journal:

Up around seven o'clock – tide almost fully in – breezy, overcast, but no rain yet. I did not want any mussels, so I ate a few clams. I then went to my giant rhubarb plant, stripped it down, and got a good fill of water.

The dogs were hanging around me, looking rather miserable and obviously hungry. Some of the steamer-duck eggs in the box were very cold and had to be dead. So I took four of those eggs and broke them for the dogs to eat, which they devoured. I thought I would keep the others until later. The fresh eggs were tempting for me to eat, but I still felt that I would be found and these eggs could be incubated once back home.

I went for a walk along the tide line like yesterday, just to see if anything had floated in overnight. I was still half expecting to find Juan – part of me wanted to, but the other half really did not. The walk took a couple of hours. I did find a fragment of glass.

The boat was in its same position; the high tide only just reached it. There were a number of logs that had washed in with the tide. I gathered up a few, just in case rescue came with the tide being down. The logs could be placed in front of the boat and would roll over them easily until it got to the water. I knew this because when I was young, we used to go down to a place called Seaton in Somerset on the south coast to go mackerel fishing. All the boats would be put into the water this way.

I came back to the shelter, decided to eat a few mussels. Unfortunately they were now having an unpleasant effect on my stomach, causing diarrhea. I decided to rest up for a bit until the tide was at its lowest. It was still overcast, no sign of the sun. The one thing I had kept dry in the Styrofoam box was my notebook, so I spent some time jotting down notes on this unwanted experience. I must have nodded off, as I looked at my watch and it was 2:30. The tide was coming back in, so I hurried to the rocks, fish spear in hand.

There were several small fish swimming in the rock pools. My spear was slightly too big; the fish could swim between the prongs. I was getting rather disheartened as I kept missing the fish. I came to a pool that held a larger fish, which looked like a mullet. I got him cornered in the pool and took careful aim. Lo and behold I had a fish on my handmade spear!

I was feeling excited and hungry, so took the fish that was still on my spear back to my rock table near the shelter. I quickly filleted the fish, took the skin off, took the meat down to the salt water to rinse it off and ate all of it. It was fantastic! It was the first real food I'd had in a long time, even though it was raw.

I went back to the rocks with the spear, but unfortunately the tide had come in and all the good pools were now under the sea. I decided since my mussel and clam supply was getting low, I should get some more, though most were under the water now. I did manage to grab a handful of both before the tide took over.

The time was now five o'clock. I had spent a good two and a half hours spear-fishing. The dogs readily ate the guts, head and skin of the fish.

I decided to go for a walk along the beach in the other direction before it got dark, again searching the high tide mark for anything useful. I came back to the shelter around 8:30 that night.

Everything was much dryer now, as there had not been any rain for a couple of days. I suddenly realized it was Thursday. I was supposed to take the boat to Puerto Montt with Eduardo on Saturday. If we missed this boat we'll have to wait another week. I have got to get off this island! I am at a loss what to do. It would be madness to push out into the sea without oars. I'll just have to hope a boat will come by soon.

Friday, November 13
Slimbridge, England

Ali Lubbock was more animated and lighthearted than she had been in a month, which is how long it had been since her husband had left England and flown to Chile. She had not heard from him after he had left Santiago to begin the journey south to Port Aguirre. All she knew was Mike was scheduled to return home soon. She missed him terribly and dared to hope this might be his last expedition for a while, if not forever. But in two days, his long absence from her would end.

She smiled at that thought and was about to head out the door for the grocery to get beef and potatoes so she could make Mike's favorite dishes once he was home.

An annoying ring of the telephone halted her exit from the house. For a moment she considered ignoring the call so she could get on with her shopping.

"Who could this be calling now?" she huffed, reluctantly picking up the receiver. It was Bill Makins.

"Ali, I received a call this morning from Max Williams, a lawyer in London," said Bill. "His office was sent a Telex from Hendricks Pugaso in Santiago."

A feeling of dread flashed through Ali's mind. Something must be wrong. "Hendricks? I've heard Mike mention his name. Is everything all right?"

A pause from the other end of the line did not boost her spirits.

"I'm sorry, Ali, but the fact is that they don't know where Mike is, really," Bill replied. "He must still be down in Patagonia, but Hendricks has received no word of him since before he left Santiago on October 28th."

"But his flight to London leaves in two days."

"I can tell you he won't be aboard that flight."

Worrying about Mike's safety during his travels was something Ali had learned to live through. This was not the first fearful episode she needed to endure.

That night, as she had on other occasions, Ali went to bed in prayer and hope that Mike would return to her yet again, safe and well. But this was the first time she wondered if he was alive.

From Mike's Journal:

It rained through the night, not too heavy. My leaf-and-log roof held up fine, although there were a few leaks. Got up at 7. The rain had stopped, still overcast, but there were breaks in the clouds. I was hoping for some sun. The wind had died down and the sea was relatively calm.

I went down to the rocks on the shore, as I was sure they'd hold some fresh rainwater from last night. I found several puddles and drank the fresh water.

At the camp, I did not feel like eating any mussels or clams, as my stomach was still playing up. I went for my usual walk down the beach, dogs in pursuit.

At about 9:30 in the morning, I was looking out to sea and could not believe my eyes at what I saw. There was a boat with two Indians rowing towards another island! I jumped up on the tallest rock and frantically waved my arms, yelling as loud as I could. At first they did not see or hear me. Then one guy stood up and waved back. They turned their boat in my direction and rowed towards me!

I was so overjoyed when they arrived I could have hugged them! They seemed a little worried at finding a white guy, two dogs, and someone else's boat. They soon surmised the situation. They knew the dogs and the boat's owner. I had the task of explaining in sign language that Juan had drowned. They agreed to take me and the dogs back to Port Aguirre and tow Juan's boat.

I ran back to the shelter and picked up my backpack, taking out the grass and repacking it with my binoculars and wet camera. I slung the pack on my back, and with Styrofoam egg box under my arm I ran back to the Indians.

The tide was high, so it was easy for us to push the boat into the water. I tied the bow line to the transom of the Indians' boat and put the dogs in the empty boat. I climbed into the Indians' boat and sat on the bottom nearer the bow end. The two Indians sat side by side on the middle thwart – each one with an oar. We took off with them both rowing in harmony – they had done this all their lives.

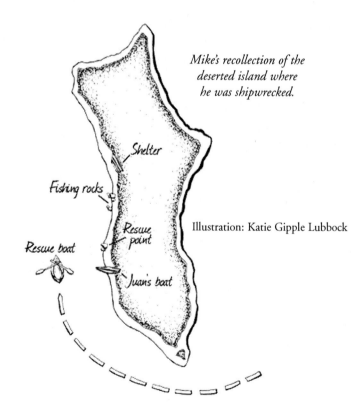

Mike's recollection of the deserted island where he was shipwrecked.

Shelter

Fishing rocks

Rescue point

Rescue boat

Juan's boat

Illustration: Katie Gipple Lubbock

The trip back to Port Aguirre took about two hours. I never thought I would be so delighted at seeing the place again.

REUNION

The dogs barked incessantly from the moment the run-down village of Port Aguirre came within view. As the boat drew near the pier, Mike became aware that many of the townspeople had jammed together on the dock. They gawked at the occupants of the tiny rowboat with Juan's boat trailing behind, empty except for the barking mutts.

It was apparent that observers in town had kept a watch for Juan's boat, knowing he had planned to return home three days ago. Once news spread that two boats had been spotted on the horizon, an outpouring of onlookers gathered to witness how the mystery would play out.

The volume of the crowd's chatter reached a crescendo once it was clear that Juan was not one of the figures seen in the boat. Mike had no clue what they were saying, but he was sure they wished he had been the one lost at sea, rather than their friend and fellow-citizen.

Mike got out of the boat and searched the faces of the assembly, trying to locate Eduardo, but couldn't find him. He thanked the two Indian rescuers for going out of their way to help him. He asked them to wait at the dock while he went to the house to get some money for their effort. But before he had climbed halfway up the hill, he turned around and saw them rowing out of the harbor. He never saw them again.

The dogs jumped out of Juan's boat and bolted past Mike at full charge. They were headed directly for their master's house with hopes for a decent meal. Mike's joy at returning safely to this isle was now replaced by the heaviness of the duty ahead of him. He had to go to Juan's home and inform the new widow of her husband's fate. Without Eduardo to translate for him, he was going to have to find assistance elsewhere.

He spotted one of the two policemen in Port Aguirre who was supposedly on crowd patrol, though more likely he was just watching the commotion like most of the town. Mike knew this man could speak English well enough to help him out.

Mike explained to the policeman what had happened at sea. The policeman shrugged his shoulders and said that it happened all the time here. None of them can swim. Mike asked the officer to come to Juan's house with him and help break the news to the family.

It was a long walk to the house, giving Mike plenty of time to become anxious about the difficult task at hand. How would the family take the news? Would they blame him for their loss?

They entered the tiny house. The dogs had arrived long before, providing Juan's wife with concern that her husband was not going to return to her. The moment Mike walked inside with the policeman, she broke down, crying uncontrollably. The officer tried valiantly to tell her the story of the incident as Mike had relayed it to him, but it was doubtful she heard a word of it. Attempts at consoling her were useless at this point in her grief.

Mike felt so sorry for her. The eldest son, José, who had been with them on the early explorations, would be expected to step up and take his father's position as head of the house. He asked José, through the policeman's interpretation, if he would come by the dock later that afternoon to claim his father's boat. Mike promised to give him some money and wished he had much more to offer.

Mike walked back to town much slower than his normal long gait was capable of traveling. The frenzied reaction of Juan's widow had deeply affected him. He was thankful at least for his earlier decision not to allow José to go with them on that disastrous trip. How much harder would it have been to break the news had the woman's husband and eldest son been lost at sea?

Eduardo greeted him elatedly as he entered into Enrique's house. He must have already heard from others that the Englishman had returned safely. Still Eduardo seemed relieved when he finally saw him in the flesh. He informed Mike that the incubators had worked flawlessly while he was away. The idea of incubating eggs jolted his mind a bit. Getting himself back to England and his family was his only concern now, although he remembered that he did have viable steamer-duck and Kelp Goose eggs in the Styrofoam box he'd managed to bring back with him. He was glad he hadn't resorted to eating those while searching for food on the deserted island.

The first thing Mike was going to do was take a long, warm shower, using lots of soap and shampoo. He asked Eduardo to fix him some scrambled eggs on toast while he got cleaned up. This was Mike's comfort food, something he always requested to eat when he felt bad or needed a lift.

After finishing the shower and meal, he felt an indescribable satisfaction at the simple pleasure of being clean, wearing fresh clothes, and having a full stomach. As a final gesture of renewal, he discarded all the clothes he had had with him on the fateful trip, except for the jacket. He would have ditched that too, were there another to wear in its place.

Mike: Eduardo had caught some fish and cooked them for supper over the fire later that night. Any food that was cooked tasted great at that moment. One thing I noticed on my arrival back to Port Aguirre was the smell of the wood fire in Marianna's house. I cannot explain it, but it gives me immense satisfaction anytime I smell a wood fire today.

Just when he thought he was feeling as good as possible under the circumstances, Eduardo shared an incredible piece of news. The ship to Puerto Montt was arriving at 9 a.m. the next day. Eduardo had already acquired two tickets. Mike was ecstatic. He could not wait to head north.

Saturday, November 14

Mike awoke in eager anticipation of leaving Port Aguirre. He made sure all the batteries for the incubator were fully charged. Eduardo made them a breakfast of eggs and bread with jam before walking down the steep hill to the docks to await the arrival of the ship to Puerto Montt. Nine o'clock came, but there was no sign of the boat. Ten o'clock passed, then 11, then 12 – still no boat. Eduardo asked the Port Captain what had happened. He said he had received a radio message that the ship had encountered some problems in Port Aisén and the crew was attempting to fix them. It should arrive in Port Aguirre that evening.

Mike knew the drill, but still wondered what else could go wrong.

From Mike's Journal:
            This whole trip south seemed to be cursed from the time we started. Every obstacle has been thrust in my way. I really think I might be getting too old for this game! I just pray that some of the eggs make it alive to

England, but I have my doubts.

Port Aguirre will do one thing for you – make you appreciate home.

The boat did not appear until 10 o'clock that night. Mike exchanged their tickets for first-class tickets. This was expensive, around 4,500 pesos, but the first-class cabin had electricity, which was needed for the incubator.

From Mike's Journal:
The ship was old and foul – even first class was disgusting. One can only imagine what third class was like. Cows and Indians seemed to fill the third-class decks.

After being told there would be 220-volt outlets to run the incubator, we found out that there were none. Maybe it was a ruse to get us to buy first-class tickets! However, the chief engineer seemed nice and helped us out. He had extra six-volt batteries which we could use once our batteries ran down. At least we have enough battery power to get us to Puerto Montt. I hope the constant vibration from the engine will not addle the eggs.

It was one o'clock in the morning when the engineer locked the door to the radio room where the incubator was kept. Mike could not check the eggs through the night, but at least he could try to sleep. He gazed once more at the dark water before entering his cabin. Port Aguirre was now long out of sight. He choked out a laughing grimace as he remembered the word "aguirre" meant "good success." If anything, it should mean "good riddance," he thought.

Sunday, November 15
Slimbridge, England

Another night of sleeplessness had worn Ali's nerves to frazzle. Two days had passed since she'd learned Mike was missing in Patagonia, or somewhere in South America.

She had already talked with Mike's mother in Oxfordshire, who called frequently to find out if there had been an update. Just as frequently Ali had called Bill Makins to find out if the lawyer in London had received another Telex message. The Telex was the only reliable communication link with South America, and not many offices had one. Other concerned persons had called and inquired if any news had been gathered, but there was none.

Through it all, Ali had remained composed, though highly anxious. As much as possible, she followed her normal routine. This morning she kept her thoughts off her worst fears by reading the newspaper. She perused the headlines of every article, but nothing interested her. Society gatherings, antics of the Royals, reports on the poor economy – she only read bits and pieces to keep her mind occupied.

She turned the page and her eyes froze on the headline of the next article.

"LUBBOCK KILLED IN SOUTH AMERICA"

Ali's anxiety exploded to full-scale panic.

"It couldn't be," she thought, in defense of her emotions. "No, it can't be!" she said aloud.

As her pulse rocketed to a frantic pace and nausea invaded her stomach, she bravely and hurriedly read the article.

She exhaled loudly as it became clear the Lubbock referred to in the article was not Mike. Oddly enough, Roger Lubbock, the son of Mike's half brother, had died of injuries from a motorcycle accident in São Paulo, Brazil.

Ali's heartbeat gradually returned to normal, but she wondered how many more expeditions she could endure.

Monday, November 16
Near Puerto Montt, Chile

The voyage to Puerto Montt was long and disagreeable. The air aboard ship smelled of animal excrement and acrid fumes from the fish and seaweed being cooked by the Indians in third class, although their food may have actually been preferable to the putrid meals served in first class.

The ship made numerous stops at small ports, taking on even more passengers and livestock. Realizing that yesterday's flight to London had left Santiago without him only heightened Mike's melancholy. He had completely lost control of the original plans and had no means to notify Ali he was safe and in route back to her. Mike attempted to keep up his spirits by acknowledging that as slow as they passed, each mile north brought him closer to home.

Mercifully, the dilapidated vessel entered the harbor of Puerto Montt and was suitably docked at 11:30 a.m. Mike and Eduardo gathered their duffle bags and the incubators and dashed down the gangway, hoping to stay ahead of the hordes of third-class passengers. Before they could hail a taxi to the railway station, the first batch of cattle was being lowered by crane from the ship's main deck to the dock.

At the railway station, Mike bought Eduardo a train ticket to Santiago, then proceeded on to the Ladeco Airlines office to book himself a 7 p.m. flight to the same destination. Eduardo rang up his friend Romero and asked him to meet Mike once he landed at the airport in Santiago.

Mike: I had decided back in Port Aguirre that once I got to
        Puerto Montt there was no way I was going to take the
        incubators on that rattling old train. I was sure the eggs
        wouldn't stand a chance of making it alive to Santiago.
        Fortunately I still had just enough money left to buy the
        ticket. Eduardo's train left at 3:30 in the afternoon. I had
        the incubators and my belongings with me at the bus ter-
        minal, where I arranged to plug in the incubators in the
        station's office. At 6 o'clock I caught the bus to the airport.

Mike arrived at the Puerto Montt airport in time to board the Boeing 727 and place both incubators beside him. Much to his amazement, the flight took off promptly. He enjoyed a good meal while gazing out the window at a spectacular view of the Andes Mountains.

The mountains, the water, and the islands below seemed idyllic. It was hard to imagine how anything down there could be the least bit threatening. Only a short time in the air and already the trials and terrors of his expedition in Chile were fading away beneath him.

Upon arriving in Santiago, he was relieved to see Romero and Alberto waiting for him in the terminal. They drove Mike to the farmhouse where he would stay until all the arrangements could be made for his departure to London.

Romero's wife, Irma, greeted him warmly when Mike entered their home. It was as if they knew the trauma he had recently experienced and treated him with kid gloves. Perhaps Eduardo had clued them in on his tragic affair in Patagonia.

After the customary pleasantries were exchanged, Mike set up the incubators and checked the eggs. He marveled at the fact that most of them appeared absolutely fine. Two of the Ashy-headed Geese eggs were nearly ready to hatch.

Irma fixed Mike a late-night meal. He was glad they did not bring up the subject of the shipwreck as part of the dinner conversation. Those memories were still too fresh and raw to talk about.

Tuesday, November 17

Sleeping late into the morning was a rare treat, but one Mike felt he deserved. Part of the need for extra rest came from his body's delayed recognition of extreme fatigue. The other was due to the frequent times he arose during the night to check the status of the waterfowl eggs in the incubator.

Two Ashy-headed Geese had hatched during the night, requiring extra care and feeding. He attended to them immediately after he showered and ate breakfast.

After his rescue from the island, Mike had lost his enthusiasm for the eggs. All he cared about then was getting home. Now, within the peaceful setting of the farmhouse, he examined the eggs again in the light of a new day far from the hardships of Port Aguirre. A different perspective emerged.

These eggs had been through much of the same trauma he experienced and survived. They were in the Styrofoam box he had used to swim from the swamped boat to the safety of the deserted island. They were exposed to the same cold, wet weather conditions, without the aid of an incubator. They did not crack despite shipwreck or the harsh vibration of the ramshackle ferry that carried them back to Puerto Montt. Mike felt a renewed sense of duty to safely transport the valuable cargo with him back to England.

The quaint farmhouse owned by his hosts was the perfect place to decompress. The cares and tribulations of the past weeks in Chile were melting away. He considered returning to bed, but there was much for him to do over the next two days and he needed to get at it.

He needed to call Eduardo to make sure he arrived home safely from his travel on the train. Mike would pay a visit as well. Perhaps Eduardo should be given the newly hatched Ashy-headed Geese. Mike could not take them to England, as he only had permits for eggs.

He also needed to visit his contact Hendricks Pugaso at his office in Santiago. Hendricks would help him obtain the veterinarian certificates required to remove the eggs from Chile. More importantly, Mike could have Hendricks' office send a Telex message to Ali and let her know he was safe and would be on the British Caledonia flight to London the following night. He imagined stepping off the plane at Heathrow airport and rushing into her arms.

Bill Makins would be there also, to take the precious battle-tested eggs with him to Pensthorpe Wildlife Park where they would hatch.

Mike checked the eggs one more time before leaving the farmhouse to take the Metro into Santiago and begin the multitude of errands before he could finally leave for home. Inside the larger incubator were eggs of the Magellanic Steamerduck, which he'd collected on various islands around Port Aguirre.

He marveled at his good fortune when he thought about those eggs having survived their time inside the Styrofoam box he was now tossing into the trash bin. The same box he instinctively grabbed from the sinking rowboat off the island of Port Aguirre. The battered yet ordinary container had saved his life. Even today, Magellanic Steamerducks and Styrofoam boxes provide vivid reminders of his narrow escape from the Port of Good Success.

CHAPTER TEN

The One That Got Away

December, 1981
Slimbridge, England

It was a difficult decision. Pros and cons were batted back and forth until the early morning darkness gave way to sunrise. The late-night session was only one of many discussions Mike and Ali had on the topic. This time, however, a final verdict had been reached.

The debate began soon after Ali and Bill Makins greeted Mike at the Heathrow Airport in London on his return from Chile. Bill took the eggs with him back to Pensthorpe Waterfowl Park. Mike and Ali returned to Slimbridge.

Mike desperately needed to find a place of tranquility after his terrifying experience in Patagonia. However, the grounds of the Wildfowl Trust was not that place. Too many questions about his brush with death were asked; too many nagging problems had accumulated during his lengthy absence. He needed to get away, at least temporarily.

Mike decided it would be best to vacate the harried environment of Slimbridge and spend some time with his longtime friend, Brent Pope, on the Norfolk coast.

Mike felt more relaxed with each of his many peaceful amblings through the marsh at Brent and Brigid's place on the seaboard. Observing waterfowl and shore birds on the marsh reacquainted him with a sense of security, purging his thoughts of the scores of troubles at the Wildfowl Trust. Brent's home had always been Mike's safe haven over the years, a place he could go to hide out. He needed this verdant refuge to successfully bury the lingering memories of Port Aguirre, of the engulfing waves, the loss of life, and the recurring sense of being lost and alone.

He had escaped with his life, not only in Chile, but on trips to the Arctic and Africa as well. Every time he trekked into the wilderness he faced the possibility of not returning home. As a young man, he was able to justify the risks – it came with the territory. But now not only was he married, he also had his son, Brent, to consider.

Mike's friendship with Brent Pope, for whom his son was named, could be traced back to his arrival at the Wildfowl Trust at the age of 17. Throughout the years, Brent was always available if Mike needed a friend to lend an ear to his problems or discuss any personal dilemmas. On this visit, Mike revealed to Brent that he was considering starting his own waterfowl collection.

Events were moving rapidly at the Wildfowl Trust. The board had set a new mission which redirected the Trust's resources toward preserving wetlands in Great Britain and away from breeding birds. Bringing new species to Slimbridge was no longer a priority. In fact, the breeding program itself, once the centerpiece of the Wildfowl Trust, was losing focus.

Mike no longer had an interest in planning expeditions to collect new waterfowl species. If the tragedy in Port Aguirre taught him anything, it was that he would no longer seek any more of these life-threatening missions. That part of his career was behind him.

He had been at Slimbridge eight years since leaving Duck Puddle Farm. He had become assistant director of aviculture, revived the breeding program that had been in disarray, brought in new species from the wild, helped save the White-headed Duck. If that were all he had ever accomplished in aviculture, it would have been a tremendously successful career. But there was more he wanted to achieve. To do it, he needed a change.

The agreement Mike and Ali reached on that early morning in December 1981 finalized the details of the next phase of Mike's avian career. The Lubbocks would leave Slimbridge; they would leave England. Their next move was to Montgomery, Alabama.

INDEPENDENCE

Doug Goode, Jr. was 17 years old when he met Mike Lubbock at the 1973 conference of the American Pheasant and Waterfowl Society in New York. Two years later he traveled to Slimbridge, England to intern at the Wildfowl & Wetlands Trust and studied advanced avicultural techniques with Mike and his staff.

Doug's father had established a waterfowl collection in Montgomery, Alabama, which also included curassows, macaws, and flamingoes. Doug eventually took over the operation of the collection from his father.

Doug and Mike stayed in contact over the years. They saw each other at avicultural conferences at various cities around the world. During one such conference, Mike mentioned that he was considering a move back to America to start his own collection. Since Doug already had a good collection of birds and wanted to do more, Mike asked him if he would be his partner in Alabama.

Doug thought Mike was half-joking about the proposal, not really expecting him to leave the world-renowned waterfowl collection at Slimbridge and relocate in Alabama. Later when Mike's call came in from England to discuss the offer further, Doug quickly agreed to the partnership.

Mike: I wanted to come back to America to establish my own
        collection. I felt it would be easier making a name for
        myself in aviculture here than in England. There everyone
        said I was successful only because I was under the shelter
        of the Wildfowl Trust. Sir Peter Scott was a big name
        there. I certainly owed him a lot, but I was always in his
        shadow. I guess I wanted freedom to do things my way.

Mike had once visited the Goode collection in Montgomery during his time at Duck Puddle Farm, while it was still managed by Doug's father. He was familiar with the facilities there. Although Ali had been to the United States before, she had never been to Alabama. For her, the launch of her husband's new career was a big challenge. But there was absolutely nothing she wouldn't do or any place she wouldn't go if it made Mike happy. His career was her priority. She was fully committed and ready to make Alabama her new home.

By the spring breeding season of 1982, the Lubbocks had relocated from the familiar surroundings of Slimbridge, not far from where Mike had grown up in Taunton, to the foreign climes of America's Deep South.

Mike added $15,000 of seed money to the venture, which was a substantial amount in 1983. He also brought his mother's private collection of waterfowl from England. These birds had been kept on her property, The Old Manor, in Shilton, Oxfordshire. In addition to breeding birds, Mike and Doug imported birds from England and other parts of Europe.

The Montgomery collection grew in size, and regular customers were established. Ali handled the administrative and accounting duties, something she had learned while working for the Wildfowl Trust. She also worked with Mike on the collection.

Lubbock family in Montgomery, Alabama

Having birds of his own was a new phase in Mike's avian career. Up to this point, the birds he collected always belonged to someone else. Often his hands were tied regarding the best way to manage the flock to attain specific conservation goals. Finally he had liberated himself from any institutional restraint and was free to pursue his own solutions for waterfowl preservation.

It was not long before Mike's credentials as an avicultural expert were called upon in a time of need in another remote location. The stakes were high and the territory dangerous. This was not an expedition to find eggs to enhance his collection. This was an assignment to save a species from the brink of extinction.

THE MYSTERY OF THE VANISHING ATILÁN GREBE

The flightless water bird called the Atilán Grebe was slowly disappearing from the face of the earth. Nobody seemed to know why. Conservationist Anne LaBastille had established a captive "breed and release" program in 1966.

Atilán Grebe
Illustration: Katie Gipple Lubbock

The population of the grebe, known locally as the "poc," was estimated to be only 80 individual birds, all of them located on Lake Atilán in Guatemala. The breeding program initiated by Anne (who was also known as Anna, and even more affectionately as Mama Poc) was successful; the population soon rose to over 200 birds.

But success turned to disaster in 1976, when an earthquake caused a major crack in the lake bed of Lake Atilán. As the water level of the lake dropped, so too did the number of grebes. By the time Anna assembled another rescue team in April of 1984, the population estimate for the fate-stricken poc was a mere 50 birds.

Anna requested that Mike attend a meeting in Atlanta where she was giving a lecture on the Atilán Grebe of Guatemala. The bird was sometimes called the Giant Grebe, but it was also called the poc because the word resembled the sound it made. It was actually a type of Pied-billed Grebe which is found in Guatemala and throughout the Americas. The Pied-billed Grebe is a flying bird, but the poc is flightless.

Mike: Anna had been studying this bird for many years, which only existed on one lake, Lake Atilán. This was one of the most beautiful lakes in Guatemala, surrounded by three inactive volcanoes. The lake had been formed long ago by an earthquake and had very, very clear water.

Anna gave a lecture about how she was trying to salvage the poc and find out how many there were left in the wild. She asked me to go to Guatemala with her and a team of researchers to attempt to save the birds by taking in eggs, rearing them in captivity, and releasing offspring in the area. She had invited other people to the meeting who she thought could help her with funding a mission to Lake Atilán to see if this bird could be saved.

She had one fairly wealthy guy there, named François Berger, who was supporting her. He had a zoological park with ponds where he kept birds, but wild birds also came in there. He said if we wanted to build a pen as a place to rear these birds we could do it.

Mike Lubbock was selected to assist Anne LaBastille's 1984 conservation mission to Guatemala. Anna requested that Mike join her to set up another breed-and-release site in order to reestablish a sustainable population of the critically endangered Atilán Grebe. She also asked him to determine the cause for the bird's decline other than the decreased water level, which by now had stabilized.

Also part of the team was Gary Nuechterlein, an ornithologist from North Dakota State University. Gary was an expert in the nesting habits of grebes and had recently been to Argentina to conduct population studies and observations of other grebe species. His role in Guatemala was to estimate of the number of poc remaining on Lake Atilán and offer any advice on restoring the poc's habitat.

The Guatemalan trip was not the first time Mike had been asked to join a team as a conservation consultant, but this adventure would ultimately have a profound effect on how he approached saving waterfowl in the future. Mike's earlier work consulting with François Berger in Guatemala for preserving the Black-bellied Tree Duck caught the attention of Anna LaBastille. Mike was also an expert snorkeler and diver, which was a tremendous asset to the rescue team. Anna was concerned that an ecological imbalance in the lake's fish and crab populations could be a contributing factor in the severe decline of the grebe's population.

Mike: The U.S. Fish and Wildlife Service had funding for Central America. I met the head of this agency at the Atlanta meeting and he authorized paying the expenses for my part of the trip.

There were political problems in Guatemala in those days, resulting in an ongoing civil war. I did not know it at the time, but the U.S. Fish and Wildlife Service had already sent people down to look into the plight of the poc, and those agents had disappeared and were presumed dead. I did not become aware of the severity of the civil strife in Guatemala until after I arrived there.

GUATEMALA CITY

The rescue team met after Anna LaBastille's Atlanta lecture in March 1984 and mapped out their plans for the expedition. Later that month, Mike flew to Miami to meet up with Anna. Together they travelled to Guatemala City and met Dickey Mata, along with François Berger.

Monday, April 2, 1984

From Mike's Journal:

From Guatemala City we all flew in François' Beechcraft airplane to his home, which was nearby the

230

Auto Safari Zoological Park he built.

The plan was to capture and breed grebes for release in nearby Lake Atilán and possibly breed them here for release at the lake. François showed Dickey and me around the park in François' brand-new ranch car. The park was not spectacular, but was fairly well laid out. I was amazed by the number of wild Black-bellied Tree Ducks. Dickey said there were 5,000 of them in the park. It was the only zoo in Guatemala, financed solely by the Berger family. It gave the Guatemalan people somewhere to go to see some interesting animals.

There was a lot of water within the park, but it was difficult to determine in such a short visit whether any of the ponds would be suitable to rear grebes. However, the staff did say they'd be willing to dig new ponds anywhere we suggested.

To get to Lake Atilán, the team drove an old van along the Pan American Highway. After traveling awhile, they had a flat tire. Mike and Dickey changed to the spare and resumed the trip, stopping at a gas station in the next village to fix the flat. Fixing flat tires was to be a daily occurrence on this trip.

From Mike's Journal:

The village where we stopped to mend the puncture had been completely annihilated by the earthquake in 1976 which killed 3,600 people. I observed the natives in the village with interest while we waited. They are all very small, only about 5 feet tall. The women wore very color-ful dresses.

There are three major villages around Lake Atilán, all populated mostly with native Indians. They were carrying things balanced on their heads, from water pitchers to bundles of sticks. Many of the men had more western-style clothes, such as jeans. Many of the elderly men car-ried great bundles of sticks. Some rode fairly thin horses. Apart from bicycles, there were a few mopeds, but most transportation was by bus. They were typical South American buses, very colorful and filled to the hilt with people. Some even rode on top, clutching their belongings – bundles of items in sacks.

The scenery along the highway was very picturesque, with lots of vegetation. We passed by several old volcanoes before arriving at the Hotel Atilán on the outskirts of Panajachel at 8:30 that night.

Hotel Atilán had been built on an old coffee plantation in a canyon outside of town. The rooms offered spectacular views of Lake Atilán, the only known habitation of the Atilán Grebe. A long dirt road connected the hotel to the main road going into town. It was an isolated area, and the members of the grebe rescue team were the only guests at the rather large, forlorn inn. In a time of guerilla warfare and civil strife, very few international tourists cared to visit remote regions in Guatemala, anymore than the locals cared about saving wildlife.

Later that night, the team added another member. Ornithologist Gary Nuechterlein arrived on a separate flight to Guatemala City and reached the hotel after Mike and Anna's group. Others living in the area were available to the team as needed, including Madelyn, an American girl who was in the village with the Peace Corps. She would help Mike and Gary with recording the calls made by the poc, and she also spoke Spanish. Also on hand was Rolando, a Guatemalan. Although his reliability was sometimes an issue, he proved to be valuable as an interpreter of the native dialect.

THE SEARCH FOR POC

The team used a small motorized boat to comb Lake Atilán for poc and possible sites to establish a breed-and-release facility with any eggs that might be collected. They cruised slowly along the shoreline all the way to an island in Santiago Bay. However, they did not spot any grebes or nests.

One of the problems they noted immediately was that the wealthy Guatemalans had bought much of the land around Lake Atilán. Because the water had receded ten feet due to the earthquake, they now had nice beaches for their summer homes. Where there weren't beaches, they cut down the rushes and trucked in sand to make one. Much of the natural habitat where the grebes would normally nest had disappeared.

They searched areas that once were reported to have grebes, even after the earthquake. They stopped at the old grebe refuge, where the birds were successfully bred and released about eighteen years prior. However, the water had receded due to the earthquake, and now the area was completely dry. Mike thought it was such a pity that the water had receded; otherwise this facility would have been ideal for rearing and releasing poc – if they were successful in finding any eggs.

The army had taken over the refuge in 1972 and built a ghastly prison. During the uprising, many people had been put in an eight-foot-square hole, about 120 feet deep. The army had since vacated the refuge, but the facility had deteriorated.

Following their first disappointing search, the team made the forty-minute boat trip to Santiago Inlet, which is at the far end of the bay. Along the way they passed by about a hundred Indian fishermen in their canoes.

There were many more reed beds in this inlet than they had seen the previous day. Numerous small bass could be seen in the crystal-clear water. The bass had been introduced years before by American sport fisherman. This non-native fish upset the ecological balance with the crabs, because bass are a foraging fish. Some biologists think the crabs were the grebe's major food source. Also apparent were many nylon fishermen's nets, which were akin to a death trap for the poc.

They continued to move the boat along the thick, dense reeds of Santiago Inlet. At last their patience was rewarded.

April 4, Wednesday

From Mike's Journal:

We saw the first poc! Anna was playing the call of a female on a tape recorder during the census we were tak-ing. The poc came out from the reeds. As we continued to move, I saw that one had crept around to the back of us – very impressive! This was the first time I had actually seen this bird, and I hadn't realized how big they truly were. After watching this one bird for a while, Anna thought it was a young male. He did not appear to be frightened, and playing the recording got him to answer back. It seemed he came out of the reeds to see why another bird was in his territory.

We moved on slowly along the reed bed, playing the recorded poc call as we went. We got several more responses. The exact number was recorded by Madelyn. Gary was taping the responses of both male and female, as he thought it would be possible to distinguish individual calls. This was the case with other species of grebes he studied. Playing the recorded grebe calls went very well and was an ideal way to do a census.

Due to the intense heat, Anna halted the census at 10:30 that morning and marked the spot where the first sightings of the grebes were made. The small, completely open boat would get uncomfortably hot, even though the temper-

Mike (left), Gary Nuechterlein (center), and Anne LaBastille (right) playing recorded poc sounds.

ature was only about 80 degrees (F). The sun is very powerful in the Guatemalan mountains, especially with the sunlight reflecting off the water. The group always took precautions to avoid severe sunburns.

Before returning to the dock, they stopped to observe some natives who were wading in the water, cutting reeds to repair the thatched roofs on their houses. After talking to the men, who happened to speak English, Mike discovered that Indians were aware of the poc nesting in the vegetation. If they came upon a nest, they would leave some reeds around it. Even so, Mike still worried about the poc nests. Gary tried to explain to the Indians that more of the reeds needed to be left in order to protect the nests.

Anna, Gary, and Mike all knew it was difficult telling the Indians what they should do. The reeds were vital to the Indians' lives. Cutting the reeds for their thatched roofs had been a part of their culture for hundreds of years, but the poc were on the brink of extinction. Many of their houses had used tile roofs in recent years, but when the earthquake occurred the roofs caved in and killed many of the villagers.

For greater safety in case of future earthquakes, they reverted to the tradition of building thatched roofs. With the potential for another earthquake looming, Mike wondered whether the reed cutters would even consider their suggestions to save the poc.

Just beyond where the Indians were cutting, a pair of grebes was on a nest. In this case, it would have been ideal to take the eggs. Gary thought just the

Native Guatemalan cutting reeds.

mere disturbance of the reed cutters getting nearer and nearer each day might cause the grebe pair to desert the nest. Mike thought it was too early to take eggs – they might hatch before there was a site established to rear them.

Once back at the hotel, Mike decided to snorkel around the bay near the main dock and then swim back to the hotel. He wanted to survey the lake's aquatic life for clues to the poc's disappearance. He was surprised at the number of crabs, though none were very big. The largest was only six inches across. They appeared to be purple in color. The crabs would disappear into a hole upon being spotted. He also saw bass, the biggest about twelve inches long. There were hundreds of bluegills around the docks. The Indians would catch them with a hook and line baited with a worm.

The team went into town for lunch. Panajachel was very colorful with all the little stalls from which the merchants sold their wares – textiles and some very nice woven shirts. Part of the fun was haggling over the price.

That night during dinner, Mike, Anna, and Gary summarized what they had learned to that point in the expedition. There seemed to be enough fish available for the pocs to eat, but the gill nets the Indians used might be playing a major role in the pocs' disappearance.

They thought the reed cutting could be done in such a way that the nesting poc would not be harmed, but would they be able to convince the locals to do this? Indians needed to cut reeds in April, when they were at the perfect length for making thatched roofs.

Unfortunately, this was the same time the poc needed the reed beds intact in order to hide their nests. Then again, the Indians have cut reeds for thousands of years and yet the pocs had survived.

The bigger problem must be that the reed beds decreased when the water level receded after the earthquake. Since then, there were not enough reeds for them to nest. They made a list of other things they considered harmful to the poc:

1. The increased number of lakefront chalets and beaches had destroyed large areas of reed beds.
2. The monofilament nets used by the Indians for fishing would trap and kill poc.
3. The introduction of bass into the lake may have reduced the number of crabs, a food source for poc, and the larger bass might be eating the young poc.

One fact they all knew and feared was that if the grebe population dropped too low, the bird would never come back, regardless of what measures were taken to save them. Unfortunately, this is what ultimately doomed the poc.

THE SUN EXTRACTS A TOLL

Early the next morning the boat was readied for another grebe-finding excursion on Lake Atilán. They searched the shoreline habitat near a mountain village called Santa Cruz. The only access to this and other such villages was by water, as the mountains were too steep for footpaths, let alone roads. Mike was amazed at how the Indians had planted corn in scattered plots so high in the mountains. Although there were a lot of reed beds near Santa Cruz, no pocs were spotted.

Continuing on, they sighted a pair of pocs a good distance from the shore. There was quite a lot of activity with the Indians working in the tule – the name of the rush-like vegetation the pocs liked to nest among. (The word "tule" comes from the Aztec word "tullin" or "tollin.") The poc did not appear nervous about the approach of Indian boats, but they were much more nervous about the researchers' boat – due to the sound and disturbance caused by the motor.

Throughout the morning several more grebes were spotted moving in and out of the tule. One pair was in hot pursuit of a coot, which had taken refuge in the rushes. Mike noted that the grebes could obviously defend their territory from coots.

An east wind came up from the mountains, causing the water to become choppy. Gary and Mike wanted to continue on with the search, especially in this area where numerous pocs were sighted. However, the waves became a big enough threat that Anna decided to return to the dock before things got worse.

As they made their way across open water, the small craft took a savage hammering from the waves, drenching the occupants in cold water. To make matters worse, the motor ran out of gas in the middle of the tumultuous lake. Fortunately, an extra drum of fuel was onboard for such an emergency. Mike and Gary managed to refuel the motor in the wavering boat without aid of a funnel or siphon. More fuel spilled into the boat than into the motor, but it was enough to restart the engine. After a long and distressing journey, they were back at the dock – cold from the icy lake water and sunburned from exposure to the mountain sun.

The next morning, the poc rescue team faced two problems. The first was the situation with the boat. The craft they had been using was too small for the number of people on the expedition. Anna wisely insisted on procuring another boat before setting out on the day's mission. That way the team could split up. One group would continue the grebe census with Anna and Gary, while the others went with Mike to finish scouting the rest of the lake for a breeding site. Although there was a second boat and motor available for hire, it came without a reserve gas tank. The motor was topped with gas, and it was determined there was enough fuel for Mike to get to the west end of the lake and back.

The second issue was the declining health of the team leader. Anna, being of fair complexion, was having more trouble with sun exposure than the others. She had not slept well that night and seemed to be suffering from sunstroke. She was unsure about going out on the boat again. After taking some extra time to rest, she ultimately decided to join Gary on the census work, which was falling behind schedule.

Rolando, the translator, was supposed to go with Mike's group, but he didn't show up. He did make an appearance later, joining the other boat, which got a later start due to Anna's illness.

Mike, with only Madelyn along, was pleased at how much better this boat handled in the waves. They headed back to where they were the previous day when Anna had called off the search due to high winds. The weather this day wasn't much better, but the team needed to get answers on how to save the poc before the mission ended in a few days.

Being out in the lake some distance from the shoreline, Mike could see how the Indians had cut the tule into little square pockets. After taking a picture of the reed patterns, he went in closer in order to count the coot in Santiago Bay.

From Mike's Journal:

> I spotted some poc. The male came out to the edge of the tule to look at us as we slowly cruised by. The sound of the motor must have made them inquisitive. As we carried on, I saw another poc swimming at least 1,000 feet away among a flock of coots. There were weeds on the surface of the water, growing from the bottom of the lake. This particular poc could have been fishing around the weeds.
>
> We finished counting coots and saw some more pocs. We moored on a beautiful beach, where we had breakfast. Afterwards, I went for a snorkel, noting cichlids and at least three or four big bass in the rocks.
>
> Once back in the boat, we continued on and found a poc in the most unusual place. There was very little tule, a house very near, and a woman washing clothes in the lake. I searched for a nest but didn't find one. The tule was fairly thick in the middle and the clump was not very wide – about fifteen feet. The reeds near land had been burnt. The area was only about 30 feet in length – a very small territory for poc.

They continued on to Santiago Bay. But the wind was getting up once again, so Mike decided to head back to the dock. He had lunch at a restaurant in town and then visited an art gallery owned by a German. The proprietor told Mike that since the rebel uprising in 1980, his business had all but disappeared.

Mike returned to the hotel and met up with Gary and Anna to discuss the mission. Anna retired early, still in distress from sunstroke. Everyone, including the Guatemalans, was feeling the penetrating effects of the sun at an elevation of 5,000 feet.

A Ray of Hope

On Sunday, April 8, Mike and Gary steered their boat to Santiago Bay once more. By all accounts, this was the best place to find poc, and more importantly, a nest with eggs.

From Mike's Journal:
> When we arrived in the bay where the reed cutters had been, we heard a poc calling. Gary and I had our wetsuits and went wading into the reeds. It was not easy walking in mud and in cold water that came up chest-high. Soon we found a nest, but they had not laid eggs yet. We came out of the reeds and got into the boat.
>
> We went to another spot where we had seen pocs previously. After much searching, I found a nest with five eggs – a big clutch! I determined they were very fresh by putting them in the water to see if they would float or sink. We took photos of the nest and then the precious cargo was securely loaded on the boat.

With great excitement, the team raced back in order to find Anna and reveal their important discovery. Speeding along the lake's surface, they envisioned the joyous response of their leader, who against the odds, without significant resources, and often working alone had invested years of her life to save the Atilán Grebe. Finally there was good news. They had found five fresh eggs. There was still hope!

Poc eggs

But soon after arriving at the hotel, the team received the news that quickly changed their countenance from joy to sorrow. Mama Poc was leaving Guatemala.

Welcome to the Jungle

Anna explained that she had called her physician in Guatemala City, who advised her in no uncertain terms to rest, rehydrate and above all, stay out of the sun. Despite the risk to her health if she stayed, the decision to leave was not an easy one. There was a lot on the line. The existence of a species was at stake. But ultimately, a heat stroke caused by prolonged exposure to the hot tropical sun while in an uncovered boat prompted her return to the United States. The team had a final meal together with Anna. A friend from Guatemala City came to pick her up, and the next morning, Mama Poc left the village of Panajachel on her way back to Miami.

The rest of the team tried to pick up the pieces and hopefully carry on with the mission to save the poc. With the discovery of the five grebe eggs, the situation wasn't really as bleak as it seemed. The search of Lake Atilán was essentially over. The census would be completed in a day or two. Except for Mike using a helicopter the next day to make a final scouting run, the poc's habitat had been methodically examined. The only major assignment remaining was to establish a site where they could hatch the eggs, rear the young, and release the birds into the lake area. But they had less than five days left to accomplish this.

However, these tasks fell neatly into the areas of expertise of Gary Nuechterlein, the world's leading authority on grebes, and Mike Lubbock, the world's leading authority in avian husbandry. If they could pull it off, it would indeed be a monumental accomplishment. With grebe eggs in hand, it was still a possibility.

But the big question remained. Where would be the best place to hatch and raise what was perhaps the last remaining progeny of this vanishing species?

There were two candidates for a breeding facility. The first, and possibly most adaptable, was the Berger family's Auto Safari Park, which Anna, Mike, and Dickey had toured prior to arriving at Lake Atilán. The park had a lot of water, but Mike could not determine on such a brief visit whether any of it would be suitable for grebes. However, the staff had assured Mike they would be willing to dig new ponds anywhere he suggested. The bigger problem with the safari park was how far away it was from the release site.

In addition, before leaving Guatemala Anna had become aware of local opposition to moving birds (and presumably eggs as well) to an area so far away from the grebe's home lake. Unfounded suspicion was brewing in the local community that Anna and her team planned to steal their grebes.

The second possibility was the old breeding refuge on Lake Atilán. Mike had made an assessment of this facility in recent days. Unfortunately, it would require substantial manpower, funds, and time to rebuild even a portion of the site. None of these were available to the team.

Neither of the two possibilities for a breeding site seemed suitable to Mike. There was still a little time before the mission ended, so he decided to check out some other lakes in the region he had heard about. In order to do this, he and the others would need to leave the relative safety of Panajachel and enter into the civil unrest of the Guatemalan jungle.

From Mike's Journal:

> Guerilla warfare remained a threat, especially in the remote areas. I actually asked someone stationed at the American embassy if it was safe for us to go. He shook his head and said immediately, "No!" I thought, "Now what do I do?"
>
> After the embassy, I went to the police and other Guatemalans to ask if it was safe to drive into this particular jungle area. I was told that as long as we took certain routes and did not go through the volcano pass, we should be okay. So I decided to go for it. I found the lake I heard about on the map and made out a route that would take us through San Lucas and then toward the coast.

On the morning of April 10, Gary and two of the locals set out in the boat with hopes of finishing the census that day. They took provisions to stay overnight on the lake, in case that was necessary. Mike, Madelyn, and Rolando the interpreter began the drive to a jungle lake that was supposedly fed underneath the mountains by Lake Atilán. The place is called Mocha, owned by an Englishman named John Smith.

From Mike's Journal:

> Madelyn drove the car through Indian villages and tropical vegetation. Once we turned off the main highway towards Mocha, the road became very rough with huge potholes and high boulders. Our travel was made worse by sugar cane trucks that nearly drove us off the road and into the jungle.

As we travelled further down the dirt road, we saw Indians coming from sugar fields and coffee plantations. One could sense the fear in their faces. Presumably, this was because they saw very few strangers and they didn't know if we posed a threat to them. A Guatemalan who was heavily armed passed us on a motorbike.

The group finally arrived at Mocha and discovered a garden paradise in the middle of a remote and troubled area. John Smith's house had a nice lawn and tennis courts. He had made the place as English as he could. There was a man-made lake and a large pond. A dam near the house featured a waterfall, which gave off the tranquil sound of running water. The setting was a bit peculiar, considering what they had passed through to get here. Because of the trouble there, John Smith would fly in twice a week and only stay at his house a couple hours each time.

From Mike's Journal:
We left John Smith's house to find the lake. As we drove on, two young people with rifles jumped out and stopped us as we attempted to cross a bridge. One came over to see what we were doing, but he could not read the papers we had. Rolando had to read it to him. The other person came over, and we were able to ask him some questions about the lake. He made it very clear that we should not stay in this area too long. They had some recent trouble with guerilla fighters on the bridge on which we were standing. There was very dense jungle in this area, making travel very unpredictable and dangerous.

We arrived at the lake and I begin taking pictures. I took photos of the lake and began judging the merits of this area as a possible breeding refuge. I spotted and photographed six Least Grebes that were fishing among the weeds. These were a smaller grebe, not a Pied-bill. I did not think the lake would be a suitable refuge for poc. It was too far into the jungle to manage, especially in such a troubled area.

We turned around and started to drive back. About five miles up the road, two armed men jumped out of the vegetation and pointed their guns at the vehicle. Rolando went to talk to them. After a short conversation, Rolando beckoned me to come down to where they stood. When I arrived the two gunmen shoved their rifles into my side and then Rolando walked back to the car.

I was terrified, as these were just kids with rifles. Rolando then came back with my camera and took a picture of me being in a state of terror. He'd actually talked to the guys and found out that they just wanted to know when we'd last seen any soldiers. He set up the gag on me. Rolando has a weird sense of humor.

After this foolish prank, Mike drove back on the rough road, making better time than Madelyn had on the way in. He had more experience than she did navigating roads of this nature. Everyone breathed a sigh of relief when they made it back to the relative safety of the blacktop road. They just wanted to get out of there.

A Race Against Time

The following day, Mike, Gary, and Dickey were closing down operations and preparing to leave the village of Panajachel. With only two days remaining before returning to the United States, they still had a major decision to make concerning the hatching of the five grebe eggs. Dickey still believed that the Auto Safari Park was a workable solution and convinced Mike and Gary to return there to have a second look. After a day of arduous travel, the trio dropped Madelyn off in Guatemala City before arriving at the safari park at nine o'clock that night.

Early the next morning, Mike, Gary, and Dickey scouted the landscape of the vast nature park by jeep. Without the benefit of a road or path, they trekked through swampy terrain and then a jungle habitat. Dickey barely avoided getting the jeep hopelessly stuck.

Mike finally spotted some ponds which he thought could be used as a refuge for poc. Dickey did not know much about how the water flowed in this area, so they talked with Philippino, the man who controlled the water throughout the park. After Mike told him what water requirements they needed to raise birds, he took them to a spot not far from the Safari Park's main fence. Gary and Mike agreed that this particular area would be ideal. As much water as needed could be diverted to this spot, since it was near the main source of water.

Even though the safari park had a suitable location for raising grebes, the amount of time to construct the area would be a problem. What would they do with the eggs in the meantime? Mike and Gary still had two more lakes to check before making the final decision.

They stopped at the first lake on their way back to Guatemala City. Immediately they knew this was not a proper place to raise grebes. The lake was very populated with people and boats, leaving the birds without the privacy they required to breed. There was also a lot of construction in the area, which could further pollute the lake.

Friday, April 13, was the team's final full day in Guatemala. Mike, Gary, and Madelyn set off to investigate what would be, by necessity, the last option for a grebe breeding site. At six o'clock in the morning, they were already making their way toward Laguna Del Pino. (Lake of the Pines). They could observe the lake for only twenty minutes, as they were due back in Guatemala City at nine o'clock for an important debriefing session. But the lake appeared to be a great site.

Mike observed nine or ten Pied-billed Grebes that were displaying and guarding territories. He knew there must be grebe nests with eggs in those territories. That gave him an idea. He devised a clever plan in his head that might just work, but he would need to return to Laguna Del Pino immediately after the required meeting in the city. Time was running out.

They arrived on time for the debriefing with a number of conservationists. The meeting lasted two hours and was a summary of the entire trip, including Mike and Gary's recommendations on what to do with the eggs they'd collected. They hoped the effort they and Anne LaBastille had expended on this project would result in a lasting future for the poc. But there was no time to dwell on the future just now. They needed to get back to Laguna Del Pino without delay to carry out the plan Mike had hatched.

Mike's plan was truly groundbreaking. He proposed swapping the eggs laid by the Pied-billed Grebes with the endangered poc eggs he found on Lake Atilán. He thought that the Pied-billed Grebes would hatch and raise the young poc as their own. Gary, the grebe expert, agreed this was the best option.

Mike: There were Pied-billed Grebes on Laguna Del Pino.
We figured that if we put the poc eggs into a pied-billed
nest, they would surely rear them. We would have to see
what would happen after that. This was the only lake I
saw that was favorable for egg swapping.
The lake would be easy for someone to watch and
follow the chicks. It seemed that most of the Pied-billed
Grebes were just beginning to nest, so the poc eggs we
found at Lake Atilán would be ideal for the experiment.
They would hatch early and be easy enough to follow, as
there would be few other pied-bills with young.

Mike and Gary explored the lake in a small rubber boat loaned to
them by Rolando. It was a very small raft and had a leak, impeding
their progress along the shore. They searched for a pied-billed nest
along the shore of the entire lake. Several nests were found, but one in
particular caught their attention. This nest had six eggs, about a week
along in the incubation period. This nest was in a far more inaccessible area, among the tule. This would be a good nest in which to swap
out the poc eggs.

The team returned to the hotel in Guatemala City that night and
discussed with Madelyn how to perform the egg swap. The young
Peace Corps volunteer was assigned the daunting task of transporting
the precious poc eggs to their final destination on Laguna Del Pino
and making the switch. Early the next morning, Mike and Gary
boarded a plane to Miami. They had done all they could with the
available time and the circumstances they had encountered. The outcome was literally left for nature to determine.

REQUIEM FOR A SPECIES

Upon leaving Guatemala on April 14, 1984, Mike Lubbock
believed that the heroic efforts of Anne LaBastille's rescue team would
save the Atilán Grebe. However, five years later, the indomitable Anna
spotted the last poc she would ever see while conducting a census on
Lake Atilán. She spent several more years searching for her lost birds
to no avail.

The number of summer homes built on the shore of the lake had
increased alarmingly since the 1984 rescue attempt, causing excessive

pollution in the water and rapid decline of vital nesting habitat. The result of these and other environmental changes brought the population of poc down to zero. The egg swapping experiment on which Mike and Gary had placed their last hope for the poc's survival ultimately failed to provide a reserve breeding stock of Atilán Grebes.

Madelyn had substituted the poc eggs in the nest of the Pied-billed Grebe as instructed, and the eggs had hatched. Madelyn and others followed the young birds for six months, and then the pocs vanished. They couldn't fly away from Laguna Del Pino. Nobody really knows what happened to them.

The unfortunate thing was that neither Gary nor Mike were available to observe the birds, band them, or follow through on the experiment during those critical first months. Anna put together another team to go to Lake Atilán the next year, but there was even more unrest in the area, which greatly impeded work on the project.

The egg swapping plan landed Mike and Gary in trouble with the conservation group overseeing Guatemalan wildlife. They were supposed to get permission from ICONA (the Nature Conservation Institute for the Spanish territories) before displacing eggs or birds on the endangered species list.

Mike: The original plan was to build a breeding site at the safari park down there. But grebes in those days, and even now, are very hard to keep in captivity. Taking eggs into captivity (the safari park) without knowing much about the birds might have been disastrous. That was the reason I wanted to place them on another grebe's nest. That would have been pioneering. I was looking at every option. We took it upon ourselves to do what we thought was best for the poc, but the authorities frowned on it.

Nearly 25 years after the loss of the Atilán Grebe, Mike Lubbock remains deeply dismayed by the result of the Guatemalan project.

Mike: The Guatemalans would continue building more houses around the lake and reducing habitat for the poc. It's very difficult to explain to people living there why they should care about this little brown bird that isn't of any real use to them. The Indians used the lake to support their way of life. We asked them to change how they fished and how they cut reeds for their homes. These are difficult goals to accomplish, especially with limited time.

The poc had vanished from Lake Atilán, and there were no more. The egg-swapping plan could have been successful if we could have had someone to follow them properly. Madelyn was not really trained for conservation work, and she had to leave six months later to go back to America.

It was a shame really, because we were right on the verge of saving the poc. It's just a shame we were too late. If we'd been down there even a year or two earlier, we could have salvaged something from it all.

So it was really sad. We had a plan, although the authorities didn't like what we did at the end.

But the bird's gone now. That one got away.

The Atilán Grebe was a beautiful and unique creature. It deserved a lasting place in this world, but instead became a casualty of development. Despite the sadness of its ultimate fate, the Atilán Grebe's contribution to avian conservation is significant.

The stakes had been raised. Mike Lubbock was not accustomed to failure, especially when it came to raising birds or saving a species. The loss of the Atilán Grebe in Guatemala became the catalyst for Mike to manage his collection as a means to preserve rare and endangered waterfowl.

With the disappearance of the Atilán Grebe permanently fixed in his mind, the new collection would not be focused on size or profit. The goal for Mike Lubbock, from the Guatemalan project forward, was to establish breeding programs that would protect waterfowl and other bird species from the harsh threat of extinction. He was determined not to let another one get away.

CHAPTER ELEVEN

Sylvan Heights

After the near miss of saving the Atilán Grebe, Mike Lubbock returned to Alabama and continued building his collection of birds with a renewed focus on preservation.

The Guatemalan mission turned out to be another brush with danger, even though his assignment was only to find fertile eggs and establish a breed-and-release program to prevent the grebe from completely disappearing. He realized he was totally responsible for the decision to go into the jungle to find a site for breeding the poc, even though he had been duly warned of the guerilla activity in that area.

Mike was not aware of the mysterious disappearance of two U.S. Fish & Wildlife agents in that vicinity of Guatemala just a few months before his arrival. Upon return to the United States he learned of their fate, which was assumed to be related to the civil war in the country.

These types of incidents always seemed to happen on his expeditions and missions. He had hoped to put these dangerous trips behind him after Patagonia. This really needed to stop, he thought. From this point on, breeding birds would be the priority. He would turn his attention to making the Alabama collection the best it could be. He would save birds through his innovative survival breeding programs.

However, Montgomery turned out to be only a two-year stay for the Lubbocks. Despite the increased number of birds and Ali's deft management, the enterprise did not gain the critical mass necessary to flourish. Without sufficient finances, expansion of the enterprise was limited. Hank Marion, one of the main buyers of their birds, recognized that Mike was struggling.

Mike: Hank Marion had a nice collection of birds in Sylva, North Carolina. He had a fair amount of wealth and knew we were having a hard go of it in Montgomery. Eventually Hank offered me a partnership.

I couldn't refuse; it was one of those things that seemed too good to be true. I thought with Hank's ability to finance the purchase of new birds, we could build a great collection. That would really allow me to demonstrate my avian breeding techniques and my new emphasis on rare species.

For example, I thought I could do in America what I had done in England by breeding the White-winged Wood Duck, which was an endangered species.

The White-winged Wood Duck was the first species he targeted for a survival breeding program. It would be the first of many he'd conduct with his newfound freedom as a conservation-oriented aviculturalist.

Mike joined with Hank Marion in November 1984. The facility was high in the Blue Ridge Mountains of Western North Carolina, in the small town of Sylva. The new company moniker reflected the name of the town and its elevation – Sylvan Heights Waterfowl.

Hank had been primarily interested in the pheasant family, but his interest in waterfowl was growing, which is why he offered to partner with Mike, one of the world's leading experts in waterfowl breeding. Sylvan Heights' facility had three major waterfowl pens and 30 side pens, using water from four different pure mountain streams.

Mike supervised the construction of winter quarters, which also contained the rearing

Mike and Hank Marion in Sylva, North Carolina.

units. The building was divided into two tiers, an upper and lower, both with separate heating units so that one could be closed off if not in use at any time during the winter.

Mike: I brought my birds from Alabama to join Hank's collection. Doug and I divided the birds equally and we parted on pleasant terms; in fact, we're good friends to this day.

Hank and I made a trip to Europe to buy new species.

250

Hank was bringing in birds and paying for the quarantine. We had 120 species of waterfowl, from the rare Meller's Duck to the bizarre Magellanic Flightless Steamerduck. Many of these birds surprised us by breeding after only a short time at Sylva. The 1985 breeding season ended up being better than we imagined at the time.

So that is how the original Sylvan Heights Waterfowl was set up. It was a pretty good collection. One of our main goals was to breed and establish some of the rarest species in captivity.

SCOTLAND NECK

Mike's new career was finally on course. Additional species and bloodlines were coming in from Europe, the facilities at Sylvan Heights were superb, the finances were solid, and plenty of buyers were coming to Sylva as a result. But Mike's plans didn't anticipate the next setback.

In 1989, Hank Marion died suddenly without warning. Sylvan Heights Waterfowl had been in operation for five years, and now its future was uncertain.

Mike: When Hank Marion died, I didn't quite know what to do. I was left high and dry. His son inherited everything and wanted to develop the land on which the breeding center was built. He had no interest in the birds, but he wanted the value of his father's share of the collection paid in cash.

The Lubbocks' financial situation could not accommodate a large cash payout on short notice. Fortunately, Hank's son was willing to consider a counter-offer.

Mike: I worked out a deal with the son where I would sell a number of birds and pay him the proceeds to get owner-ship of the remaining collection. I got my pick of any materials, such as the fencing and pumps, for nothing. He was going to bulldoze all the buildings and anything else left there, so we had to act fast. Anything I couldn't remove in time would be sold for scrap.

But where would the collection go? There was not much time to make a decision. The answer came from Toad and Hanna Herring, a couple who made frequent trips to Sylva to purchase birds for their own waterfowl collection in Scotland Neck, North Carolina.

Toad Herring was in the lumber business. The couple owned some property behind their home that had yet to be cleared. On the trips he made to Sylva to buy birds, Toad recognized that Mike Lubbock was far more than the typical waterfowl collector. He had bird sense and a vision of how to make a collection valuable. With Hanna in agreement, Toad offered to lease an eight-acre parcel of land to the Lubbocks and assist them in relocating operations to Scotland Neck.

Scotland Neck is on the opposite end of the state from Sylva, some 380 miles toward the Atlantic Ocean in the rural farm region of northeastern North Carolina. The town of just over 2,000 residents has a Scottish heritage. Not far from its current location, Scottish Highlanders, led by Lord Nairn in 1722, formed a colony near the "neck" (or bend) of the Roanoke River. On a good map, the bend even seems to resemble the curve of a swan's neck, very much like the current Sylvan Heights logo.

The peak elevation in Scotland Neck registers just 98 feet above sea level, far below the 2,040 feet in the mountain town of Sylva. Though both cities are in the same state, the climate in Scotland Neck is much milder, especially in winter. But summers there can be brutally hot. This required Mike to consider which of his birds might not adapt well to the warmer environment.

He sold most of his arctic birds to raise money to pay Hank Marion's son. These birds in particular might not breed well in Scotland Neck. He kept all of the rare and endangered species he had at Sylva. This included some bloodlines of species he had found in the wilds of Africa and South America, which were bred at the Wildfowl Trust.

Many trees had to be cleared before any fencing or birds could be moved to the new property.

Mike: Toad and I were surveying the property to see how the
        breeding center should be laid out. We were walking near
        where the parrot house is now. We were in the woods
        when suddenly we heard an almighty crash. An enormous

oak tree fell down – out of nowhere! There was no wind or anything that should have caused it to topple over.

We went over and looked at it – bees were flying out from the trunk. I turned to Toad and said, "Well, that's got to be a sign that Sylvan Heights should be right here."

The move from Sylva to Scotland Neck was made hurriedly. The long distance between the cities complicated the relocation. Fencing had to be taken down and driven across state along with a portion of the birds, then erected at the new site. Ali, along with James Ballance of Zoo Atlanta, directed the dismantling of the pens in Sylva, while Mike assisted another crew in assembling them at the new site. However, the birds had to be temporarily housed while their new aviaries were being constructed.

Mike: Toad cleared a lot of the property, but before we could build anything we had put up holding pens at Toad and Hanna's place by the ponds. Birds were everywhere. It was a nightmare until we built the new aviaries.

The first ones we finished were the Middle Pens, below where the barn is now. We eventually finished the barn, with an incubator room, plus a little duckery and a big duckery, patterned after the ones I had in Sylva. It took awhile to build it.

Today I look around and think, "This is quite a collection of birds."

Mike and helper Stuart Kennedy ready cranes for trip to Scotland Neck.

Mike and Ali christened the new avian breeding center as Sylvan Heights Waterfowl II, named after its predecessor in Sylva. The avian preserve established in Scotland Neck in

253

1989 marked the beginning of what was to become the largest and most biologically significant waterfowl collection in the world.

* * * * * * * * * * * * * *

The Lubbocks' avian preserve was aptly complemented by the region's wealth of natural resources and wild birds. Eastern North Carolina is the winter home to approximately 75,000 Tundra Swans, about half of the species' population. Every winter, thousands of Tundra Swans fly south from their nesting sites in the Arctic and descend upon the open fields just outside the town of Scotland Neck much to the delight of local residents and visitors. Mike will often take special guests to view the flocks of swans, which cause entire fields to appear to be painted white.

Scotland Neck is near the Roanoke River, a protected scenic waterway that wends like a snake through the Carolina coastal plain on its journey from the Virginia mountains to the Albemarle Sound. In addition to providing valuable wetlands for migratory waterfowl, the river also hosts a large heron rookery and a wintering area for bald eagles. The adjacent woodlands offer seasonal roosts to neo-tropic migrant birds.

The Lubbocks' new hometown included an important quality that gave Mike great comfort and a feeling of familiarity. Scotland Neck serves as a hub to the farming community, encompassed by hundreds of square miles of rural landscapes and agriculture. The agrarian feel of the area brought back fond memories of his days growing up in the Blackdown Hills near Taunton, England.

Mike knew the language of farming and respected the down-to-earth character of his neighbors. Many of them raise crops, such as cotton and soybeans, while others raise livestock. Breeding birds requires many of the same attributes as farming – a strong work ethic, a readiness to endure extreme weather conditions, and a willingness to put the needs of the animals first. In fact, the staff and volunteers working at Sylvan Heights often refer to the preserve as "the farm."

Mike Lubbock had found the perfect rural home to build his avian breeding center. He was surrounded by birds at every hand, not only in the aviaries, but also as he traveled throughout this region of North Carolina. At Sylvan Heights, he could breed the species of birds which he determined were important to preserve, without interference from any institution, partner, or authority.

Duck Mecca

The combination of the warm eastern North Carolina climate, top quality facilities, and Mike and Ali's penchant for breeding and acquiring birds resulted in an avian population explosion at Sylvan Heights Waterfowl II. Every spring the broody hen boxes and incubators were full of freshly laid waterfowl eggs, and the rearing units in both the large and small duckeries were filled with fluffy hatchlings.

Mike and Ali worked closely with other conservation and avicultural groups to help private breeders and zookeepers develop advanced avian husbandry skills and participate in survival breeding programs for rare species. They held important positions on the boards of the International Wild Waterfowl Association and the Carolina-Virginia Pheasant and Waterfowl Society, among others.

New species and bloodlines were imported. Mike was especially keen on acquiring some of the rare and endangered species he had brought in from the wild to the Wildfowl Trust. He eventually acquired and bred Pink-eared Ducks, African Pygmy-geese, Maccoa Ducks and White-backed Ducks, as well as White-headed Ducks and Magellanic Steamerducks.

He also obtained the critically endangered White-winged Wood Duck, which was originally brought into breeding collections from the Saam River region of northeast India, near Tibet. These particular birds came through a contact Mike had established at the National Zoo in Washington, D.C.

Possibly his biggest coup was bringing the Freckled Duck to Sylvan Heights. This is the same species for which he was denied permission to collect eggs on his 1979 expedition to Australia. These birds initially came into the Wildfowl & Wetlands Trust after the Australian government changed its policy on exporting native birds. With assistance from the Wildfowl Trust and the Wildlife Conservation Society, Mike Lubbock was granted permission for Freckled Ducks to be shipped to the Bronx Zoo and then to Sylvan Heights Waterfowl. This soon resulted in a North American First Breeding Award.

By the late 1990s, Sylvan Heights was home to nearly 3,000 birds representing 161 species. The eight-acre refuge was teaming with activity in the woodlands just outside the city limits of Scotland Neck, but few of the town residents were even aware of their existence. Mike and Ali had little in the way of assistance. Only two of the staff members were paid; the others consisted of volunteers and interns from around the country and world.

Nick Hill came to Sylvan Heights from England to be curator of aviculture. Nick brought with him 20 years of avicultural experience, once serving as assistant curator at Birdland Park and Gardens in Gloucestershire, England. Birdland was founded by Nick's grandfather, Len Hill, known as the Penguin Millionaire.

Very quietly, Sylvan Heights was becoming known by waterfowl experts and hobbyists as the place to go if avian husbandry was an interest. Interns came from Texas, Florida, Oregon, and other states far from North Carolina. Mike Lubbock's fame and legacy was even better known by folks outside the United States. Interns traveled to Scotland Neck from the United Kingdom, the Netherlands, Spain, Germany, Australia, Singapore, Venezuela, and Chile.

The mostly foreign staff at Sylvan Heights often caused a stir in Scotland Neck's shops and businesses. Yet for the most part, the avian breeding activities conducted on the hill behind Toad and Hanna's property went unnoticed and somewhat unappreciated. Mike and Ali were just "the bird people."

SEEKING SUSTAINABILITY

By 1996, the business of breeding waterfowl had changed significantly. Fewer people were keeping waterfowl as a hobby, and most zoos and nature centers were decreasing the size of their waterfowl displays to make room for more popular animal exhibits. Hobbyists and zoos were Sylvan Heights' biggest customers. Revenues were going down at the same time that the number of birds and the cost to rear them was increasing.

Mike's endangered species breeding program was continually expanding, adding to the decline in profits. Only a few of these birds would ever be sold. He also bred an increasing number of species that were rare in captivity. Many of these birds were not popular with collectors. They usually did not have attractive plumage, and therefore the buyers of these "little brown ducks" were very few. Mike did not breed them to sell, anyway. Nonetheless, they were an important part of his conservation program.

With their income in decline, the expense of feeding the 3,000 birds at the breeding center and the utilities cost for operating water pumps and incubators around the clock was threatening the sustainability of Mike's collection. It had grown to be one of the largest waterfowl collections in the world, but it appeared to be too expensive for a private individual of very modest financial means. Collections this large were normally funded by wealthy individuals or zoological institutions. Most individuals were selling their collections.

Mike: When I arrived in Long Island, New York, in 1969 to supervise the sizable collection for Winston Guest, there were seven major waterfowl collections just on this one island of New York. Now none of them remain. The same thing has happened with the major private collections in New England. Except for the Ripley collection, they have all disappeared. During this time, no new large waterfowl collections have come into existence anywhere in the country, except for Sylvan Heights and Paul Dickson's Pinola Preserve in Louisiana.

Even zoos in recent years have significantly downsized the number of waterfowl they display and breed.

Mike: Most of the major waterfowl collections that once existed at many zoos have slowly gone down in numbers. The San Diego Zoo, Bronx Zoo, Philadelphia Zoo, Saint Louis Zoo, and San Antonio Zoo all once had very extensive collections of waterfowl. During the past 25 years all of these zoos have drastically reduced their holdings of waterfowl.

SeaWorld San Diego, which once boasted the world's largest waterfowl collection, currently has only a modest number of birds compared to their zenith. Few zoos conduct any substantial breeding program for the few species they maintain. The only American zoos that have added significantly to their collections in recent years are the Central Park Zoo in New York and the Palm Beach Zoo in West Palm Beach, Florida.

The writing was on the wall. Sylvan Heights required help or the world's largest and most biologically relevant waterfowl collection was in danger of being broken up. If it were to be lost, it would be very unlikely anyone, including Mike Lubbock, could ever again build another to match it. Getting permits to take birds and eggs out of the wild in the manner Mike did during his expedition years is now nearly impossible in most countries except in the most dire of circumstances.

Something needed to be done to sustain the collection, not only during the lifetimes of Mike and Ali, but also for future generations who would benefit from the important waterfowl conservation programs developed at Sylvan Heights.

THE WATERFOWL SOCIETY

One reason Sylvan Heights Waterfowl II struggled financially was Mike's insistence on breeding birds which had a high level of conservation value but little or no monetary value. Many of these birds never left the preserve.

Ironically, the rare and endangered birds which drained the coffers provided the most persuasive argument for others to get involved in support of Sylvan Heights.

Mike and Ali had received a great deal of assistance from the Bronx Zoo in New York City. Having once been curator of Duck Puddle Farm on Long Island, Mike had provided many birds to the Bronx Zoo and was well known by the zoo's director and curator of birds, as well as many of the zoo's donors through the Wildlife Conservation Society. However, such donations were complicated by the fact that Sylvan Heights Waterfowl II had not been incorporated as a non-profit organization; therefore donations were not tax deductible.

The contributions made by the Lubbocks to the global preservation of waterfowl spurred influential conservation organizations to aid in sustaining the operations at Sylvan Heights.

William Conway, President of the Association of Zoos and Aquariums, took notice of Sylvan Heights' sustainability issue. Conway was concurrently president of the Wildlife Conservation Society, which serves also as the not-for-profit arm of the Bronx Zoo and the other New York City zoos. He was well aware of Sylvan Heights' importance in breeding waterfowl, as a training site for avian husbandry, and for providing research opportunities.

Conway also knew that the biological diversity assembled at Sylvan Heights attracted attention from many institutions involved in various types of zoological, environmental, and medical research. Permission to utilize Sylvan Heights' collection of birds had been granted to reputable organizations such as the National Zoo Conservation and Research Center, the U.S. Fish and Wildlife Service, and the University of North Carolina, to name only a few.

With such an essential conservation resource being on the verge of collapse, Conway approached Dr. David Jones, director of the North Carolina Zoological Park, about developing sustainable funding for Sylvan Heights.

Mike: I knew Dr. Jones from when he was the director of the Zoological Society of London. He and Russ Williams, the executive director of the North Carolina Zoological Society, came from Asheboro to visit Sylvan Heights.

They determined that it was vital to sustain a collection of birds having such a high degree of biological significance.

In 1997, the North Carolina Zoological Society accepted the challenge and designed a plan that would help the waterfowl breeding center continue functioning and providing future generations an opportunity to see and learn about waterfowl.

Sylvan Heights became an essential part of the Zoo Society's campaign to positively impact affect the future of rare and endangered species globally. A partnership was formed, and the transformation from being primarily a bird-breeding business to a conservation-oriented avicultural, research, and environmental education non-profit entity began for Sylvan Heights.

As the first order of business, the new partnership established the Sylvan Heights Waterfowl Society, a non-profit fund offered through the NC Zoo Society. Sylvan Heights finally had a tax-deductible entity that attracted donations from proponents of global waterfowl conservation through aviculture.

The Waterfowl Society, as it was often called, funded various breeding projects and defrayed overhead costs, especially the astronomical expense required to feed 3,000 birds twice each day. It also provided an avenue to expand Sylvan Heights' public reach beyond eastern North Carolina. After the original website was established in 2003, waterfowl enthusiasts from across America and the world became aware of Mike Lubbock's accomplishments and could lend their support through the Waterfowl Society.

While the website was successful in spreading the word about Sylvan Heights, it was apparent that something on a grand scale would be needed if Mike Lubbock's irreplaceable waterfowl collection was to be preserved.

Mike: We worked for several years with Russ Williams and Cheryl Turner of the NC Zoo Society, coming up with various ways to raise funds for Sylvan Heights. The main plan was to build some additional infrastructure so that visitors could tour the breeding center.

Many people already wanted to see what we were doing at the breeding center, but it was difficult to show them around. The grounds are often muddy, there are no paved paths for visitors to walk on, the fences are electrified to keep out predators, and it's much harder to see the birds because there's so much vegetation needed in the aviaries to provide cover and nesting material for the birds. Also we had some issues with how the extra activity may disturb the birds and affect their breeding.

So the idea to conduct tours at the breeding center never got past the planning stage. Ultimately it was decided that opening a visitor's park at a separate location from the breeding center was the way to go.

Soon after Mike and Ali settled on opening a new waterfowl park, a remarkable series of events occurred in very short order.

One possible site for building the park became the early frontrunner. A local businessman who owned a track of land just outside Scotland Neck offered it as a location for Sylvan Heights' new project. He also proposed having a lodge built for use by members of Ducks Unlimited, as well as a new School of Ecology, an alternative-study form of high school education. All three entities would interact. The students of the school would use the park as an outdoor classroom, Sylvan Heights' guests could stay at the lodge, and Ducks Unlimited was involved with the other sites in various ways advantageous to its members.

Initially, this concept garnered a great deal of support from all parties, including the NC Zoo Society. It appeared to be a win-win situation for all concerned. Discussions and terms of agreement progressed nicely throughout the fall of 2003.

However, Mike and Ali began to have second thoughts about the project. Mike recalled past problems he'd had whenever partners were involved. He could already imagine the kind of complications that could emerge from such a complex union and wondered if the plan was in the best interests of Sylvan Heights' future.

Late in December 2003, Mike and Ali concluded that even though no other plan was on the table for consideration, this one was not the best for them. They pulled out of the discussions with the cooperative.

Ali agreed completely with the decision. However, she had deep concerns if perhaps this action may have spelled the end of the waterfowl park. Already they had turned down two relatively solid proposals – the NC Zoo Society's plan of upgrading the breeding center for tours, and now this combined effort that would give rise to a separate park for Sylvan Heights. How many other available locations could there be in the small, remote town of Scotland Neck?

* * * * * * * * * * * *

The traditional New Year's Eve party at the Lubbocks' home produced all the fun and frivolity of past years. But as the assembled guests gathered to welcome in the year 2004 with cheer and hilarity, Mike and Ali were far more subdued. The normally optimistic Ali wondered if at some point during the upcoming year the day of reckoning would come, and Mike's prized waterfowl collection would have to be sold off in pieces.

She had fervently supported her husband's dream throughout the years. After each arduous expedition, she comforted him when he returned home battered, physically and mentally drained. She encouraged him when changes at the Wildfowl Trust caused him anguish and disillusionment. Since coming to America, she'd seen him through the financial frustration in Montgomery, the heartbreak of losing his business partner in Sylva, and the frantic rush to bring the collection to Scotland Neck.

For many years, she had taken all the financial and administrative pressures off his shoulders, all the things she knew he could not handle without getting upset or discouraged. She did it all so Mike could be wholly focused on his first love – caring for the birds, saving them from the cruelty of extinction. She shared this love with him and would do literally anything to see that his dream continued, even to the detriment of her own health.

She dared not even think what the loss of his birds would do to him. She must go on believing for a solution, although she had no idea what that solution would be or from which direction it would come. On this night of merriment to ring in the New Year, she found nothing worth celebrating. She raised her glass and offered cheers to her beloved friends, and thought that somehow the looming disaster would be averted. Something would come along to save them. It always did.

Little did Ali realize, as the clock marched toward midnight and Mike's favorite music from the '60s blared amidst the revelry, that yet another opportunity was afoot to save Sylvan Heights. Her believing prayers had already been answered.

SYLVAN HEIGHTS BIRD PARK

It had always been in plain sight, yet the possibility never crossed Mike or Ali's mind. Standing adjacent to Sylvan Heights Waterfowl was a tract of undeveloped property. The nearly 20 acre swath of land bordered a cotton field to the north and stretched west to the cemetery and east to the old beaver dam. It was the perfect location to build a waterfowl park.

A few days following the New Years Eve party, Ali received a call from Toad Herring, informing her that the E. A. Walston land which straddled Clark's Branch had just been posted for sale. Toad had assumed Sylvan Heights was already committed to the cooperative property, but thought she would want to know about this parcel anyway. It was as if heaven had opened up and dropped the solution square in their laps.

They needed to act fast, and secrecy was of utmost importance. No one outside a small insider group of Sylvan Heights' supporters could know of Mike and Ali's desire to obtain the property. If word were to get out, the asking price of the land would surely double.

Russ Williams of the NC Zoo Society was contacted, and he quickly crafted a plan. The property was right next to Sylvan Heights – not only a convenience, but practically a necessity for managing the park once it was built.

There was not nearly enough money in the Waterfowl Society's coffers to make such a purchase. This fact did not discourage Ali even a little. Now that she knew the perfect property was available, nothing could sidetrack her from obtaining it.

Russ Williams and Cheryl Turner, his senior grants writer, had already established the groundwork for a $1.5 million capital campaign designed to finance the development and construction of the waterfowl park under the auspices of the NC Zoo Society. However, the campaign needed a big contribution up front in order to swiftly and quietly purchase the Walston property.

Ali knew who could be counted on to make a financial commitment large enough to save Sylvan Heights. Without hesitation, a call was made to Nancy Collins in northern Ohio. A charitable waterfowl enthusiast and breeder, Nancy had made it her business over the years to see that Mike remained in a position to raise his birds.

She was willing to help Mike and Ali buy the property through the NC Zoo Society's Sylvan Height Capital Campaign. She wanted her contribution to remain anonymous, not seeking adulation for herself but giving of her resources to save wild waterfowl from extinction anywhere in the world they were in trouble. Nancy had helped Mike many times before, but this was big, and it went a long way towards assuring the collection at Sylvan Heights would be seen by future generations of people who appreciate wildlife and the environment.

According to Mike, without Nancy Collins' generous donations over the years, the waterfowl collection at Sylvan Heights would have been broken up and likely never reassembled anywhere in the world – a significant biological resource lost forever.

Mike: We need more people like Nancy, those who recognize the grave dangers these birds face in the wild and are willing to step up and do something to help them. I can't do it myself.

We have the collection and survival breeding programs in place. But it takes many others who are willing to play a role in preserving these species. I'm just thankful Nancy got involved, or we wouldn't be here today.

* * * * * * * * * * * *

Mike's 60th birthday party on January 17, 2004, doubled as a celebration for the purchase of the Walston land. The Lubbock's close friends had come from far and wide to mark the special occasion.

Brad Hazelton, curator of birds at the Fort Worth Zoo and former Sylvan Heights intern, commented to Mike during the party, "You must be nuts to be 60 years old and still have a dream as big as this. Most people your age are making plans to retire."

Mike led the party attendees on a vigorous walk through the new property, describing in detail where he envisioned the main building would be located, where ponds would be dug, which stands of trees needed to be preserved.

The well-wishers all nodded in agreement, though most had great difficulty envisioning any of it. All they could see was a dense forest overgrown with brush and other entanglements, which made navigating the land more of a struggle than a walk in the park.

Mike had already surveyed the property many times. His ability to "see" the natural resources through a simple visual inspection provided vital insight as to how the new park would be designed. Several features of the land struck him upon initial reconnaissance.

One major problem with the land was that it did not have any natural springs. A plentiful supply of clean, fresh water for ponds was vital for a park featuring waterfowl.

Mike: The biggest gamble in buying the Walston land was the
        water. We would have to drill wells and hope that we'd
        find water in enough abundance and clarity to sustain the
        birds. As the park was being built, we drilled three wells
        and hit water each time. That was big relief.

The landscape was aesthetically pleasing and heavily wooded, including several magnolia trees that were near the state record for size and age. The pathways would be placed in a manner that all significant plant species would be preserved.

The property was bordered on two sides by wetland areas. Over time, these important environmental gems had become obstructed by invasive species and were not able to perform their natural role in providing adequate food and shelter for the area's native wildlife.

Mike and Ali developed a plan that would reclaim the wetlands to their natural state and provide an "ecological laboratory" for students to explore, as well as stunning vistas for visitors to observe wildlife.

By all accounts it was a perfect location for the birds and visitors alike. Mike and Ali were about to embark on their most exciting and meaningful endeavor since the foundation of their work in Scotland Neck.

Mike: We set a mission we could only dream about a few years before – to make Sylvan Heights not only the premier waterfowl collection in the world, but also an ecological center for educating students and families about wildlife and the environment.

Landscaping plans and architectural drawings for the Waterfowl Park were in place by the spring of 2005. Mike designed the aviaries in a manner that allows visitors to walk inside the netting and have unobstructed views of the birds as they interact in a naturalistic environment.

He also decided to use a continental theme to display the birds. Waterfowl species would be grouped to represent Australia, Africa, Eurasia, North America, and South America. Wherever possible, plant species native to each continent were acquired for planting. Mike made certain these aviaries provided the birds all the protections and natural elements they would need to be at ease and content.

The design of the large continental aviaries was unique. It had never been seen in zoos or anywhere else. They would be covered in netting to protect the birds from predators and also allow Mike to display fully winged birds. Mike knew it would delight visitors to walk inside the aviary with the birds and have them fly above them. Visitors would likely forget that the netting was even there. All the poles holding up the netting were on the outside, allowing photographs to be taken without any obstructions inside the aviaries.

An Endangered Species Exhibit, sponsored by the International Wild Waterfowl Association, was also included. This display would feature the world's largest group of White-winged Wood Ducks, a critically endangered species found in the Far East and which had become a focal point of Mike's conservation effort since developing his own collection.

Other exhibits were designed for the many non-waterfowl birds Mike wanted visitors to experience at the park, such as the Eurasian Eagle-owl (the worlds' largest owl), as well as the Toco Toucan,

Laughing Kookaburra, Australian Brush Turkey, Black Crowned Crane, Lady Ross' Turaco, and Emu. There would also be a variety of parrots, pheasants, and endangered curassows.

Mike: There were two reasons why I wanted the park to show more than just waterfowl. Having been at the Wildfowl Trust, which was open to the public, I always felt sorry for the visitors during the summer because that's when many of the birds went out of color. The males looked like females because they'd lost their breeding plumage. So I chose other bird species that would provide lots of color for visitors to enjoy year-round.

I also wanted visitors to come away with an educational message about preserving birds and the habitats in which they live. So I chose many of the bird species we put in the park on the basis of how that message could best be demonstrated.

Construction on the two-story log structure at the Waterfowl Park began in the fall of 2005. The Eco-Center, or Visitor Center as it has became known, would be the entry point for guests to begin their immersion into Sylvan Heights' avian world. Mike designed a Multinational Aviary presenting a variety of waterfowl from all corners of the world to greet visitors as they emerged from the Visitor Center.

Soon, over 1,000 birds would make the park their home, in addition to the 3,000 that were across the valley at the Avian Breeding Preserve.

DUCKLING DAY

After numerous construction delays and setbacks, it became apparent the park would not be ready to open in the spring of 2006 as projected. However, enough of the building was completed by May that the Lubbocks decided to hold the annual Duckling Day celebration at the Visitor Center, utilizing the outside deck overlooking the Multinational Aviary as well as inside in the Golden Leaf Education and Reception Room.

Duckling Day is a Sylvan Heights tradition, when higher level members of the Sylvan Heights Waterfowl Society can visit the Avian

Visitor's Center from Multinational Aviary prior to Grand Opening

Breeding Center, which is not open to the public. The event normally occurs during the peak of breeding season, and members get a full tour of the facility. The highlight for most members is the having the rare occasion to go inside the Little Duckery, which is packed with freshly hatched ducklings, goslings, and cygnets, all peeping and squeaking inside the brooders. It is not unusual for members to be offered an opportunity to hold one of these little ones in their hands for a short time.

The event was also a good dress rehearsal for the Lubbocks, their staff, and volunteers. From this point forward, they would need to learn how to accommodate large crowds of visitors at the park every weekend, as well as other special events throughout the year.

THE GRAND OPENING

For those who toiled and planned to help Mike and Ali open their waterfowl world to the public, it may have seemed that October 7, 2006 would never arrive. The ups and downs, starts and stops, and assorted frustrations of the project had appeared endless.

The morning of the Grand Opening dawned with rain threatening, but never making good on its warning. The caterers had set up the kitchen the night before and were busy in their preparations by first light. Special guests of Mike and Ali had gathered in Scotland Neck from all around North Carolina, North America, and other faraway places in the world. Scotland Neck had become a worldwide destination on this weekend. Visitors from Zimbabwe, South Africa, the Netherlands, Germany, Spain, Scotland, England, and Venezuela were in attendance for the grand opening ceremonies.

It was a day of great significance for the Lubbocks and their extended family of supporters. It marked a new phase in the career of the Waterfowl Man, and a new hope for the preservation of the world's wild waterfowl.

The official festivities began at 9:30 with Mike and Ali giving greetings, handshakes, and hugs as guests walked into the brand-new Visitor Center for the first time. All were amazed, many actually stunned, by the beauty and luster of the building. Live music wafted softly through the rooms and an elegant brunch was served.

At noon, the guests assembled outside in the parking area and were joined by members of the public to witness the official opening of Sylvan Heights Waterfowl Park & Eco-Center. (This was the original name prior to being renamed Sylvan Heights Bird Park in 2011.)

The morning threat of rain had ceased, although in near perfect weather for ducks, a light mist had permeated the air as the crowd of well-wishers focused their attention upon the podium resting on the front porch of the Visitor Center.

The grand opening ceremony opened with a series of heartfelt tributes to the importance of Sylvan Heights Waterfowl Center and the contributions made by Mike and Ali Lubbock to the future of wild waterfowl.

Dr. Mel Levine, noted child psychologist and author:
> Last line from the Robert Frost poem, "A Minor Bird" —
> *"And of course there must be something wrong, in wanting to silence any song."*

I urge you as you walk around Sylvan Heights to close your eyes and just listen to the choral music at each one of these displays, because it is really extraordinary.

So much of the mission of Sylvan Heights is to make sure that future generations can share in this extraordinary music of wildlife.

Frank Todd, ornithologist and author:
> *This tiny little town of Scotland Neck is on the global map with respect to waterfowl. Over the last several decades, the Who's Who of the waterfowl world have made the pilgrimage here to meet the guru and see the duck mecca.*

Peter Kooy, aviculturalist:
> *Mike Lubbock and the Lubbock family have been working with us in the field of aviculture for more than forty years. In that time we've shared many of the same dreams. One of those dreams was developing an eco-center to teach others the knowledge we've gained over the years on how to care for birds and the environment. I've learned a lot from Mike and I admire him. The techniques he developed at the Wildfowl Trust in England were so great for the future of waterfowl.*

Russ Williams, Executive Director, North Carolina
       Zoological Society:
> *The effort to make this park a reality began in 1997 when the Association of Zoos and Aquariums recognized Sylvan Heights' importance to zoos, avian collections and to the welfare of waterfowl everywhere. As one very special donor said, "If not for the work of Mike and Ali Lubbock, some waterfowl species would not exist today."*

Last to speak was Mike Lubbock. He came to the podium with Ali on his right and Brent, who was in charge of public relations and development, at his left. Mike thanked his family, Toad and Hanna, Russ and Cheryl of the Zoo Society, volunteers, donors, and supporters who made the opening of the park a reality.

With those words of thanks still ringing in the ears of the massive crowd, Mike and Ali walked down the porch steps to the ceremonial ribbon, and using a large pair of scissors, together they cut the final barrier between the public and their new waterfowl world.

Together, as they had worked for all the years since the early days at Slimbridge, they had toiled, endured, overcome, laughed, planned, and dreamed. Together they had done it; they had given the world the finest waterfowl conservation, education, and entertainment facility in North America, and quite possibly the world.

Mike delivering speech at the park's Grand Opening with Ali and Brent standing beside.

Mike: Ali's been the backbone of Sylvan Heights. I'm sort of the bird brain and she does everything else brainy. I've been very fortunate.

Mike and Ali built an avian-lover's paradise. And they built it in Scotland Neck, North Carolina, the little farm town the Lubbocks call home.

CHAPTER TWELVE

Saving Wild Waterfowl

Sylvan Heights Waterfowl Park quickly became a destination for all those interested in seeing birds and enjoying a walk in natural surroundings. School groups came in droves for the wetland educational programs, and families found the park the perfect place to spend a day together. Bird enthusiasts were enamored with the variety of species on exhibit, as well as abundant photographic opportunities.

Visitors streamed to Scotland Neck from surrounding communities such as Roanoke Rapids, Rocky Mount, and the thriving metropolitan areas of Raleigh-Durham and Richmond, plus the five-city area of Norfolk, Virginia. Over 12,000 visitors made the journey to the remote bird haven during the first year of operation.

Before very long, accolades began rolling in for the new park. Mike and Ali were named the NEER 2007 Entrepreneurs of the Year for the development and success of Sylvan Heights Waterfowl Park. (NEER stands for NorthEastern Entrepreneur Roundtable.)

Mike was finding that having the park and the avian preserve provided the ideal combination of education and conservation programs he needed to assure that endangered species were given an opportunity to survive in the wild.

Mike: With the park, I can show people waterfowl which they would never see unless they went into the wild, which is impossible for most people to do.

I understand there is a lot of resentment with zoos taking animals out of the wild and putting them on display. But it's a thrill when a child or kids from inner city communities see a wild animal up close for the first time.

My saying is, "I'd rather see a live animal in captivity, than to see one dead and stuffed in a museum."

THE NEXT GENERATION

The primary purpose for building the park was to have sustainable income for perpetuating operations at the breeding center. But Mike knew he needed help managing all the responsibilities. He was serving as executive director, involved in conservation projects, and promoting Sylvan Heights while still maintaining a major role at the Avian Breeding Center. He needed to find someone he could trust to manage the birds and the day-to-day operations at the park.

After a great deal of thought, Mike knew there was only one person who met the criteria he had set to become curator of Sylvan Heights Bird Park. He turned to a former intern at the breeding center, Brad Hazelton.

Mike knew that Brad had a special skill for rearing birds because of the time he spent at Sylvan Heights learning advanced avicultural techniques. After his internship, Brad joined the staff at the Fort Worth Zoo in his native Texas, where he worked as a bird keeper before eventually being promoted to curator of birds.

Mike: No one else met the qualifications I needed for this
        important job. I knew he didn't want to leave his home
        in Texas; however, I asked him to come here and he did.
        It was a difficult decision for him to leave a good position
        at the zoo and relocate his young family in rural North
        Carolina, but we really needed him at Sylvan Heights to
        carry on the work into the future.

* * * * * * * * * * * *

Mike always hoped that his only son would one day follow in his footsteps and carry on his avicultural work. But Brent did not share the same interest for breeding birds as his father. He was fascinated with birds and worked with Mike at the breeding preserve growing up. However, he found the solitary life of raising birds not to be to his liking. Brent prefers to be around people, constantly engaged in conversations. He is a social seeker, much like his mother. Mike knew that Brent cared about the birds and wildlife conservation, but didn't share his love for breeding birds.

Brent's people skills come naturally. Once he reached his teen years, he traveled throughout the world every summer, staying with his parents' friends who kept birds. Spending time in England, Holland, Spain, Africa, and elsewhere, Brent became a well-traveled young man.

Brent was awarded an Associate's Degree in English from Edgecombe Community College, after which he redirected his studies toward a degree Marketing and Communications at East Carolina University.

By the time Brent graduated from ECU in 2003, plans for establishing a waterfowl park at Sylvan Heights were being put into motion. Brent was interested in working in the new venture with his parents, but was unsure as to whether those plans would actually come to pass.

In the summer of 2003, Brent went on a visit to the family of Peter Kooy, a friend of the Lubbocks and a major exotic bird breeder in Holland. Mike had recommended that while he was in Europe, he should also go to Spain to see Beltran De Ceballos, Mike's friend and a seasoned conservationist. It was Beltran who provided Brent with a sage piece of advice that ultimately steered him to Sylvan Heights.

"You have the skills, the knowledge, and the passion for conservation work. You just have to put it to use," Beltran told him. "The new bird park is your opportunity."

Beltran went on to explain to Brent that an important aspect of managing the park, besides the birds, would be his expertise in public relations. With this new perspective, Brent knew he could utilize the degree he received from East Carolina to help his family and also foster the passion that burned within him – conservation.

Whether it was his experiences with rhinos in Africa, orcas in Alaska, sea turtles on the Atlantic coast, waterfowl, or wetlands, Brent had developed a keen concern for the loss of natural habitat and the detrimental effect that had on the earth's wildlife.

During his extensive travels around the world, he had witnessed firsthand the struggle animals endured in a world with a shrinking natural environment. His own world view had been changed. He knew with certainty that his calling was the preservation of wildlife – the waterfowl species in particular.

At Sylvan Heights, Brent could leverage his father's past achievements and also publicize the new conservation mission that the combination of the park and avian breeding preserve afforded him.

Inspiring others to be involved in the protection of waterfowl and one of their primary habitats, wetlands, become the primary focus for Brent Lubbock.

"We can all do something to help waterfowl and the environment. The education component of visiting Sylvan Heights shows people they are needed to step in and make a difference," says Brent.

"The park demonstrates to visitors that the breeding programs contribute greatly to preserving all species of waterfowl, but especially those which are rare and endangered. Prior to the existence of the park, only a few people ever knew what we were doing. Now the world can know and help us in our mission to save this valuable natural resource."

Mike was delighted when his son decided to take a marketing and public relations position at Sylvan Heights. It was a different side of the equation than what Mike first thought he might do, but he was happy that Brent had found a zeal for preserving waterfowl. It stemmed from the same basic passion Mike had when he began breeding birds in the early years at Wildfowl Trust in Slimbridge. It had all worked out in the end.

Brent Lubbock

Mike: Brent is very knowledgeable on birds, knows all of them, and that makes him very good at his job. But communicating with people is what he does best. Whether he's speaking to the locals in town, the mayor, or the visitors, he's comfortable. It doesn't matter if he's talking to one person or a thousand, he doesn't have any qualms about it. He does a radio program every week, and many television shows. He's a natural at it; we rely on him to do it all.

For me, it's satisfying to know that if I die tomorrow, Brent will take the reins and keep Sylvan Heights going.

Mike, Brent, and curator Brad Hazelton mapped out plans to expand the park in a massive Phase 2 campaign. Phase 2 would bring three flamingo species to the park, including the rare lesser flamingo from Africa. In addition, the wetlands portion of the property would be opened up to visitors, while preserving the critical environment for native plants and wildlife to thrive.

First, a large tree house was constructed which provided guests with a panoramic vista of a wetlands habitat. Later a blind was opened on another part of the wetland near a pond that would eventually attract beavers. Here visitors are eye-level with wildlife coming in view of the blind.

Within a few years, the name of the park was changed to Sylvan Heights Bird Park to reflect the expansion into bird species other than waterfowl.

SURVIVAL BREEDING PROJECTS

With the majority of the staff's attention focused on the park, Mike made certain the husbandry efforts at the Avian Breeding Preserve didn't get ignored. Breeding birds had always been at the heart of Mike's career.

Mike: When the park opened, a lot of people thought my dream had come true. But having a public park was never my dream. I'd already done that at Slimbridge. My dream was to spend my life breeding birds.

Awards for avian husbandry success still flowed Mike Lubbock's way. In August 2007, Mike Lubbock received the prestigious Jean Delacour Avicultural Award from the International Symposium on Breeding Birds in Captivity. Named after his mentor, who recommended he go to America to try new husbandry methods, Mike was humbled to be the recipient of the award.

That same year, he was presented the North American First Breeding Award for the critically endangered Madagascar Teal. Using funds raised by the Sylvan Heights Rare & Endangered Species Fund, Mike was able to import a few Madagascar Teal from Europe.

The birds were easily bred and established at Sylvan Heights, with some of the birds being sent to a few zoos in North America. As a gesture of goodwill, Mike officially presented the rare ducks to the government of Madagascar.

Now there are a sufficient number of Madagascar Teal in survival breeding programs around the world, so that if a protected habitat is found for them in Madagascar, there are plenty of birds to send back to the wild.

Mike: I was not worried about who actually owned the
        Madagascar Teal at Sylvan Heights. I just want to save
        the bird.
        We want to save wild habitat for these birds, but
        that's becoming harder and harder to do. Without sur-
        vival breeding programs in place as a backstop, someday
        the birds here might be the only ones around. If the habi-
        tat isn't protected, you can't put the birds there. But if
        you haven't got the birds in the first place, there's little
        hope they can be saved.
        We've reached the stage when the birds become very
        rare in the wild, right down to the last few, maybe, that
        you've got to say, "Yes, we're going to take them into cap-
        tivity," or "No, we're not." And if you don't take them in,
        they'll probably die out.
        If we're really honest about it, it won't be many years
        in the future until many of the birds are gone in the wild
        – even though we're trying to save their habitat. But if we
        maintain survival breeding programs like we have at
        Sylvan Heights, at least those birds won't become extinct.

CONSERVATION MISSIONS

In 2012, Sylvan Heights formed an alliance with the International Wild Waterfowl Association, making Sylvan Heights Waterfowl Center the new home of the IWWA. This alliance for waterfowl strengthens the reach of Sylvan Heights' survival breeding programs and endangered species missions. Mike Lubbock continues to expand his horizon on his lifelong quest to be involved in saving as many species as possible.

Mike: I'm really focused on how to help birds in the wild,
        because now you can work within many of the countries

where endangered birds are found. Before, we were pioneering. We'd go into these countries and find that nobody else was interested in saving the wildlife – that made it very difficult.

But you can give money to the local people and help protect an endangered bird. I've seen that work over the years. In an impoverished country like Cambodia, where they were trying to protect the White-winged Wood Duck, one can give the head of the village $100 to protect a pair of birds, rather than take the eggs or hunt the birds. That $100 has more economic benefit to the village than the pair of birds. It gives them an incentive.

We're involved with a survival breeding program in Brazil to save the critically endangered Brazilian Merganser, but it's being done in Brazil. In the old days, I collected birds or eggs and took them to America or England to breed them. Those days are over. That just shouldn't happen now.

JASON ISLANDS NATURE RESERVE

For many years prior to the opening of the Sylvan Heights Bird Park, the Lubbocks had worked in near anonymity, breeding birds, with Mike making a number of international consulting missions in an effort to help save species in the wild.

One such mission launched in 2001. Mike's good friend Frank Todd became aware that two small islands in the Jason Islands archipelago had been offered for sale. Grand Jason and Steeple Jason Islands are near the Falkland Islands, which are located off the southern coast of Argentina.

Mike had collected birds and eggs in the Falklands as part of his 1973 expedition to Argentina. Part of his exploration included some of the small islands, similar to Grand Jason and Steeple Jason Islands.

Mike and Frank recognized the conservation opportunity these islands offered and sought a way to make them a wildlife preserve. Mike was well acquainted with Wall Street investment manager Michael Steinhardt. Mr. Steinhardt maintained a sizable waterfowl collection in his state-of-the-art aviculture facility. He also supported numerous wildlife conservation projects through the Bronx Zoo and

Wildlife Conservation Society, as well as playing an important role in establishing Sylvan Heights Bird Park.

Mike spoke to Michael about the idea of buying the Jason Islands and establishing them as a nature reserve. Mike was given permission to explore the project and present a proposal for buying the islands.

Mike: The world's largest breeding colony of Black-browed Albatross and 60 percent of the global population of the Striated Caracara are found on the Jason Islands. [The Striated Caracara, also called a Johnny Rook, is one of the rarest birds of prey in the world.]

Over the two islands there are at least a million penguins – Rockhopper, Gentoo, Magellanic, plus a few Marconi and King Penguins.

Just those birds alone made preserving these islands very important.

The Jason Islands are an ecological treasure trove, which also includes Falkland Steamerducks, Ruddy-headed Geese, Southern Giant Petrels, Blackish Cinclodes, Cobb's Wrens, and White-bridled Finches.

Mike: The price turned out to be approximately half a million dollars for both islands. Once we knew the purchase price, Frank calculated what a million penguins would cost. It came out to be 13 cents per penguin or something like that. Presenting it that way made a penguin look really cheap!

Michael Steinhardt rather liked the way we'd done it and said he'd be interested in purchasing the islands.

As soon as the discussions began for the acquisition of Grand Jason and Steeple Jason Islands, a substantial roadblock was encountered. After performing more research, Mike discovered that the islands could not be sold to anyone who was not a British citizen. He told Michael Steinhardt that in the worst case scenario, the ownership of the islands could be titled to Michael Lubbock, who was a British citizen. Details for establishing a nature preserve could be worked out afterwards.

However, Michael Steinhardt had already enlisted the services of a top-flight English lawyer. He had chosen the legal route to deal with the roadblock.

After much haggling with the government over the need to protect the islands, the negotiations remained at a standstill.

Steinhardt's lawyer then posed the notion to the British Government that if an American owned some islands in the Falklands, it could be a benefit if any disputes over ownership of the Falklands arose. Shortly afterwards, Michael Steinhardt was signing the deed for ownership of Grand Jason and Steeple Jason Islands.

About a year later, Mike, Ali, Frank, the Steinhardts, and the English lawyer all went down to the islands, which were now a wildlife preserve, to see this ecological treasure themselves.

During the trip, the formal ceremony for the transfer of the islands was held. It was an elegant affair, steeped in the vestiges of British tradition.

Mike: We had a formal dinner as part of the ceremony. There was a lot of protocol involved. After the dinner, Steinhardt had to toast the Queen, and the Governor of the Falkland Islands had to toast the President of the United States. I sat near Michael to prompt him on the proper protocol.

In 2002, Michael Steinhardt donated the islands to the Wildlife Conservation Society as a measure to assure that the preserve will remain in pristine condition. He also funded the building of a conservation research station.

Mike: This was one of the most rewarding things I've done in conservation. I feel that I played an integral part with forever protecting those islands and the wildlife there.

VENEZUELA'S FOREST GOOSE

The Orinoco Goose is found primarily in the llanos of Amazonia with its wetland areas and open grasslands interspersed by jungle-lined rivers providing ideal habitat for the endangered bird.

Known as the world's only true forest goose, the Orinoco Goose requires large hollowed trees for building its nest during breeding season. The trees in the Venezuelan llanos only grow in abundance along the tributary rivers of the Amazon, such as the Orinoco River, from which the bird gets its name.

Mike Lubbock's first conservation mission to Venezuela came in the late 1990s. He had been asked to perform a census of the Torrent Duck, which were believed at the time to be rare in the rivers of the Andes Mountains. On his first trip, he formed a team of Venezuelan conservationists to conduct the survey, the first ever done for the Torrent Duck. Sylvan Heights became a founding member of the Venezuelan Waterbird Foundation.

While making additional visits to Venezuela to update the Torrent Duck project, Mike took a side trip to the llanos region near the Orinoco River. It was here that he became familiar with the environmental problems affecting the Orinoco Goose. He had bred the bird at Sylvan Heights but had never visited their stronghold habitat in Venezuela.

What he saw was widespread deforestation of the jungle areas to make room for the expansion of cattle ranching, placing the population of Orinoco Geese at extreme risk.

In the rainy season the llanos floods and the cattle are moved back to the dry land. But as the floods recede in the dry season, big lakes are formed which attract hundreds of thousands of waterfowl and other birds.

Because the trees have been cut back far away from the lakes, the Orinoco Geese and their young must travel long distances to get to the water from their nests in the forest. As a result, many of the hatchlings fail to survive. Being an expert in nest box design, Mike had already made progress on a solution to the problem.

Mike: Before I went down there the first time, an American field researcher who worked in Venezuela came to Sylvan Heights to learn what type of nest boxes Orinoco Geese would use. He had been to the llanos to study them. He placed the boxes in the llanos near the lakes and the results were encouraging. They were boxes I designed and he proved that they worked.

Mike visited the researcher on a trip to the llanos to observe first-hand how the manmade nest boxes were working in the field. He was convinced this was the best approach to support the dwindling population of Orinoco Geese in Venezuela.

Mike: I thought placing more nest boxes in the llanos for Orinoco Geese was a good project to maintain. The researcher was in the last year of his study. I recommended that our foundation continue the work he started. With financial help from the IWWA, nest boxes were placed strategically in the llanos. Orinoco Geese didn't have to go 14 miles from the water, as they did in some cases, to find trees to build nests. Having nest boxes near the water areas brought the losses of the hatchlings down tremendously.

Mike made his last trip to Venezuela with Brent in 2006. Political strife in the country has made it too difficult to return. However, if the situation improves, Mike is anxious to return to the llanos to check on the geese and place even more nest boxes for them.

THE BRAZILIAN MERGANSER

Serra da Canastra
National Park, Brazil
July 2011

A cloud of flies continued to annoy the biologists who crouched uncomfortably in the tall, dry grass along the bank of the San Antonio River.

Mike was glad he chose to wear his long trousers, as he would have already been eaten alive by the swarm of ticks had he chosen short pants. It was still morning,

Mike searching for Brazilian Mergansers in Serra da Canastra National Park.

281

but the temperature had already climbed above the 80 degree mark.
"What an odd winter season they have here," Mike thought.
"There's little to no rain, but it rarely gets below 50 degrees. The perfect climate for these pesky insects."

Mike was by far the oldest member of this small team. He was there as an avicultural consultant along with Livia Lins and Flávia Ribeiro, biologists from the Terra Brasilis Institute, and aviculturalist Robert Kooy.

Their mission was to collect eggs from Brazilian Merganser nests and bring them to a newly built merganser rearing unit at the avian collection of Dr. Moacyr. Robert Kooy, son of Mike's aviculturalist friend Peter Kooy, was overseeing the collection as well as the special merganser breeding project.

The Brazilian Merganser not only ranks among the most endangered of the waterfowl, but of all birds as well. Possibly fewer than 250 birds remain, and some field researchers fear that even this estimate may be optimistic.

The river habitat required by the Brazilian Merganser has suffered from staggering deforestation and permanent flooding from dams. The dwindling population of these fish-eating ducks is perhaps most numerous in Brazil's Serra da Canastra National Park, 500 miles northwest of São Paulo.

The Brazilian Merganser, one of the world's rarest animals.

As a member of the Brazilian Merganser Recovery Project, Mike Lubbock was personally invited to Brazil in 2000 to discuss what actions should be considered to save the merganser from extinction. Mike had returned to Brazil several times, most recently in 2009 to discuss the project with the head of the Brazilian Merganser project, Luis Silveira, and introduce him to Robert Kooy. Mike would also aid in designing the special rearing unit that was now in place at the breeding facility.

The group had settled in their viewing position on the river bank, directly above a Brazilian Merganser nest. They waited for the appearance of the young male on his favorite rock, from which he could guard the nest and eggs from intruders. Once he took his position,

Mike knew the female would come off the nest for a feed.

The Terra Brasilis team had been observing this nest site and the different pairs of birds using it for the past three years. Mike also had observed this particular male earlier in the trip and was well aware of his habits in protecting the nest.

As expected, the male swooped into position on his rock and began his ritual.

From Mike's Journal:

> It was very interesting to watch the male sleep for a while, and then go upstream for an hour before returning to his rock to preen and sleep again. What was extremely interesting about this particular male was that the Terra Brasilis team had banded him along with his mother on the San Francisco River after the breeding season last year. Terra Brasilis have been banding birds on the San Francisco for the last three years. Around twenty young mergansers have been banded, as well as a number of adult pairs. Most of the adult birds had returned or never left their territory, but this male is the first of the off-spring birds to be located in three years.
>
> Not only was it interesting that he had changed rivers, but he had also paired up with an older female. None of the other merganser species breed in their first year, so we were wondering if the eggs in the nest would be fertile.

Mike was observing the river when he heard the unmistakable call of a female merganser. "Grr-eee'-cht, grr-eee'-cht ." At 12:15, she had come off her nest with a great deal of vocalization. The male responded with loud calls until the pair flew upstream together to feed.

The team left their observation position and climbed down the bank to the nest. They had brought the equipment needed to dig down through a portion of the bank to where the nest and eggs were located at the end of a long tunnel.

Mike had noted during his observations of the Brazilian Merganser that the birds had changed from their typical locations for building nests. He thought he knew the reason why.

Mike: Brazilian Mergansers had always preferred hollow trees as nest sites, but those became vulnerable to predation from the long beak of the Toco Toucan. Apparently, toucans have increased in number over the years and found merganser eggs to be an easy food source to pilfer.

So what the mergansers do now is find a hole in the river bank, probably made by an armadillo or something. The birds can get their nest back in the hole far enough so that the Toco Toucans cannot get to the eggs.

My idea is to design a nesting hole in the bank that predators can't walk into and the toucans can't reach their bills into. It would be pre-dug for the mergansers to nest. And they'd use it.

Digging into the nest was not an easy job. They could not dig with much force without disrupting the nesting chamber. Rob propped himself against an overhanging tree for leverage and used a post-hole digger to make headway. Flávia shined a light into the nesting tunnel so Mike could see how to direct the digging.

Even though they made the opening big enough to reach into the hole, Mike's long arm still could not reach the eggs. More digging was needed to allow Mike to get part of his shoulder into it. Both Mike and Rob tried reaching into the expanded hole, but neither could quite touch the eggs.

Flávia, however, being much more petite than either of the males on the team, managed to reach the eggs. Mike candled the first few eggs – they had been incubated no more than a week. This was not ideal, but he thought they might be viable.

The digging operation had taken nearly an hour. Livia, in the meantime, had been sent down to the river, crossed over, and was standing upstream, trying to stop the ducks from returning to the nest. Despite all of her frantic waving, and even falling into the water, the pair was not deterred. The female attempted to enter the nest while Flávia was still removing the eggs.

From Mike's Journal:

After seeing the female try to get into the tunnel hole, we thought about returning the eggs to the nest. But we decided that with the disturbance made to the hole, the nest might fail. We determined that the best decision would be to take the eggs. Even though they were not as advanced as we would like, they would be fine in the incubator we had brought with us.

Rob and Flávia carefully covered the new nest hole with the piece of concrete and then covered it back with the dirt they had dug out. Mike took the eggs immediately to the incubator, which was set up in the car.

From Mike's Journal:
> Rob and Flávia returned later and were pleased with how the blocking of the hole had been done. They left the original nesting tunnel intact so it could be used again.
> It wouldn't surprise me if the pair just downstream takes over this territory and uses the nest site.

Once the portable incubator reached the required temperature, the team began the journey back to the town of Pocos. Mike sat in the passenger seat and supported the incubator between his hands to absorb any sudden jolts from the extremely rough dirt roads. Every so often they stopped so Mike could rest his arms and breathe a little fresh air instead of dust. It took two hours to get back to the hotel.

They all went to Rob's room and candled the eggs. There were six eggs in total – two were infertile, one had died very early in incubation, and three were fertile.

Mike: Knowing that the male was not even a year old, it really was not a surprise that two of the eggs were infertile. What was interesting is that most of the clutch was fertile. It is more than likely that the first two eggs laid were the infertile ones – perhaps the male lacked experience in copulating with the female at that point. Livia said that six eggs is a very unusual clutch size – the average is usually between eight and nine.

The next day the team was scheduled to return to Moacyr's Pocos facility with the merganser eggs. Livia suggested that before they go, they should all get up very early and go to another nest site on the San Francisco River. The team had been monitoring the nest, so Livia knew the female should be leaving the nest with her hatchlings around 7:00 a.m.

They arrived in the area just before first light and set up two camouflage sheets so the birds wouldn't spot them from their viewing position across the river from the nest hole.

As the morning light emerged over the horizon, Mike identified the male, which was on guard on the river not far from them. The sun continued to rise and light shone over the nesting hole at around 7:15 a.m. The female came out with lots of vocalization, immediately followed by six squeaking babies that rolled down the steep bank onto the water to join the male, with the female not far behind. The whole extraordinary event happened very quickly. Mike had witnessed the initial emergence from the nest of six precious offspring of one of the rarest animals on earth.

After the pair had gathered their ducklings on the river, they swam upstream out of sight. Rob, Flávia, and Mike waded across the river to the nest site. Livia had originally counted seven eggs. She wanted to know what happened to the last egg.

This nest hole was not very deep, so it was easy to reach the one egg that was still there. Mike candled it and found that although it had not pipped the shell, the beak of the duckling was in the air cell.

Mike, as he had learned to do many years before, held the egg lightly to his lips for a few seconds. The egg did have a small amount of heat in it, and he detected a little movement inside. Mike knew the duckling was still alive, but that would not be the case for long if it were left in the nest. They had not come prepared to take any eggs from this site and had no incubator with them. Improvising, Rob stuck the deserted egg in his underpants.

By the time the team returned to the hotel, the egg had warmed up, but there was still very little movement. Rob placed it in the incubator with the other eggs, hoping that it just might make it.

Later, the eggs were packed in the portable incubator and the team drove back to Pocos. The return trip took over five hours, but at least the roads were better than the team had experienced in the field. Mike still supported the incubator in his hands, but he was able to rest it on the seat much of the time. On arrival at Moacyr's collection, the eggs were transferred to a standard incubator.

BRAZILIAN EPILOGUE

Unfortunately, the abandoned egg from the San Francisco River did not hatch. It was not strong enough, which was probably the reason the female had left it in the nest. After Mike left Brazil, two of the Brazilian Merganser eggs taken from the nest on the bank of the San Antonio River hatched and were successfully reared to adulthood. Those eggs, parented by a very young male and an older female, served as the foundation of the Brazilian Merganser breed-and-study program, and quite possibly the best hope for this species to escape extinction. It is hoped that eventually the second phase of the plan can be implemented – to release the offspring of mergansers at the Moacyr facility into the wild.

Mike: I was very pleased to work with the Terra Brasilis team. Flávia later came to Sylvan Heights to be trained in advanced aviculture as part of our Avian Husbandry & Management Program. She was excited to return to Serra da Canastra and put her new skills to use in the wild.

      We now have a team of dedicated Brazilian biologists doing conservation work and saving the birds in their own country. That's exactly what I like to see around the world. That's the way it needs to be.

      There are a lot of waterfowl species that need this kind of help. I can assist with the field studies and discuss the issues with the local experts. This is what happened with the Brazilian Mergansers, but it took ten years before we took any eggs in to start a breed-and-study program.

      I hope they get permission soon to take in more merganser eggs from the wild.

      Looking back on it, one of the greatest thrills in my career was seeing those baby mergansers rolling down the bank, following their parents into the water for the first time.

A Walk Around The World
Sylvan Heights Avian Breeding Preserve
October 7, 2013

The first light of morning peeks through the boughs of the tall pines surrounding the breeding preserve. Mike Lubbock is in his dusty office inside the immense avicultural barn. The coffee maker emits its final gurgle, signaling the availability of freshly brewed java.

Wearing his signature outback hat, Mike rises from his dusty green padded desk chair. Instead of reaching for his unwashed coffee mug and filling it as he usually would with the steamy beverage awaiting him on the cluttered work table, he exits the office and makes the short walk around the corner to the Little Duckery.

It is a day of remembrance, the seventh anniversary of the opening of the Sylvan Heights Bird Park, which is nestled in the valley of Clark's Branch less than a quarter mile from the barn. Within a few months, it will also be the 30th anniversary of the founding of Sylvan Heights Waterfowl. Mike is rarely sentimental about his accomplishments, but today just feels like one of those days he needs to reflect.

He enters into the Little Duckery and gazes down the two rows of rearing units, 12 on each side, all painted royal blue. Even the concrete floor is blue. Only the cream walls above the units and the white ceiling brighten the space enough to make it gleam as he turns on the lights.

Nick Hill, the curator of aviculture and Mike's trusted right-hand man at the breeding center, has only five of the heating lamps glowing warmth over selected units. Being October, the rearing units are not full of hatchlings like it would be during the peak of breeding season in May or June. However, a few of the southern hemisphere species breed early, so there is always something in the Little Duckery at any given time of the year.

Mike moves down the rows, glancing inside to identify which species Nick has hatched during the past few days. Ancient-looking Magpie Geese from Australia are in the first occupied unit. They appear more like birds from the age of dinosaurs than any waterfowl seen today.

The muted din of alarmed peeping greets him as he moves to the next unit. A large batch of White-faced Tree Ducks scurries to one corner of the rearing unit and huddles for protection. These birds are a reminder of a very recent conservation success in the Caribbean island of Trinidad.

In 2012, the American Embassy in Trinidad had requested that Sylvan Heights help restore the populations of White-faced Tree Ducks and Bahama Pintails to the island where they were once abundant, but now nearly extinct. Mike agreed to bring a flock of each species to the Pointe-à-Pierre Wildfowl Trust, operated by his old friend and colleague, Molly Gaskin. These birds were bred at the Trust and the offspring eventually released in a preserve, where it is hoped they will become established.

Mike flew to the islands with the ducks, along with Brent's wife Katie, to check on the health of the birds and advise Molly and her staff on techniques for breeding these species. Nothing really was more confirming about the career he had chosen so long ago than to know that offspring from the birds he had raised at Sylvan Heights would be released back to their natural habitat.

The next two units harbor Coscoroba cygnets of South America's southern waters and the Hartlaub's Ducks – a bird which is so subtly beautiful, and threatened in its native Africa.

At the end of the row is the last occupied unit. Mike glances inside and laughs. On this day that he has chosen to mull over his career, there certainly couldn't be a bird he associates with discomfort more than the African White-backed Duck. It was while wading in Jeff Lewis's pond in Nairobi, Kenya, to catch this species that he contracted schistosomiasis and that terrible itch that put him in the hospital for a week in London. "Lovely bird," he thinks, "but a bad memory today."

Mike leaves the Little Duckery and finds his olive-drab Ranger motorcycle in the long dirt isle inside the barn. He straddles the well-used bike, giving it several hardy kick-starts before it roars to life. Slowly coasting down the hill from the barn, he stops at the Magellanic Steamerduck pen, with his bike's idling motor in need of frequent snaps of the throttle to keep it revved.

Mike observes the large flightless ducks floating stoically in the small rectangular pond. He struggles to subdue the memory of the horror endured off the coast of Port Aguirre – and of Juan, lost beneath the cold sea of Patagonia. Mike can't help but wonder how Juan's son, José, has fared as head of the household. He must be in his 40s now.

Shaking his head to remove the gloomy reminiscence, Mike re-engages the clutch, moves through the gate of the breeding center, turns right, and accelerates down the gravel road leading to the Bird Park.

Climbing off the bike and reapplying his hat over his silver-white hair, Mike enters the lobby of the Visitor Center long before the first guest arrives at the park. A familiar image on the far wall of the lobby beckons Mike to linger. The original painting, named "Back from the Brink," donated by local artist Dorothy McLennan, depicts the plight of the White-winged Wood Duck in the wild.

Mike has passed by this painting a thousand times without stopping to reflect. It has hung in the lobby since the grand opening seven years ago. But today, Mike pauses to remember one of the greatest successes of all his survival breeding programs.

Once found throughout Southeast Asia, the striking bird now clings to life in isolated areas of Sumatra and Cambodia. For now, at least, it is safe from extinction thanks to the survival breeding program at Sylvan Heights, where it is estimated one-fifth of the world's population of White-winged Wood Ducks reside. But much more work is needed before the duck's long-term future is secure.

A panicked call of a bird from outside the lobby interrupts Mike's train of thought. He immediately recognizes it as a Freckled Duck call and goes onto the porch overlooking the Multinational Pond.

Leaning with both elbows on the hewn-log porch rail, he searches the large pond and discovers the reason for the disturbance. A Freckled Duck has been uncomfortably pursued by a far more aggressive White-headed Duck – no real problem.

Mike watches the aggressor swim toward him on the porch, perhaps expecting some waterfowl pellets to be tossed his direction, as so many visitors do at this spot. The preservation of the White-headed Duck represents one of his greatest achievements – helping the Spanish conservationists return the stiff-tail duck to its natural habitat. The revived population of birds has held its ground for over 30 years.

The cool autumn temperatures and clear Carolina blue sky lures Mike to explore his avian world even further. Exiting the porch to the right, he takes the pathway down the hill and enters the Africa exhibit.

The aviary is alive with excitement, as one of the staff has recently finished putting out fresh food bowls throughout the exhibit. On the grassy areas, the Abyssinian Blue-winged Goose is squawking directly at a pair of interloping Cape Shelducks. On the pond, a passive female Madagascar Teal is being chased by a Cape Teal, with both the pursuer and the pursed flapping their wings and accelerating upon the water. "None of that, now," Mike thinks, as though to admonish the Cape Teal as the pursuit continues around the island. "She's critically endangered."

The squabble on the pond continues, causing all the birds to react one way or another to the commotion, either moving out of the way or joining the fray. The cacophony of bird sounds is music to Mike's ears.

And there, treading lightly and quietly through the pond, as if immune to frantic disharmony, is a pair of African-pygmy Geese. To Mike's mind, it is perhaps the most attractive of all the ducks.

He recalls his Botswana adventure and how he'd schemed for two weeks to catch them, remembering the ancient Gong and Flare tactic he'd used at night in the lily pads of the Okavango River. He is proud to have been the first to breed this magnificent bird.

Mike checks his watch. Only 30 minutes until the park opens for visitors. He still wants to inspect the lower pond of the North America exhibit, where there has been some issues with the water level.

Taking the side exit out of Africa, Mike heads toward North America, but first he has to go through the Eurasia exhibit. Nearly alone on the lower pond are a pair of Baer's Pochard. Mike pauses to check the birds to make sure they are acting normal. It is a requirement for all Sylvan Heights staff members who care for the birds to observe them carefully to detect any health problems early. By the time a bird looks really sick, it's usually too late. And the Baer's Pochard are some of the most important ducks in the collection.

Mike has high hopes that this rare bird will eventually be another candidate for a breed-and-release program. A conservation group working in eastern Russia has contacted him about obtaining birds from Sylvan Heights to release offspring in the wild. Mike has had discussions before about release programs that have never panned out. The habitat has to be right and be protected before the birds can be released there. But at least the Baer's Pochard project is a possibility for reintroducing a bird to its native environment.

Walking through another set of gates, Mike finally enters the North America exhibit. The largest aviary in the park, it also has the largest variety of birds. Two species of mergansers, two species of eiders, two species of swans, two species of goldeneyes, two species of Canada Goose (neither one being the commonly seen Atlantic Canada Goose), three species of tree ducks, the show-stopping Emperor Goose, the colorful American Wood Duck (or Carolina Duck), several teals, Roseate Spoonbills, and other birds. Yes, North America is the happening place.

Yet Mike's attention is captivated today by one of the least grace-
ful and somewhat dull species – a White-fronted Goose. His memory
floods with visions of sliding around on the Arctic ice of Victoria
Island with Charlie Fix, the insanely great bush pilot, both of them
chasing a flock of flightless White-fronted Geese. How crazy were the
things he did on that expedition? Why didn't he just take the flight
back to Edmonton along with his birds after that incident? How many
times had he narrowly escaped serious injury or death?

He was too young to be scared and too adventurous to be wise in
those days. But somehow, some way, he survived the Arctic and many
other dangerous situations throughout his life with birds. Someone,
something, maybe God's benevolent hand, had intervened on his
behalf and kept him safe. Safe so that he could eventually find the love
of his life in Ali, have his wonderful son and ultimately his partner in
Brent, and build the world's largest and most significant waterfowl collection. Alive and well to help save as many species from extinction as
possible in his lifetime and develop an organization that would do the
same after his own time has passed.

He tugs the brim of his Outback hat and lowers it nearly below his
eyes. There are visitors in the park now, and he fights to suppress the
lump in his throat before his emotions become visible.

A small group of visitors enters the aviary and recognizes Mike's
signature hat from a television program that featured Sylvan Heights.
Mike answers their questions and proceeds to identify for them many
of the birds in the North America Aviary, providing plenty of details
on migration and other behavioral traits of each species.

The guests seem genuinely delighted by the encounter and express
their gratitude for the beautiful park he built and the birds he made
available for them to view. As they take their leave and walk toward the
Eurasia Aviary, Mike recognizes a truth he has previously denied.

"Perhaps," he reflects, "having the park was my dream all along.
I just didn't recognize it until it became a reality."

The water level of the lower pond seems fine. He needs to get back
to the breeding center where there are many birds he needs to see. He
will make sure they are cared for the way that only the Waterfowl Man
can do.

* * * * * * * * * * * *

Mike and Ali Lubbock at the time of printing.

About the Author

Dale True is from Dayton, Ohio and became fascinated by the world of nature at an early age. He is a graduate of Wright State University and has been a volunteer at Sylvan Heights Waterfowl Center since 2002, primarily as a media writer. Dale lives in High Point, North Carolina.